Queen of the Road

The True Tale of

47 States,

22,000 Miles,

200 Shoes,

2 Cats,

1 Poodle,

a Husband,

and a Bus with a Will of Its Own

Queen of the Road

DOREEN ORION

Broadway Books
New York

BROADWAY

PUBLISHED BY BROADWAY BOOKS

Published in the United States by Broadway Books, an imprint of
The Doubleday Broadway Publishing Group, a division of
Random House, Inc., New York.
www.broadwaybooks.com

BROADWAY BOOKS and its logo, a letter B bisected on the diagonal,
are trademarks of Random House, Inc.

Library of Congress Cataloging-in-Publication Data

Orion, Doreen.
Queen of the road : the true tale of 47 states, 22,000 miles, 200 shoes,
2 cats, 1 poodle, a husband, and a bus with a will of its own / Doreen
Orion. — 1st ed.
p.   cm.
1. Orion, Doreen—Travel. 2. Voyages and travels. I. Title.

G465.O73 2008
917.304'931092—dc22
2007048066

ISBN 978-0-7679-2853-3

PRINTED IN THE UNITED STATES OF AMERICA

5 7 9 10 8 6

To anyone longing to pursue his or her inner bus.
(It's not necessary to have your own driver, but it doesn't hurt.)

Contents

Queen of the Road

Chapter One

DETHRONED

Prevost Princess

3 parts vodka
1 part peach schnapps
1 part raspberry liqueur
1 robust whine (optional)

Recline on couch; command husband to assemble and shake.

When my long-dreaded thirtieth birthday arrived, I really wasn't as upset as I imagined I'd be, for I had achieved a much more important milestone: my sartorial centennial. I owned one hundred pairs of shoes. Then, at age forty-four, I found myself trying to cram a mere half that number into a living space of 340 square feet.

The whole thing was Tim's fault.

When he announced he wanted to travel around the country

in a converted bus for a year, I gave this profound and potentially life-altering notion all the thoughtful consideration it deserved.

"Why can't you be like a normal husband with a midlife crisis and have an affair or buy a Corvette?" I demanded, adding, "I will never, ever, EVER, not in a million years, live on a bus."

Something less than a million years later, as we prepared to roll down the road in our fully outfitted, luxury bus, it occurred to me that Tim had already owned a Corvette, long ago when he was far too young for a midlife crisis. While I pondered who he might be seeing on the side (and whether his having an affair might prove less taxing than living in a metallic phallus on wheels), I wedged and stuffed—and, oh my GOD! bent—the cutest little Prada mules you've ever seen into my "closet," which was really not a closet at all, but much more resembled the cubbyhole I'd been assigned many pre-shoe-obsession years ago at Camp Cejwin. How had I let myself go from "never ever" to . . . this? Both Tim and I are shrinks, but he's obviously the better one. It took him five years, yet he whittled down my resolve, no doubt with some fancy, newfangled brainwashing technique ripped out of one of our medical journals before I could get to it.

That wouldn't have been the first time my sneaky husband tricked me into doing something I didn't want to do. Well, OK. It was only the second time (that I know of), but the first was a doozy: Almost twenty years before, Tim lied to get me to go on our first date.

We met in 1984 when we were both married to other people. I was a fourth-year medical student living in D.C., but doing as many rotations in Tucson as I could, because that's where my first husband had just moved for graduate school. (He wanted to be an archeologist and put his studies on hold so I could finish my medical training. In return, I told him I'd do my residency wherever he wanted to get his Ph.D., not for one moment thinking he'd pick a city with no Nordstrom.) Tim was a second-year psychiatry resident in the Tucson program, and I was assigned to his team.

Although he was terribly nice and we got along well, I was, after all, happily married and didn't give him a second thought when the rotation was over. As for Tim, his marriage to Diane (or D1; I'm D2. There'd better not be another upgrade) was already crumbling. Two years later, I was the second-year resident, Tim was about to graduate, and we were both divorced.

Tim and D1 had been high school sweethearts and their marriage was more a function of inevitability than compatibility. As for my ex and me, we just got married too young. Shortly after I graduated from medical school, I could see that our two-year union had been a mistake and vowed not to marry again for a long, long while.

Seven months later, I ran into Tim.

I was at a bar with a group of friends, drinking, dancing, and having a grand ole time. Tim walked in with a friend of his. Since we hadn't seen each other in nearly a year, we chatted briefly, but apparently enough for him to realize I was no longer married. Again, I didn't give him another thought—until he called a few days later.

"Hey, Doreen. It's Tim." *What is this guy calling me for?*

"A bunch of us from my class are getting together Saturday night to go back to the bar. You know, me, Mike, Walt, Ann . . . Dave. I wondered if you'd be interested in coming?" *Did he say Dave?*

"Uh . . . sure! See you then." Seems innocuous, right? But, you see, Tim had dangled Dave in front of me because he knew I was attracted to him. How did he know? Because every woman with a pulse was attracted to Dave. And I snapped up the bait with no more thought than the many times I'd gone home with a designer dress that didn't fit, just because it was on sale. Tim hadn't dated much since his marriage had broken up and was not in a place where he wanted to risk rejection. So, you might ask, what's wrong with arranging to go out in a group? Determine if we're compatible? Have an out if . . . ? See how good that man is at deception? There was *never* a group going out. It was always just going to be me and Tim.

That Saturday night, a few hours before we were to meet, the phone rang.

"Hey, Doreen. It's Tim." *What is this guy calling me for?*

"I'm really, really sorry, but everybody's flaked out. Nobody can come tonight. I thought I'd show up anyway, hang out, have a beer. You're welcome to join me . . . if you're not doing anything."

"Uh, sure. See you, then." I couldn't make other plans that late on a Saturday evening. *Guess I might as well go.* And that's *exactly* what Tim knew I'd be thinking when he'd concocted his evil plan.

We met at the bar (aptly named "The Bum Steer"), where we talked, laughed, ate, talked, laughed, drank, and talked and laughed some more. *Hey. This guy's kinda . . . wonderful.* Of course, I didn't know that he'd hoodwinked me, yet. He waited a few weeks to tell me. By then, I was so smitten, I was actually flattered he'd gone to all that trouble. If only I'd realized it was the start of a pattern—sure, one that recurs only once every twenty years, but a pattern nonetheless. I shudder to think what he'll make me do in another twenty.

That first night, I found myself falling. *What is going on here?* Then I remembered my vow. *I don't want to get involved with anyone.* So I strengthened my resolve. *I can't get involved with him.* But, all too soon, there it was: *How . . . can . . . I . . . not?* That first "date," which wasn't even supposed to be a date, lasted eight hours. We've been together ever since, progressing through the all-important M's—Monogamy, Moving in, Mortgage, and Matrimony.

And then, unfortunately, motor home.

As a pampered Princess from the Island of Long, I have always been smug in my position as role model for my friends. They marvel at how I get Tim to do:

1. all the ironing (by exiting the house in horribly wrinkled clothes);
2. all the laundry (by washing everything together, so his favorite baseball shirt turned pink);
3. all the dishes (by being incapable of stacking the dishwasher in an energy-efficient manner).

He also walks the dog (I'm a cat person), cleans the house (I'm a pig, but in fairness to me, the first time he suggested we split chores on a weekly basis, I said, "That's fine, honey, but on my week, I'll write a check"), and takes out the garbage (are there really any married women who still do this?). But once we announced we were doing the "bus thing," as we came to call it, my friends started viewing me with disgust. They insisted I'd let them down. As their husbands eyed mine with envy and tried to get him to divulge his secret recipe for spousal capitulation, the wives shunned me as if the decision to chuck everything and live in a glorified tin can was a symptom of some contagious insanity.

The most curious reaction from our married friends, however, was incredulity—not about the bus, but about the amount of togetherness the bus would require.

"How in the world can you spend twenty-four/seven with each other? We could NEVER do that!" they'd say, shaking their heads in a unison of misery at the thought. Tim and I would just exchange knowing looks and try not to smile. Twenty-four/seven was actually the one aspect of bus life we were both looking forward to. I even think there are a few of my friends who believe I'm rather quiet, just because I never have much to contribute on the "let's bitch about our marriages" front. I know I'm lucky. Unfortunately, Tim knows it, too.

He loves when Joanne, one of my best buddies from residency, calls. She's one of the absolute nicest people I have ever met (second only to my husband). But she also has the absolute worst luck with men. Tim can always tell when I've spoken to her during the day, for as soon as he walks through the door at night, I invariably hurl myself into his arms and beg, "Don't ever leave me!" He'll shoot me a smug little smile and ask, "How is Joanne?"

Twenty-four/seven? No problem. Bus? Well . . . I tried to convince myself (really I did) that my living on one was a natural fit. Although I love the idea of travel, in practice I don't particularly like doing it; the closets are never big enough and there's always the risk of ending up on a hotel's first floor, which smacks way too much of camping for me. I loathe camping. In fact, my idea of "roughing it" is to stay at the Holiday Inn.

Tim and I lived in Boulder, Colorado, for ten years before we hit the road. Boulder is always at the top of every "Most Nauseatingly Healthy/Active Cities" list—though many in surrounding towns refer to it as "Nestled Between the Mountains and Reality"—so sure, I can appreciate natural beauty. I just don't want to have to walk around in it. Besides, the whole fresh air thing is overrated. I'm a physician. A scientist. Stale air, fresh air, it's all the same molecules. I had so shunned the "great" outdoors, in fact, that I had never even been stung by a bee until the age of forty-three—and that was in my own house. I just like being inside. I like not getting dressed. I like not putting on makeup. I like not brushing my . . . well, never mind. Some might call me lazy. I can't be bothered to disagree.

I'd never even realized how strange my love of the great indoors was until one February, when I heard Tim talking to a neighbor in our yard. I poked my head out the door to say hello.

"Doreen! It's nice to see you!" she exclaimed, as if I were a burn victim, finally emerging from the hyperbaric chamber. Tim, of course, couldn't resist singing out, "Guess it's six more weeks of winter!"

I had even gravitated away from patient care to doing insurance reviews so I could stay home all day, in my nightgown, with a cat on my lap. For years, Tim used to come home and exclaim in amazement, "Don't tell me you haven't gotten dressed all day!" But I was proud of my record: 118 hours without leaving the house. Once I perfected the art of not even leaving the bed in the morning, it took Tim a while to get used to this new development. But I figured he'd come around. How could he not be impressed? I found out just how one day when, seeing me sitting up against the headboard, typing away on my laptop, cell phone standing by with papers strewn about, he exclaimed, "Look at you!" At first I didn't quite get his meaning, and asked with considerable pride, "Yep. Who else doesn't have to get out of bed to work besides whores?"

"Even whores have to leave their beds to get johns," he said with disdain.

In fact, however, I always managed to get out—technically speaking—at least once a day: In the neighborhood, I'm known as "the Mafioso" because I'll venture outside to pick up the mail or the paper in a bathrobe, like Vinny the Chin, who roamed Greenwich Village in his pajamas so if the Feds ever got anything on him, he could plead insanity. I tried pleading insanity when I first told my girlfriends about the bus. Although they agreed with the diagnosis, it didn't seem to make them any more forgiving.

I also tried to convince myself that on a bus, I could do what I really loved (stay at home in my pajamas), while doing what I thought I should love (travel). How in the world could I ever have thought this was a bad idea? I even came to view it as a promotion of sorts: from Long Island Princess to Queen of the Long Narrow Aisle.

Tim, on the other hand, never had any reservations about the bus thing from the moment he stopped at the local newsstand and happened upon *Bus Conversions* magazine. He had found his people and his cause.

Ever since he started his private practice nearly fifteen years before, Tim would come home from work at seven or eight in the evening, then make an hour or more of patient calls he hadn't been able to get to during the day. While he often counseled people to take better care of themselves, it was not something that he himself seemed able to do with any ease, largely because he was working himself to death taking care of them. He also tried to be as available to his patients as possible and if someone asked him to take a very difficult case, he always said yes, just because he believed he could help. His practice was killing him.

As I railed against the bus thing, I accused Tim of wanting to do it just so he could escape psychiatry. If he really needed out, I was all for it, but why should I have to give up my life (which I was perfectly content with) for a year? While he assured me this wasn't the case, that the bus thing was something he truly wanted to do, I maintained my skepticism, although the most he would admit to was hoping the bus year would help him "mellow out." Eager to change the subject, he proceeded to ask how I myself might like to be different by the end of the year. I cocked my head and batted my eyes, relishing this rarest of moments when my darling husband was the one to walk into a trap.

"Why?" I asked with all the sweetness I could muster. "Do you think there's something I need to change?" Tim must have seen his bus dream flash before his eyes.

"N-no," he stammered. "I-I just thought maybe you'd like to . . . you know . . . well . . ." His eyes seemed to roll back into his brain, desperately searching its contents for a way out of this one. Finally, he sighed.

"It's just something I really want to do—while we're young and can still enjoy it. I've done everything right all my life, the way I was supposed to do it. Now I want something for me. And I want it with you." I suddenly had the same gooey feeling as all those years before, when he fessed up about tricking me to go to the bar. I gave him a kiss and said, "I'll think about it," but we both knew: Tim had me. Again.

He also had a point. Like many people, until we reached our late thirties, Tim and I went through life feeling rather invincible. Not only was it inconceivable that something bad could ever happen to us, even our very mortality seemed suspect. When we hit our forties, this changed, as our contemporaries experienced sudden, unexpected tragedies: A friend was diagnosed with breast cancer. A colleague died of a heart attack in his sleep. Both of us, for the first time, could feel creaks and aches in bones we hadn't thought about since anatomy class. Over the years, we each treated people in our practices who looked forward to all they planned to do in retirement but, when the time came, were too ill to travel or too devastated by the death of a spouse to live out their dreams.

Those lessons started hitting home as we officially breached middle age. We knew we were fortunate in that we would always have jobs; neurosis is a growth industry, after all. We could afford to do this now and go back to work later.

All these considerations weighed on me, swinging my decision back and forth like a fifth wheel dragged down the road. In the end, Tim finally got his way when he pointed out, "Look. We didn't have kids so that we wouldn't be tied down, so that we could do whatever we want, when we want. I won't miss out on having kids without getting any of the benefits."

Tim and I always assumed we'd have kids. It just never felt like the right time, for either of us. Yet, as the years went by, we both came to realize we didn't miss not having them. And through seeing how much work our friends put into child rearing (particularly the necessity of leaving the house on a regular basis, for things like driving them to and then having to sit through—oh, God—soccer games), I gradually came to the conclusion that maybe motherhood just wasn't for me. Since Tim didn't feel strongly that he wanted kids either, at some point we agreed (especially after what we'd seen in our line of work) it wasn't fair to a kid to have it, if we weren't motivated to. Instead, our pets have become our kids and through them, we've realized that our decision was most definitely for the best. And not just for us, but for all of mankind.

Living in our house is like living with furry little Helen Kellers before the arrival of Annie Sullivan: Our two cats walk all over the table while we eat, grabbing what they can, jump on and off the bed all night, sticking their paws in our faces demanding snuggle (yeah, it's cute—the first time), and blackmail us with bloodcurdling screams while we're on the phone (and thus not paying attention to them), resulting in more than one potential Animal Welfare investigation.

As for our standard poodle, he has gotten used to going everywhere with us. If, for some reason, we absolutely cannot take him, he shoots us a glance of utter despair as he drags his curly butt to the couch, which he knows very well he's forbidden to sit on. Of course we don't have the heart to make him get off, since he's already being so cruelly abused.

If we'd had kids, they'd be little monsters. Then they'd grow up to be big monsters. It's a benefit to the entire planet that we have chosen to remain childless. Really, the U.N. should give us a humanitarian award.

Since we had vowed years ago that not having kids would mean we would take advantage of the freedom other people our age didn't have (something we had yet to do), I finally realized Tim was right about the bus thing and agreed to his plan.

Although I wouldn't exactly say I was enthusiastic about it.

On a cold, dreary Sunday in January 2002, Tim lugged me to an RV show in Denver. Even though he had already been tainted by *Bus Conversions* magazine, he was still thinking it would be simpler to just buy some sort of trailer to live in. So we trekked through the convention center for hours and hours, holding hands. Tim always holds my hand while we walk, but for once, it felt less like affection and more like fear I would run away. Up and down the aisles we went, in and out through the various rigs: class A's, B's, and C's, fifth wheels, pop-ups, and, Lord help me, camper vans. I suspect he started with the latter, just to get me to the point where I'd be begging to live on a bigger vehicle.

The very last booth of the day, the one we nearly skipped (my

Manolos were killing me), was that of Vanture Coach Manufacturing, Inc. The owner, Chris Brown, and his business partner, John Frank, jovially entertained prospective clients, proudly displaying examples of their craft—the conversion of various types of vehicles (which unfortunately included buses) into motor homes.

While Chris took another poor deluded man (who stupidly hadn't been clutching his wife's hand, as she was nowhere to be found) aside, John walked up to us with a wide smile and explained why converting a bus was a much better idea than buying a ready-made RV.

"For a little more than buying one new, you can get a bus made to your very own specifications!" he enthused. Tim nodded, transfixed by the wall of bus pictures lining the Vanture booth. John continued, "They're bigger than most RVs, and of course, for men, big is always better." Tim licked his lips, images of converted school buses, double-decker buses, and flexible buses barreling down a one-way road deep into his psyche, ripping up the carefully laid foundation of my contented life in their wake. I needed to find a detour. Fast.

"In a bus," John confidently intoned, "when you take out the lavatory, the old waste tank makes a great safe!" Drool dribbled down the side of Tim's mouth. As I sized up the rapidly deteriorating situation, John sensed he had to win me over. I was just about to sink to the depths of desperation with a demure "Honey, let's go. I have cramps," when John seemed to figure he had me figured out.

"With a bus," he said, eagerly turning my way, "you can have exactly the kind of kitchen you want—" I cut him off with a withering look. What was I worried about? This was going to be *too* easy.

"I don't cook." Undaunted, he narrowed his eyes, studying me.

"In a bus," he said evenly, hands on his hips, "you can design a washer-dryer combina—" I nodded toward my husband, who had by now let go of my hand to better study the bus pictures with the same rapt attention he'd used preparing for his medical board exams.

"He does the laundry," I said, challenging John to up the ante. He took a deep breath, pursed his lips, and dropped his eyes to the floor. Slowly, his gaze rose as he took in my swollen feet, unaccustomed to a full day of wearing shoes, their twin cousins, Righty and Lefty Love Handles, and, finally, the trace of an afternoon bonbon lingering on my lips. A smile crept over his face. He folded his hands on his chest and looked me right in the eyes with all the confidence of Ralph Kramden.

"In-motion satellite TV" was all he said.

"I . . ." My hesitation sealed my fate. While most people would assume the man is the vidiot in the family, in ours, Tim hardly ever watches TV. He's too busy outside, doing stuff. I, on the other hand . . . John continued with a rush of words, circling in for the roadkill.

"Your husband can be up front doin' all the drivin', while you lay in bed, all nice and cozy . . . in your pajamas, snuggling with your . . ." He noted the trace of white fluffy fur stuck to my black Gucci purse.

". . . cat?" He shot me a questioning look. My eyes widened. John stepped back and beamed at me, triumphant.

"Tim," I cried weakly. He seemed not to hear, as he stood before the display of buses in various stages of being stripped down to their skins. All that was missing were the front-end pasties, fishnet hubcaps, and tantalizing glimpses under the hoods. This called for my favorite whine: full-bodied and piercing, with much more than a hint of provocation.

"Ti-im!" Still nothing. Forget the finesse.

"TIM!" He, and the rest of humanity, turned toward me. He could see how shaken I was, but still had trouble peeling his eyes away from the bus porn before coming over.

"Take me away from the bad man," I whimpered. He gave John a quizzical look. John gave him a barely perceptible wink and a nod. Then Tim steered me away, as he slipped a Vanture card into his pocket.

People often wonder how Tim and I could have ended up together. We count ourselves among them. Other than our occupations, I doubt you could find a more disparate pair: Tim loves the outdoors, treats everyone he meets with kindness, and has an intense need to keep busy, to accomplish things. I am more of a misanthropic couch potato. As a clinician, Tim provides care to patients. Through my insurance review work, I deny care to them. When it came time to hit the road and Tim had to give up his practice (which included being medical director of a psychiatric hospital), his patients cried. The staff cried. I even detected tears in the eyes of the janitors, for Tim is a kindred spirit to Everyman.

On weekends, this mild-mannered psychiatrist sheds his suit and tie, slaps on his safety goggles, laces up his steel-toed boots, and assumes the guise of . . . Project Nerd, Domestic Superhero. Tim tackles everything around the house. I call it his Pesky Protestant Work Ethic, and give thanks every day that I have not been given that cross to bear myself. Whether it's installing landscaping (complete with drip irrigation), cleaning gutters (repairing any leaks), or felling sick trees (chopping them into firewood for the winter), by 9 a.m. on a Sunday, my husband has done more than I'll even think about doing the entire week.

(I never did understand that Army commercial. Is getting up before dawn to work your butt off really supposed to be a selling point?)

I don't want to give the impression that Tim is an angel. Far from it. He takes full advantage of his knowledge of, well, everything. Not only that, he turns my slothfulness against me every chance he gets. For example: I'm always too hot. Unless it's winter; then I'm too cold. Yes, part of the problem when the temperature drops outside is that I get around even less, but still, regulating my body heat is just not one of my strong suits and I don't think I should be penalized for having a disability. Tim, however, thinks I should get bundled up in the winter. He says I should walk around in a sweater—in my own house! To me, that smacks too much of getting dressed. Besides, why should I suffer? I maintain I should be able to wear only my pajamas to keep comfortable and I'm more than willing to make the concession of switching to flannels, but Tim says just because I'm lazy down to a cellular level doesn't mean he should accommodate me.

When we first lived together, he noticed the temperature on the thermostat was always higher when he got home after work. But a real superhero doesn't argue, he swings effortlessly between buildings, flies around the earth to change the course of time, and thwarts armed divisions without any artillery of his own. A domestic superhero simply waits his wife out until she finally has to leave the house to get her hair done. Then he installs a fancy, new, totally-incomprehensible-to-the-double-X-chromosome thermostat. It took me months to figure out where the "override" button was. By then, he had brought home a newer, even more incomprehensible gadget.

Thus began the Thermostat Wars, which continue to this very day. Just when I seem to have finally bested my enemy, Tim escalates the conflict by procuring more advanced technology, and the skirmishes begin all over again with my small arms desperately trying to defuse the situation. Détente does not work with my husband. He simply refuses to negotiate, even when I force him to bear witness to my pathetic attempts at staying warm by snatching up an unsuspecting cat and sucking the heat out of my nonhuman shield. My royal title is no match for Tim's superpowers and I fear I shall forever be consigned to a state of perpetual nonthermostasis.

I did achieve, however, a small victory after a deliciously satisfying escalation in hostilities the time we visited his father in Arkansas several years before the bus thing.

Maybe that's where Tim gets his crazy ideas. Bob worked his entire life as a mail carrier, finally got to retire, and what does he do? Buys a small farm in a small town in Arkansas, running it by himself, to work harder than he ever had in his life. The first time we visited him was in July. July in Arkansas. In fairness to Bob, he did have the air-conditioning turned on. Just not nearly high enough. Tim had the gall to point out the irony of the fact that the number that would have made me positively ecstatic in winter was reducing me to abject misery in summer.

"What do you want from me?" I cried. "Everyone knows that seventy-six degrees in winter is *not* equivalent to seventy-six degrees in summer." Project Nerd was unmoved. Fortunately for me, farm life requires that one go to bed right after dinner. So after Bob retired that first evening, I lowered his pitiful thermostat, a relic from a preindustrial past I had no difficulty whatsoever decoding after years of warfare with his son. Unfortunately for me, however, farm life also requires getting up much earlier than I could possibly consider, and the luxuriating in bed I looked forward to on vacations was marred by rolling around in my own sweat by morning. Bob had been up for hours and had raised the temperature to a post-nuclear level.

How could two men who had not been particularly close be so alike? We were planning to go to Arkansas again during our bus year. I prayed that spending more time with his father would not mean repairing the distance between them to the extent that Tim's next harebrained scheme would involve the milking of large, dim-witted mammals.

By winter of 2003, I was calling all over the country. Because I worked at home sitting at my desk (with two cats vying for my lap), reviewing cases on the phone, and Tim saw patients all day, it was logical that I be the one to search for a bus. Tim determined to teach me about all that mechanical stuff as best he could, and as usual, when my husband puts his mind to something, he gets the job done. No matter how impossible the task.

I simply can't abide mechanical things. Still, Tim sat me down in his den, amidst stacks of *Bus Conversions* magazines, and the lessons began. A lesser man would certainly have thrown in the shop towel. I can't even tell a Chevy from a Ford from a Honda. Whenever Tim wants to point out a car on the road, he has to say something like "The green one, with four doors." How could I ever tell buses (which all tend to be painted the same, after all) apart?

A lot of couples are annoyed by their differences. Tim and I are fascinated by ours. For us, rooting around in each other's psyches is like studying exotic animals in a zoo. As a result (and partly, I'm sure, because we're both shrinks), there's not much we let each other get away with. When nothing was sinking in during our first bus lesson, I tried to pass off my resistance as stupidity. "I just don't have the head for this stuff," I protested. Tim would have none of it.

"You just don't want to be bothered learning it," he maintained. As I whined that I really was trying, he got up, went into my office, and returned with one of *my* magazines. He riffled through the pages and settled on a picture at random.

"What's this?" he demanded as he shoved it under my nose. I glanced down and reflexively blurted out, "Badgley Mischka. Spring runway collection." Tim slammed the magazine shut with a self-satisfied grin and I shut my mouth during the remainder of his painstaking, excruciatingly detailed classes.

Tim prepared me well—maybe too well, in fact. A typical conversation with a potential seller about his older bus went like this:

"Is it a 6V92 or an 8V92?" I asked with much more confidence than anyone who had no idea what either one was had a right to possess. I had a suspicion that the latter was more powerful, or maybe it just had two more parts. Or maybe they both had ninety-two parts, but the 8V referred to a volt thing. (Or maybe it was a vixen thing? Mud flaps on big rigs always seem to have saucy silhouettes.)

"It's a D Deck," he answered. Momentarily stumped, I suddenly recalled something Tim had mentioned which had managed to sink in.

"D Deck two or three?" I probed.

"It's a three," he answered.

"Hmm," I mused, toying with my prey. "I've heard the threes are less reliable."

"Well, ah . . ." he struggled to respond, but I was off and running.

"Aluminum wheels? Rust problems? Five- or six-speed?" I finally threw him a bone. "Sounds interesting. I'll have my husband give you a call. He knows a lot more about this stuff than I do." The man paused.

"Ah, ma'am." He hesitated. "It sure seems like you know enough."

I finally happened upon a '98 Prevost on a Volvo website. Even I knew that a Prevost was the Holy Grail of buses. Rock stars travel in Prevosts. So why not Princesses? When I called, the already low price posted on the Internet had been cut by a third.

By May 2003, the Prevost was finally parked at Vanture. We had spent nearly six months just finding this bus that now had to be renovated before we could leave on our trip in the summer of 2004.

I consoled myself with the one bright spot thus far to the whole bus thing.

Decorating!

It's easy to fool yourself when things are on a small scale. A twelve-hundred-dollar handblown glass sink for the bathroom? Well, if it were a house, we'd be buying two, so in a bus, we're actually *saving* money! Of course we had to have granite countertops in the kitchen, but did we have to get the most expensive granite known to mankind? We fell in love with the Blue Bahia when we first spotted it at the warehouse; its intense, sparkling azure vein seeming to pulsate as it called out to us from amongst the more mundane slabs.

"What's that?" we asked the saleswoman. She hesitated, then whispered its name with a mixture of reverence and fear worthy of one of my ancient forebears daring to utter The Name of Yahweh.

"It's the most expensive we have," she apologized.

"How much?" Tim asked.

"Three-twenty a square foot" came the reply.

"Oh, that's not so . . . Wait a minute. You mean three *hundred* twenty dollars a square foot?" She nodded sheepishly.

"What do they do, mine it on Mars?" I demanded.

"Close," she replied. "Underwater." Then she added in an even more hushed tone, "If any of the guys drop it, they're summarily . . ." Her eyes darted about the warehouse as Tim and I waited, holding our breaths.

". . . fired," she finally confided, barely audible.

We were duly impressed. Even more so when, as designers are wont to do, she held up a sample of our lush cherry cabinets to the granite. It was an irresistible combination, but we were prepared to resist. Tim and I pride ourselves on being able to put up a united front on most anything. There was no way we would be daunted. Until she sealed the deal.

"Oooh!" she exclaimed. "It's really going to pop your cherry." With a promise like that, after nearly fourteen years together, we had to have it.

For the granite, the stainless steel tiles, and the custom appliqué ceiling, it was just too easy to reason, "Well, we'd never get it in a house. But, in a bus? How many square feet could we possibly need?" The answer, when it came to the merino wool window coverings from the Netherlands, was so over the top, I couldn't help but ask, "What do they do? Fly the sheep over first-class and then shear 'em?"

Cost, it turned out, was to be only the first of many, many aspects of bus life we would underestimate.

Chapter Two

THE MELTDOWN CRUISE

Phobic Friar

1 part Frangelico
1 part raspberry liqueur
⅔ part Baileys

Hold martini shaker firmly with both hands; tremble violently; pour down throat.

efore we headed off for the year in the summer of 2004, the Vanture guys had encouraged us to take a "test run," a shakedown cruise, to "work the bugs out." Tim and I had no idea what they meant. Unfortunately, we were to find out.

The day before the launch of our three-week mini-adventure, Peter, the custom electronics guy, still hadn't finished. Throughout the yearlong bus conversion project, it was evident that Peter had serious issues with time management. (It was only after living in the bus that we discovered he had even more serious issues with custom electronics.) In addition to his time management difficulties, we had also become used to his creative attempts at responsibility management.

"Ya know, Doreen, it's just like doin' a house. The AV guy always gets pushed to the side. In a bus, it's even worse, 'cause there's less room. I was in there the other day . . ."

Peter finally showed up at 5:30 p.m. It took him four hours to get the Internet up and running, but then there was no TV signal. By 12:30 a.m., I was the one who called it quits.

"I can live without TV for three weeks," I told an astonished Tim. "Peter can fix it when we get back."

"Are you sure? That's like normal folk going without food or water," Tim said, reaching to touch the back of his hand to my forehead.

The morning of June 18, 2004, dawned sunny and bright. Tim and I were well rested as we left our home in Boulder for our shakedown cruise. First stop: Reno, Nevada.

At least that's the way it was supposed to be.

Here's how it was: We awoke late, to pouring rain. Since ours was a narrow street on a cul-de-sac, I was charged with directing Tim as he backed down the hill and making sure no traffic was coming as he swung the rear end of the bus into an intersection. No problem, I thought. I've flown many a time and studied the guide men out on the tarmac, with their staccato ballet of arm signals, easing pilots onto the runway.

I quickly discovered why those gentlemen wear sneakers.

The rain had paused momentarily and things were going smoothly as I walked backwards, behind and slightly to the side of our forty-foot-long behemoth of a bus so Tim could see me in his mirrors. I guided him down the hill, my arms perpendicular to the ground, forearms in unison, alternating perpendicular, vertical, perpendicular, vertical . . . until my adorable little slip-on sandal slipped off on the slick street. I quickly made the universal signal for "stop," or what should be the universal signal—wildly flailing arms—as I stepped behind the descending 40,040 pounds of Prevost, reached down, and retrieved my little orphan Annie Klein. The sound of what I would later learn were air brakes hissed in my ear. I completed the rest of the maneuver and climbed into the bus, feeling pretty proud of myself, until Tim, white as the cute little camper van I would soon wish we had gotten instead, gave me a horrified look.

"NEVER step behind the bus while I'm backing up," he said with a shrillness I hadn't heard from him before.

"But, sweetie," I replied, "you were going to run over my favorite sandal."

"NEVER step behind the bus while I'm backing up," he repeated, his new mantra. This would not be the last time he would raise his voice fearing for my life that day.

After Tim hooked our tow vehicle, a Jeep, to the back of the bus, we got safely under way, traveling without incident, until we hit the highway ten minutes later. At 60 mph, the bus door flew open. I, of course, was in the "buddy" seat, just to its left.

"SHIT!" Tim screamed. "You're belted in, right?" Indeed, I was. Did he think I was crazy? He'd only practiced driving the thing a total of six hours.

"I can get it," I calmly replied, not wanting to distract the driver. After all, there must be a reason for the sign up front that says, "FOR PASSENGER SAFETY FEDERAL LAW PROHIBITS OPERATION OF THIS BUS WHILE ANYONE IS STANDING FORWARD OF THIS WHITE LINE." I unbuckled my seat belt, climbed down, and stood in front of the door (and the white line). I grabbed the handle with my right hand.

One. Two. Three. As I swung the door in toward me, the lift of the wind pulled against me, flinging the door open even wider, this time with me attached.

"SWEETIE! NO! STOP!" Tim screamed. It wasn't so much the castrato-like octave of his voice as the slap of the cold, wet rain on my face that shocked me into Sandra Bullock mode. I clutched the handrail along the entry stairs with my left hand, my right still on the door handle. My slide to a certain death (or, at the very least, vast array of new prosthetic devices) ceased.

"LET GO OF THE DOOR!" Tim barked as he wrestled the bus into the emergency lane.

"No," I cried, "I think I can do it!" Reasoning that Ms. Bullock had been able to do all those stunts in *Speed* wearing a simple sundress, while *I* was sporting a brand-new designer tracksuit and all I had to do was shut a door, I kept my left hand on the rail, braced myself, and tried again. No dice—not even fuzzy ones. I just could not get it closed until Tim stopped the bus. At that point, he pressed a button on the dash that actuates the door's air lock, bolting it shut.

"I am so sorry, sweetie," he said, as white as the line on the shoulder of the road we were now straddling. "It won't happen again," he promised.

"Better not," I snapped, "or I'll have to invoke the 'two strikes and you're a dimwit' rule." Tim nodded, his face solemn. That would be the second to last thing he'd ever want me to do, right behind flying out the bus door.

The two strikes and you're a dimwit rule was decreed one night when Tim left his wallet at home and couldn't pay for dinner. When we go out, if I bring a purse at all (what are husbands for, anyway, if not to take care of the bill?) it's to make a fashion statement, not to carry anything practical, like money or credit cards. For weeks afterward, every time we'd leave the house, I'd ask, "Do you have your wallet?" Finally, Tim begged in exasperation, "If I only forget something once, do you really have to remind me every time?" Hence, the two strikes and you're a dimwit rule. Came in real handy the second time he left the ignition on in my car overnight, draining the battery.

Things did start to look up when we crossed the border into Wyoming. The rain was now merely a drizzle and I was beginning to enjoy my perch up high, as well as the waves and stares of pedestrians and passing drivers, unaccustomed to seeing such a large tour bus on their streets, especially one painted ocean blue with red, turquoise, and green stripes, all outlined in gold.

"Look! They think we're celebrities," Tim exclaimed.

"No," I corrected. "They think *I'm* a celebrity. They think *you're* a bus driver."

"At least they think I get to drive a celebrity," he mumbled under his breath. By the time we reached a truck stop in Laramie to gas up, the rain had started in again, hard. As he stood out in the downpour, Tim realized he didn't know how to operate the diesel fuel pump. He called over to the driver of a big rig next to us.

"So, is this pay at the pump?" The trucker gave him a condescending look. "No," he growled, "push the intercom and tell 'em which pump you're on." Two hundred twenty dollars later, our 179-gallon tank filled, Tim climbed back in, his hand dripping blood.

"What happened?" I asked, alarmed, thinking perhaps he'd come to blows with the trucker over the not too subtle slight to his manhood.

"Oh, I noticed the tow cable for the Jeep was frayed. It's been dragging on the ground. I had to shorten it," he said. I gave him a worried look. "I don't think I remembered to pack Band-Aids," I said.

"I did," he replied, ripping a paper towel. "They're in the bay." He wrapped his hand as best he could and we headed back to the highway. As soon as we hit 60 mph, the door flew open again. Since, after the previous incident, Tim (who likes to lord it over me that I took Physics for Non-Majors) had painstakingly and with excruciating detail explained the concept of camber, by which the angle of the door away from the bus creates lift, thus precluding any hope of my being able to close it, I didn't try to.

Tim eased the bus to a stop and I slammed the door shut. As we looked deep into each other's eyes, we both had flashbacks to my near-death experience of only a couple of hours before.

"Two strikes and you're a dimwit rule," we chimed in unison.

Night fell. So did the hail. Tons of it, the size of the tassels on my last-season Cole Haan loafers. Tim's face was as white as the paper towel bandaging his hand had been before becoming soaked in blood. Even the truckers were pulling over on the shoulder. We did, too. The sound of the hail pounding into the steel skin of our bus was deafening. I was certain the windshield would crack. Or worse. The storm let up after five interminable minutes, resuming the pelting rain we had begun to long for. Our dog, Miles, and our male cat, Morty, were both sitting at attention on the sofa. Before Tim started up the bus again, I went into the back to check on Shula, our female cat, who had spent the entire trip thus far cowering under the bedcovers. *I bet this scared the pee out of her.* It had. Right through to the mattress.

Neither of us wanted to venture outside to inspect the damage. While Tim struggled to remember if we had coverage for hail under our new RV policy, I wondered how in the world we could ever break the news to Manny, Vanture's paint and body-work man who had painstakingly detailed the bus at our house only the day before. Miraculously, as we later found out, we didn't have to worry about either, as the hail had not left even one tiny dent.

Our plan had been to make it to West Wendover, Nevada, just across the Utah border, for our first night. There was a very convenient truck stop we had spotted many times on our car trips to Reno. Tim's mother, Dorothy, lived there and was turning eighty in two days. We had organized a surprise party brunch at her favorite restaurant, so we really could not be late. West Wendover was a twelve-hour drive from Boulder, very doable had we gotten an early start. But as we headed into Rock Springs, Wyoming, it was already 11:30 p.m. (a normally six-hour drive had taken us eight) and we were both drained. We decided to stop for the night at another landmark we'd taken note of, the Flying J truck stop, just off Interstate 80. There it was. And . . . there it went. We took the next exit, intending to turn right back around, but somehow ended up in the deserted parking lot of a college campus. Tim stopped the bus so we could catch our breaths, make a plan, and wait for some improved visibility.

"I think we should just stay here for the night," I said, my voice shaky.

"I don't want to. A deserted parking lot isn't safe." Since Peter had also failed to hook up the security cameras, it really didn't seem like a good idea to stay. We ate a quick snack and headed back to the Flying J.

One might think a truck stop would be clearly marked, but there was construction, the rain was still going strong, and somehow we missed the exit, again. As we barreled down the wrong street, trying to find a place to turn around, the bus door flew open for the third time.

"SHIT!" Tim exclaimed, his face now white as the cotton atop the new Tylenol bottle he'd popped open after the second door incident. This time, I couldn't help but laugh as he stopped the bus to airlock the door.

"You know, honey," I said, "the only bad thing left to happen is to get the bus stuck somewhere we have to back out of so we have to unhook the Jeep in this weather." And that's exactly what happened a few minutes later, with the Jeep sticking out into a four-lane road.

We finally made it to the Flying J, Tim driving the bus with me following behind in the Jeep. Since it had been bad enough unhooking it in the storm while watching for traffic, we decided not to bother rehooking it just then. Unfortunately, the only spaces available at the truck stop involved Tim backing up the bus into a narrow space between two trucks. The side view mirrors were completely fogged up from the rain and he just could not see to do it. (As for the backup cameras, they were tied to the nonexistent security cameras, so . . .) We got out of our respective vehicles and conferred in the downpour. Well, maybe "conferred" isn't exactly the right word. I begged.

"*Please*, honey. Let's go back to that school." And we did, finally parking for our first night at 1:30 a.m. God bless you, Western Wyoming Community College.

As we turned the mattress and hand-rinsed the pee-soaked linens in the sink (we didn't know how to use the washer-dryer), I had my darkest moment of the day, as I spied a still-traumatized Shula huddled in a corner. *She's not going to adapt to this bus thing. Maybe we should leave her with Dorothy. Maybe she'll take me in for the year, too.*

Our bus has three temperature zones, one for the main living area, one for the bathroom, and one for the bedroom. We cranked the heat in zone three and climbed into a sheetless bed. We awoke an hour later, shivering.

"Something's wrong with the heating system," Tim said. "I'm freezing."

"Me, too," I answered, teeth chattering. We grabbed an extra blanket (mercifully not left in the storage bay under the bus) and somehow managed to sleep a few more hours. It was only sometime the next day, after I kept turning up the air-conditioning in zone one (not that Tim minded this time; he was sweltering by the windshield), went back to the bedroom to check on Shula (still in full cower mode), and noticed how much cooler it was in there, that we realized zone one, not zone three, was actually the bedroom.

Surely the karma gods intended that we get all the bad luck out of the way that first day.

Yeah, right.

The next morning, Tim started up the bus at 8:30 a.m., with me still asleep—for about a second. I had thought sleeping on our bus would have that familiar, comforting feeling, harkening back to all the snoozing I'd done on Greyhounds traveling back and forth to college. However, lying flat in a queen bed in the very back was anything but reassuring. All of the turns, bumps, and ruts were amplified. I felt as if we were careening off the road while swerving to avoid Godzilla during a meteor shower.

I bolted out of bed, but stayed in my pajamas (the one bright spot thus far). At first, I was glad I had risen, as the weather was clear and the mountains ahead in Utah were stunning. But once upon those treacherous beasts, destroyers of confidence with their "runaway truck lane" and "steep grade ahead" signs, I longed for the insecurity of the bed in the back. I tried to calm myself. I was being ridiculous. Then Tim seemed to be having trouble with the brakes. His frantic pumping was a good clue. I asked what the matter was.

"Nothing, sweetie," he reassured between clenched teeth. When Tim won't even tell me what's wrong, I know it's something really, really bad.

I might have tried to believe him in this instance, but soon there was the unmistakable smell of smoke. Then there was the minor added detail of our bus taking the turns way too fast.

I clutched Morty to my frilly flannel chest and realized Shula had the right idea all along. As I pondered our imminent, fiery demise, Tim finally figured out the problem. Rather than turn the Jake Brakes on high, he had turned them off.

As he later painstakingly explained with excruciating detail, diesel engines don't normally slow with compression (i.e., when you take your foot off the gas in a car, it slows down; with a diesel engine, it just keeps going). Our diesel engine bus, however, was equipped with Jake Brakes (God bless you, Jacobs Vehicle Systems), which bypass the regular brakes to decelerate the bus, thus avoiding overheating on such steep grades, slowing such massive tonnage. To operate the Jake Brakes, the driver toggles a switch with his left hand. Unfortunately, Tim had assumed that "up" was high, when in fact, "up" was off.

"Much better, huh?" He laughed, realizing his mistake. *You could say that.*

We arrived in Reno that evening and parked in front of Dorothy's house for the night. We were overdue at Tim's brother's for dinner. The bus door, however, was still misbehaving. On the road, it wouldn't stay shut—now, it wouldn't lock.

Project Nerd got his tools from the bay and took the door lock apart. Meanwhile, I tackled figuring out the ice maker in the fridge. I needed a martini. Bad. (Yeah, I know it's "badly," but

I didn't need it "badly," I needed it bad, see?) While he got the lock working as well as he could, I saw that, in fact, there were a few ice cubes already in the tray. Unfortunately, the manual said to discard this first set. Something about chemicals, dirt, growing a third eye . . . I didn't know and I didn't care. I needed my martini and I needed it. Bad.

Soon, some nieces and nephews returned to drop Dorothy home from the dinner we'd missed. They all came in for a look and were duly impressed. After the tour, one nephew, a strapping twenty-two-year-old I had always been close to and who knew me much better than the others did, took me aside and said, "Aunt Doreen. You're a really good sport."

"Yup," I burped, feeling no pain, sucking down the last, fruity, tranquilizing drop.

The next morning, Sunday, brought with it a new day . . . and a new mattress. Tim spent most of the morning working on that darn door lock, this time with the help of his brother and nephew, while I stayed in bed with Shula. I hadn't been sleeping well since the night before we left Boulder.

Doing a project with his brother and nephew was something I knew Tim would greatly enjoy. He was the first in his family to go to college, and frankly, they didn't know what to make of him. That, coupled with being ten and eleven years younger than his only siblings (who were actually half brothers), had made Tim feel like an outsider—a welcomed, even adored outsider, but an outsider nevertheless. Fixing our lock was something Project Nerd, Project Nerd-in-law, and Project Nerd Light could do together. One of those male bonding things, like shopping is for women; just as strenuous, requiring just as much problem solving and teamwork ("Where should a blazer hit on a skirt this long?"), and somehow just as fulfilling, even without anything stylish to show off in the end for the effort.

I hadn't had many close relationships with non-Jews until after my divorce. I grew up on Long Island, stayed in New York for college, and married a Jewish man. As an only child, especially an only Jewish child, I had felt the burden of expectation. Tim's family was nothing like that. While I often lamented growing up feeling as if someone were living through me (having a Jewish mother is akin to having a Siamese twin who's older), Tim lamented the opposite: His family never encouraged him to be a doctor, nor even to go to college. While both his parents had occasionally expressed regret at not having had an education, it was seeing them struggle that spurred Tim into becoming a professional. (He always loved science, and assumed he'd be some kind of researcher, but found that he also enjoyed interacting with people, hence his decision to become a doctor.) Of course, Tim's family wanted him to succeed, but after generations of rural poverty, it was programmed into their DNA to expect him to fail and they only hoped to spare him that pain. Failure—in fact, anything less than greatness—is just not an option for a Jewish child, even if that necessitates certain fabrications.

When my cousin in her thirties announced she was finally getting married, her very Orthodox family rejoiced. So did I. I knew how much she wanted children.

"What's her fiancé do?" I asked my mother.

"Oh, he's in electronics," she replied with a wave of her hand. I found out later that being "in electronics" meant he was a counter boy at 47th Street Photo.

Not that it mattered to me. It's just that I was so used to the pressure to succeed, to strive, to get degrees (another cousin, a rabbi yet, has seven—including an M.D. and two Ph.D.s) that, as maddening as Tim found his family's attitude, I found it liberating. Through Tim, I felt a kinship with people who had always seemed "other." And connecting so deeply outside my comfort zone allowed me to separate, just enough, from the parts of my own upbringing I found suffocating. (Little did I know this year would also make me feel a kinship with another group, one I never even knew existed—"RV people.") It's a testament to Tim that my parents accept and love him as much as they do. They call him the Goy Wonder.

As the boys played with the door lock, I lay awake—again. I was too wound up to sleep, even after days of sleep deprivation. All we had been through since leaving Boulder, not to mention that it was dawning on me how drastic my change in lifestyle was to be for the year, left me strung out, on edge, and way too wired. With only a couple of hours to nap before Dorothy's birthday brunch, I was also desperate. I sat on the floor of the kitchen and perused the liquor cabinet. My exhaustion precluded shaking ingredients into a martini. I needed to figure out what would taste acceptable without flourishes. I spied my prize.

"Ah, Frangelico! Come here, my nutty little friar friend," I cooed. I had that monk unfrocked so fast, he didn't know what was sucking the life out of him. I drank the sweet, hazelnut nectar straight out of the bottle, then grabbed his chocolaty, if misnamed buddy crème de cacao (who's not creamy at all. Why is that?) with my other hand, gulping it down as a chaser. Tim walked in.

"What are you doing?" he exclaimed, looking at his watch. I'm not a big drinker. I'll have a cocktail on the weekends, maybe a glass of wine with dinner then, too, but that's about it. Here it was, barely noon on a Sunday, and I was well on the road to getting soused. *On the road. Oh, God. Better have another.*

"Honey," Tim said gently, prying my hands loose from my new best friends. "I am really sorry for dragging you on this trip. This whole bus thing was my idea. I can't believe I'm putting you through all this. Say the word and we stop." I looked up at my husband, his face a mixture of concern and hope. He does so much for me—everything, in fact. I'd always felt the unevenness of it all, not that he ever complained (or that I ever wanted it to change). But now, this was something he desperately desired. It seemed the least I could do.

"Look, it's your dream, but I don't blame you. I did agree to it. And," I lied, "I'm not ready to quit just yet." He gave me a grateful hug.

This first leg of our trip was proving even more stressful to Tim than to me. Dorothy wasn't doing all that well. Although they spoke regularly on the phone, Tim hadn't seen her in about a year, and in person, the difference was startling. We knew she was getting more forgetful, but it was much easier for her to hide the extent of her decline when interacting long-distance.

Spending time with her in Reno, however, it quickly became obvious: Her house was in disarray. Bread and jelly sat by themselves in the otherwise empty fridge. She was confused by the dishwasher. During her birthday brunch, she seemed anxious and uncomfortable around that many people, even though we were all family. (Including not only her three sons and their spouses, but her eight grandchildren and their significant others and kids.) Even more disconcerting, she didn't really seem to understand why we were all there.

Tim and his brothers stayed by her side all during the meal, and she did seem to enjoy herself after a little while. The rest of us did as well. I particularly delighted in noting that one of her great-grandchildren, an adorable three-year-old named Ileana, wore a lovely blue satin frock for the occasion. I was even more impressed, however, when she chose a perfectly matching balloon to take home. Now, there's a girl who knows how to accessorize.

One of Tim's brothers offered to have Dorothy come live with him and his family. She would have none of it. We offered to have an aide come stay with her. She would have none of that, either. But Tim was able to convince her to at least see an attorney with him, so when the time came, he could be appointed guardian. For now, however, we couldn't force her to stop living on her own. With a son and several grandkids in town, someone would at least be looking in on her every day.

Tim had always been close to his mom. For many years, after his parents divorced when he was thirteen and his much older brothers moved out, it was the two of them against the world. Now there was no escaping that she was in trouble and there was very little he could do—that she would let him do—about it.

Although Project Nerd sure tried: He cleaned her house and even rented a carpet shampooer, bought her groceries and clothes, did the laundry, and easily found a host of repairs that needed to be done.

None of it made him feel any better about leaving her like that when the time came for us to go.

As we prepared to depart Reno for New Mexico, Tim procrastinated. I figured he was just hesitant to leave Dorothy, but in addition to that, he finally admitted he was wary of the next disaster down the road. An insecure driver behind the wheel of twenty tons of bus is not a good thing. I tried to console him.

"I know," he said. "Nothing's going to happen." An irrational bus driver is even worse than an insecure one.

Once we got on the highway again, Tim relaxed as he always did while driving. He loves anything with a motor, particularly old cars; he thoroughly enjoys tinkering with them, driving them (when they work), even cleaning them. For me, a car is just a means to an end.

When we first dated, I had a ten-year-old "shit blue" (as Tim dubbed it) Toyota. It was my first car. I had gotten a deal on it from the lot (why no one else wanted it, I'll never understand), and I couldn't have been happier. It was reliable and got me where I needed to go.

"At least let me clean the thing!" Tim begged.

"Why bother? I don't care and you never ride in it. We always go in your Corvette, which, I might add," I pointedly informed him, "is ten years older than my car." He rolled his eyes.

"At least let me change the oil for you."

"What oil?" His eyes stopped in mid-roll.

"You've never changed the oil? You've had that thing for nearly two years!" I shrugged.

"I don't know what you're talking about. It runs on gas, not oil." The very next day, he was under my car doing the oil change thing. It looked like a crappy job, so I offered to do his laundry.

Growing up a Princess, I had never learned to do laundry. As an adult, I taught myself. And as a big proponent of not wasting energy (mine, not the electric company's), I figured it was good enough to throw everything in together on cold. Worked for me. Unfortunately for Tim, that particular load included his favorite baseball shirt—and my new red blouse. As we sorted together afterwards, he surveyed the damage, grumbling, "No wonder all your underwear is pink." That was the last load I ever did.

On the drive out of Reno, Shula spent the entire day sitting in the buddy seat with me. It wasn't that she'd suddenly gotten courageous, but rather we had decided to keep the door to the bedroom shut (we really liked our new mattress). As soon as the engine started to rumble, she climbed up on my lap and dug her face in against my stomach. See no evil, hear no evil, be no evil, I guess. Occasionally, she'd lift a terrified eye in my direction for a quick, accusatory glare.

"Looks like she's saying, 'Mommy! Make the nightmare stop!'" Tim said. But I couldn't wake her—I was sharing the same bad dream. After a little while, I actually thought she was purring, but soon realized the "purr" was coming from her haunches. Trembling was more like it.

Miles and Morty, on the other hand, seemed perfectly content hanging out together on the love seat. I started thinking that maybe there was some bus-related weakness on the double X chromosome, especially as we continued onto Carlsbad and a new problem arose: bus phobia.

On the slightest downhill, I'd try to mind-meld with Tim, to get him to put on the engine brake, my foot stomping on air. At every turn, I'd clutch the seat, anticipating a rollover. At every dip in the road, I'd hold my breath, listening for the sound of bending steel, a portent of our imminent, albeit mercifully swift, midsectioning. It didn't help that the glasses in the wine rack clinked. *What was I afraid of?* I kept asking myself. The answer was always the same: careening off the road amidst the sound of our belongings crashing. I didn't even get so far as to imagine my own or anyone else's demise. It was the careening and the crashing. Careening and crashing. Phobias aren't rational.

On a particularly hilly, winding, and dipping road, I became particularly scared and particularly quiet. As a good shrink, Tim noticed.

"What's wrong, honey?" he asked.

"Nothing." I realized I'd better start talking about something, anything, before he caught on. Just then, we happened to pass a highway sign announcing the number of miles to Albuquerque. Without even thinking, I launched into a rousing rendition of that old Partridge Family hit:

Point me . . . yee
In the direction of
Albuquerque-e-e-e . . .

And, then, with a bit too much feeling:

I want to go home.
I need to get ho-o-o-ome.

Sometimes, a song is just a song. Not in this case. By the end of that line, I was sobbing.

"What is wrong?" he asked again, more insistent. I mulled over my response. I've always found that it's just not worth keeping things from my husband, for not only does he eventually find out, but I also always somehow feel better after confiding in him. I guess that's why he had such a busy psychiatric practice. Yet this appeared to be a special case; telling him I was terrified of riding in the bus, *while he was driving the bus,* did not seem like a particularly good plan. On the other hand, he knew something was wrong, and keeping it from him would let his imagination run wild, although how he could possibly think something worse was beyond me. I took a deep breath and plunged in.

"OK. Look," I began. "I can tell you what's wrong, if you really think you want to know what's wrong, but if you don't," I breathlessly continued, "you should tell me right now, because I don't really have to tell you. Especially while you're driving." After an introduction like that, how else could he respond but "Tell me, already!"

"Fine," I said, continuing in a rush of words, "It's not that I don't trust your driving. You're a great driver. It's just that people are idiots!" I never for an instant included my idiotic self in that assertion. "What if someone makes a sudden stop? What if we hit an elk? What if the brakes go out? I keep imagining us careening over the edge of the road. I don't even imagine the dying part, just the careening. The screeching of tires, the shattering of glass. But, most of all, the careening. The CAREENING. I can't take it anymore!" He gave me an incredulous look. I nearly lost it.

"HEY! Hey, driver! Eyes on the road! You're getting too close to that car!"

"And to think, I almost bought a system with radar," he said. I ignored his comment.

"What about the overpasses! And the WMD?"

"What WMD?" he asked, exasperated.

"Exactly!" I cried, triumphant. "The government lied about WMD, they could lie about the overpasses! How do we know they're as tall as they say? Whenever we go under one, I keep thinking, 'It's going to sheer our heads clean off!' "

"I can't believe it!" Tim exclaimed. "You're phobic about the bus." So much for making me feel better. I guess he gave at the office. I certainly didn't need a shrink to tell me I was phobic, especially when his solution was to pull over to a deserted parking lot so I could learn to drive the thing, to "feel its power." *Yeah, maybe in my next life.* Just my luck, I'll come back as John Madden's wife.

Before the bus had even been converted, Tim asked if I'd want to drive the thing.

"Are you insane?" I asked. He couldn't understand why I

wouldn't at least give it a try, but he also couldn't hide his plea-sure: Not only did he love to drive, but he didn't particularly like when I did. Whenever we went anywhere, he always drove and, inevitably, would comment on some cockamamie maneuver by some other driver.

"Look at that!" he'd exclaim. Then, on hearing my noncom-mittal "Hmm," he'd shoot me a sideways glance.

"You don't do that, do you?"

"Uh . . . kind of . . ." was the most I might allow. Tim was only too thrilled I didn't want to drive the bus. I even started a blog on our journey to keep our friends and family apprised of our whereabouts and called it "Leave the Driving to Him."

Although I remained fearful the rest of our trip to the camp-ground, the welcome sign outside a small town in New Mex-ico did manage to bring a smile to my face: "Portales, home of 12,000 nice people and 2 or 3 grouches." Once we landed in Carlsbad, we toured the caverns and stayed for the evening flight of hundreds of thousands of Mexican free-tailed bats. I didn't even scream as they spiraled out of the cave. I guess that's one plus of my newfound bus terror: Even a phobic's gotta prioritize.

I calmed down after several days spent safely docked, until Tim decided to fire up the stereo for the first time and couldn't get enough bass. He thought perhaps it had to be adjusted through the TV, and lowered the 42-inch flat screen from its tucked perch in the ceiling . . . right onto the only ever so slightly ajar stereo doors. They and their glass inserts cracked into hundreds of splinters. I should know; I was still pulling shards out of my feet when we got home.

The next day, he decided to tackle doing laundry in our Comb-o-matic 6200, an unholy joining together of a washer and dryer into one space-saving unit. Up until now, this mutant machine had slumbered in our closet, awaiting animation from its first jolt of 110 current. I cringed as he got out the instructions for the Frankensudser.

"Don't worry, honey," Tim reassured me. "What's the worst that can go wrong?"

"Flood? Locusts? Pestilence? And for that matter, rioting townspeople?" I offered. He started perusing the manual.

"Christ! This isn't a washer-dryer. It's the control panel to the space shuttle!" I relaxed, figuring it would take a while for anything to implode, pondering the relative horrors of a lumbering nineteenth-century monster who couldn't squeeze through our side aisle versus the malevolent machinations of an artificial intelligence wrought by some evil genius with a cleanliness fetish. My reverie was soon interrupted.

"OUCH!" While probing around the machine, Tim hit his lip. It was bleeding. I guess HAL didn't feel like washing clothes just then.

Soon we had a name for yet another cabinet-dwelling computer: "the bitch." She was a system Vanture had installed, but we hadn't paid any attention to. Until now.

"Alert!" she'd squawk. "Fresh water system, three-quarters . . . gray water system, seven-eighths." She apparently lived in the kitchen, along with all the master controls for the bus. Tim and I dubbed her "the bitch" because she never said anything really useful, like "Alert! Front door about to fly open!" Or, "Alert! Cat about to pee in bed!" Or more useful still, "Alert! This bus thing is the stupidest idea you've ever had! Abort! Abort!" Within a few days, after we realized that the pronouncements she did make weren't even true—i.e., we had far less fresh water than she said we did—we started calling her "the lying bitch."

Tim, Miles, Shula, Morty, the lying bitch, HAL, and I settled into a routine while parked in Carlsbad for the week. I would do insurance reviews and write during the day (my blog and screenwriting, which I had taken up a few years before), while Tim did paperwork to close out his practice, some bus or Jeep maintenance, or hiked with the dog. We'd rendezvous late in the afternoon and do something together: a walk or a bike ride, a swim or a trip into town. Afterwards, we'd have happy hour. Tim had discovered some local beer, and back in my pink designer tracksuit, I loaded up my fairy godmother (which, I understand, some people refer to as a "martini shaker") and, in a silvery flash or two, was transformed into a Princess once again. We'd drink, have some snacks, sit on lawn chairs near our rig, Miles lying by our sides, and watch the sunset. It was always so spectacular that I started bringing out my camera and discovered a new passion—photography. I found myself actually getting my butt off the chair, even lying on the grass to get the perfect shot. Tim enjoyed watching me enjoy my new hobby.

"I've never seen you so active!" he marveled. "And outside to boot!"

After the sun set, we'd cook . . . er, thaw dinner. Then, sit inside our new home and talk. It didn't even matter what we talked about: sights we'd seen that day, what we were going to do the next, even wondering what friends at home were up to. I was reminded of that first "date" in the bar, talking for hours and hours about who knows what, just feeling close and laughing with one another. Spending time this way, without any of the distractions I used to consider essential (TV, going out to fancy restaurants, wearing high-end clothes) made me start questioning just how essential they were.

I quickly pushed those thoughts aside.

But then, I noticed Tim mellowing. He started taking pleasure in little things. We had splurged (of course) on a new set of dishes for the bus, one with a travel theme, each plate depicting a different place (Mount Rushmore, San Francisco, even a spaceship on the moon). As I watched Tim set the table for dinner each night, I could see his boyish delight as he discovered where we would be dining next. And I couldn't help it. I thought about downsizing, again.

And quickly made myself another martini to forget all about it.

The days and nights passed pleasantly. At home, we would have watched a network evening news show while eating dinner, then both worked for a couple of hours before watching some other show before bed. It seemed Peter had done us one good turn by screwing up the TV. Cocooned in our own little steel and fiberglass world, it finally felt . . . right.

Until we started moving again.

Chapter Three

QUEEN OF THE ZARCONS

Hurlatini

1 part rum
2 parts Midori
1 splash pineapple juice
1 splash sweet 'n' sour
1 white-knuckled squeeze of lime

Pound martini shaker against emergency exit until window breaks or ingredients sufficiently mixed for tasty self-medication.

On July 1, we began the next leg of our meltdown cruise, sallying from the serenity of Carlsbad to the surreal of Roswell, New Mexico, for the annual UFO Festival. I had first heard of the festival from the short-lived WB series *Roswell*, about a group of stylish alien teens trying to keep their otherworldly identities secret from government agencies eager to dissect them, while still managing to look fabulous for prom. (I'm a sucker for teen dramas, but I'm not embarrassed by that fact at all: Since I write screenplays, it's easy to rationalize it as "working.") Tim and I had both eagerly anticipated the festival as a rare opportunity to observe weirdness recreationally, without the expectation that we do anything about it. Once there, however, we quickly felt compelled to unlearn years of professional practice making eye contact with people.

We had tickets for the UFO Festival concert (Willie Nelson was headlining. You don't suppose . . . ?), so stayed at its venue, the Eastern New Mexico State Fairgrounds, which provides RV hookups "around back, by the swine barn." *Oh, Princess from the Island of Long, how far hast thou fallen?*

As we rolled in on the bus, everyone at the fairgrounds—campers, staff, and cowboys alike—stood on their feet, waving at us with what can only be described as stares of reverence. We were used to the "celebrity" treatment, but this was a bit much. It was only when we parked, got out, and were approached by several people who asked, "Is Willie in there?" that we realized what all the fuss was about. I pulled Tim aside, managing to murmur to him while keeping a Stepford-like serenity on my face, "If we say no, they're liable to turn ugly."

"What do you suggest?" he whispered back.

"Let's tell 'em Willie's sleeping, but we can get them his autograph for five dollars apiece," I replied, opting for the practical. Tim shook his head, ever opting for the plausible and walked back to the crowd to explain.

"We'll say it's for Farm Aid!" I called after him weakly. *Guess we won't be enjoying diesel on Willie this trip.*

In the end, we spent only one day being assimilated into the UFO fold (hold the anal probe, thank you), as a little seemed to go a long way. The main events took place at the Roswell

Civic Center, where, in the exhibition hall, a dozen or so authors wearing plasticine smiles congregated to hawk their books. One such scribe, as detailed in the conference brochure, "retired early to a mountaintop in southern Arizona to explore his relationship with reality." As shrinks, Tim and I could have spared him the damage wrought on his 401K from early retirement by pointing out that if reality is something you have to explore your relationship with, the two of you probably went through a messy divorce long ago.

We strolled around the floor, passing various booths, and soon found ourselves at one manned by a couple, where I made the mistake of making eye contact with the wife. She immediately launched into her well-practiced—some might even say android-like—spiel.

"My husband"—she nodded over at her partner, whose wild-eyed look I'd seen before in many a padded room—"kept his abduction from me for eighteen years. He never talked about it with anyone, even though *they* didn't tell him he had to keep it a secret," she confided, woman to woman, as if I could not help but concur with the punishment she undoubtedly meted out for such a marital infraction. Well, actually I could. Concur, I mean. Infractions are infractions, after all, especially when committed by husbands. But then, she continued, picking up his tome, "This book is in large print for older people." *Saleswoman of the Year, this one.* Then, "And I made him take all the profanity out so it's suitable for kids." Now she'd really lost me. Fortunately, a true believer arrived and distracted her with a question while I made my escape.

"Why didn't you rescue me?" I hissed at Tim accusingly.

He was just as fierce back. "Don't you be making eye contact with these people," he admonished.

We stayed to hear a lecture by the "original civilian investigator of the Roswell incident," who actually put forth an intriguing theory as to why aliens have returned to our planet so often to take so many of our citizens: We're someone's crop. Does make you stop and think now, doesn't it?

We left New Mexico none too soon, for after spending only a few days in the Southwest (and especially after buying my first cowboy hat—well, I needed something to wear to Willie's concert), I started speaking with a distinct twang. Now I know what got into Madonna after she moved to London.

Once back on the road, I couldn't help noting again how Tim seemed mellower, as if he were starting to "detox" from his many years of medical director and patient care duties. His boyishness and sense of fun came back in full force. One day, we took a break from a long drive at an empty highway rest stop that had a grassy picnic area with shaded benches and room for the dog to run. As we ate our sandwiches, we talked, threw the ball to Miles, and watched the traffic go by. Just as we were about to get back on the road, Tim belched, then farted.

"All systems go!" he cackled. That's my Timmy.

The rest of the trip to our next campsite was uneventful. Tim even managed to navigate through aggressive rush-hour traffic without skipping a beat, although unfortunately for my bus phobia, showed me his shaking hands once we stopped. He also recounted how, during his bus driving lessons with an RTD instructor, they had encountered heavy traffic on the freeway. The instructor told him to take an upcoming left-hand exit, but Tim balked. She said that was fine, but "sometimes you just have to change lanes." Now it was hearing that refrain, playing over and over in his head, that got him through. (As did remembering that if cars wouldn't let him in, just allowing the bus to drift over caused a simply divine effect, as if magically opening up a space, like the parting of the Red Sea.)

When we stopped for the night at an RV park in the desert, we high-fived each other, exclaiming, "Another leg without a disaster!" We spoke too soon. It was over a hundred degrees and when we plugged into shore power, we got none. We tried to fire up the generator, but after an eight-hour drive, it was over-heated. So were we. So were Miles, Morty, and Shula. The main-tenance guy for the campground came by and said the entire line of campers went down as soon as we hooked in. We don't know what he did, but in about a half hour, it was fixed. He came back and assured us he would monitor the problem. Good thing. The power only lasted another five minutes.

I called the office and got us moved to a different site. As we made our way to our new spot, everyone came out of their rigs, shooting us the same looks obese people get when boarding air-planes. Fortunately, we were able to plug in without incident.

We soon discovered another heat-inspired near calamity: Since the RV park was nearly all asphalt, the ground was way too hot for Miles's paws. So, rather than walk to the dog walk area, Tim lifted the poodle out of the bus, deposited him directly into the Jeep, and drove him over to the designated grass whenever it was potty time. Frankly, Miles seemed to enjoy the royal treat-ment. I could relate. I tried to get Tim to carry me into the Jeep as well, but it's hard to get good liveried help these days.

The next morning, we headed to Tim's father's house in rural Arkansas—Van Buren to be exact—the last stop of our three-week meltdown cruise. He and his dad had had their struggles; Tim always felt abandoned by Bob after his parents divorced. For decades, he and his father spoke to each other by phone three times a year and no more, on their birthdays and Christmas. Tim had a similar relationship with one of his half brothers, although they spoke three times less a year.

I could never understand just cutting someone off like that, no matter how upset you were with him, and eventually chalked it up to cultural differences: Apparently, in WASP families, if you don't get along with someone, you have as little to do with them as possible. In Jewish families, if you don't get along with someone, you move next door to make them as miserable as possible.

As Bob got older, he reached out more to his only child, but Tim still felt awkward with the whole situation. Being too busy with work to visit became a convenient excuse, as much to Bob as to himself. After Bob got ill with cancer a few years back, however, Tim tried to make more of an effort even though work continued to remain an obstacle, like it was to nearly everything in his life, taking up most of his time. Now, at least for the year, we had nothing but time. Hence, the decidedly meandering and indirect route of our meltdown cruise: Colorado, Nevada, New Mexico, and now Arkansas.

This leg, however, would prove the most challenging yet.

We made the mistake of following MapQuest directions to Bob's house. The Internet instructions *seemed* easy enough, but what we soon learned about MapQuest is that it gives the most direct route—not necessarily the most drivable one. When we got off the highway several miles from Bob's house, the roads kept getting smaller and smaller. Soon we were traveling over tiny, one-lane bridges perched precariously over creek beds. Then we passed a "no trucks" sign.

"We should turn back!" I protested.

"We're not a truck," Tim blithely responded. "Besides, there's no place to turn around." He was right. We had no choice but to continue. We arrived at a bridge with the sign "Limit 30 Tons."

"How many are we?" I cried, reeling with bus phobia.

"Twenty," he replied. "Don't worry." We made it over that bridge, only to quickly come to another, this time with the sign "Limit 13 Tons." That was all I needed to turn my reel into a full-fledged centrifuge; I could feel my lunch quickly separating itself from my intestinal tract.

"WE'RE TWENTY TONS! WE'RE TWENTY TONS!" I screamed, contorting to grab something, anything to steady myself, even as my eyes remained glued to the road. That there are no armrests turns out to be a serious design flaw when the buddy seat is inhabited by a bus phobic.

"Don't worry," Tim assured me, a manic gleam in his eyes as he barreled onward. "It's too small for us to have all three axles on at the same time." He hit the gas and we lurched to the other side. Then we came to an obstacle that would even have lent the *Simpsons'* Otto pause: a washed-out culvert. Tim stopped the bus, climbed down, and inspected the impasse firsthand.

"We need to back up," I moaned weakly. The lack of airsickness bags was another huge design flaw. That this was probably due to the absence of a seatback in front of me was little comfort. "We won't make it."

"I might agree," Tim said, "but we still can't turn around." He was right again, of course. We were on a single-lane road, with no room to park the Jeep, let alone turn the bus around. Predictably for Tim, rather than get a tad out of sorts like me (OK, maybe I should just go with the streamlined "hysterical" here), this was just one more technical puzzle to solve. Not to say, however, that my husband wasn't mightily embarrassed by the entire incident. Bob had, after all, offered to give us directions, but Tim demurred, saying, "We'll be fine. We've got a computer!"

After he positioned himself back behind the wheel, Tim gingerly maneuvered us through the stream and got us on a larger road. Then he promptly dashed right by his father's house, completely missing the place. This occasioned a frantic call to our cell phone.

"Was that you? There's no place to turn around where you're headed!" Indeed, there wasn't. We unhooked the Jeep, Tim managed to find a spot to do a K-turn, and I followed him back to the house. I think I kissed the ground when we arrived, but I can't be sure: It's all a blur, in large part due to the green-tinged drink I invented to commemorate the occasion, the Hurlatini. Bob and his wife, Frances, had a good laugh when they heard about our ridiculous route.

"We won't even drive our cars that way!" Bob informed us.

Tim parked the bus on Bob and Frances's front lawn. The first evening, as we said goodnight and left the house to go to bed in the bus, Frances, who is one of the kindest souls on the planet, eyed my capri pants and exclaimed, "You better watch out or the chiggers'll git you!" I couldn't believe my ears. This woman I had thought so lovely was nothing more than a disgusting racist! My eyes grew wide and I was just about to open my mouth even wider to allow some choice words to escape, when she grabbed a small aerosol can and offered it to me. Now I was stupefied into silence. Did she really expect me to mace these . . . these . . . Well. I was not about to use the C-word. Seeing my expression, Frances repeated her admonition slowly, as if I had ridden into town on a short bus.

"The . . . chiggers! The . . . chiggers . . . 'll . . . git . . . you!" she insisted. I examined the can. Bug spray. Chiggers, I soon learned, are nearly microscopic dots of torture that lie in wait in grass to burrow under your skin, causing itching and unsightly blemishes. If I'd had jurisdiction, I surely would have banished them from this strange kingdom.

While we were on Bob's farm, I asked to drive the tractor. I may not have been willing to get behind the wheel of my husband's precious Prevost, as he thought I should, but at least I could attempt to partially counter my bus phobia by driving some type of big rig. Bob readily obliged after being assured by his son that a high entertainment value could be had. I was not daunted, but rather filed Tim's glee away on the complaint form for the mythical home office I'd concocted in my head, devised on our first day out, at about the time the door flew open for the third time, in order not to feel we were so very out there, so totally on our own. Now "insulting passenger" joined "nearly killed passenger," "nearly killed passenger," and "nearly killed passenger." Maybe they'd send a replacement driver.

Poor Bob must never have been in the presence of royalty before, as he actually began the process by showing me the clutch and seven-speed pattern with high-low differential. As usual, I was possibly able, though most definitely unwilling, to comprehend mechanical gadgets and simply asked, "Don't you have anything with an automatic?" He looked at me as if calculating the increase in insurance premium I was about to cost him. But donning my new cowboy hat (not to mention adorable black-and-white cowboy boots and designer jeans), I drove the thing and not only didn't stall it once, but moseyed across the length of the cow pasture and back with nary an injury to man or beast. To Bob and his son's dual expressions of amazement (if not disappointment) upon my return, I simply imparted the obvious lesson that should have been gleaned by those foolish menfolk:

A Princess can do anything she puts her mind to—provided she's wearing the right outfit.

Arkansas left me in a state of perpetual moaning, à la the Hindenburg disaster: "Oh, the humidity!" The resulting hair debacle was on an order of magnitude neither Tim nor I had seen since almost a decade earlier, when, after a horrendous perm, I'd immediately gone swimming in a highly chlorinated pool in an even more highly misguided attempt to commit permacide.

It had been raining in Van Buren for the past week (the same rains that had washed out the narrow roads on our way there), causing a far worse problem than that to my coif. Turns out, parking in Bob and Frances's front yard was probably not the brightest idea: We started sinking. By our second day, we were pitching distinctly starboard. Since we had no intention of touching the stereo electronics again anytime soon, my *Titanic* CD was out of the question. I simply had to provide the illustrative background music myself and sang "Nearer My God to Thee," in my best falsetto, every chance I got, alternating with an even more overwrought rendition than the original "My Heart Will Go On." I still have a mark on my chest from the climactic thumping part. Where was Celine Dion when I needed her?

One morning, we were awakened by Frances banging on the bus door.

"Tim! Tim!" she cried. "Come quick!" We both assumed something terrible had happened to Bob.

"Cousin JT's been run'd over by the tractor!"

Seventy-something Cousin JT, who lived down the road a piece, had been tinkering with the dead engine on his tractor when he reckoned (as Tim later explained in excruciating and painstaking detail) he'd take a screwdriver to touch across its battery's poles to see if it would spark. It did, although he hadn't counted on simultaneously hot-wiring the engine—especially with him standing in front of it. Fortunately for Cousin JT, the same rains that had so vexed my hair and our bus's equilibrium were precisely what saved his life, for as he was mowed down, the soft earth underneath his body gave just enough to keep him just enough alive. It was his head, however, that was fixin' to prove his undoing: He refused to go to the hospital. Naturally then, Bob and Frances wanted the doctor in the house to make a house call. *OK. I guess my husband the psychiatrist can ask JT how he feels about his near-death experience.* Before I even finished the thought, Tim dashed out the door.

During the four hours before he returned, it started to pour. Now the bus was seriously listing. Would we ever be able to get out? Did the local AAA have a flatbed truck to rescue us with? Was there even a local AAA here in Van Buren, Arkansas? Would the entire earth swallow us whole, and if it did, how would I rescue the pets? I decided that with Tim AWOL, I was acting captain and had to go down with our ship of fools. The only thing to do, then, was huddle under the covers with Shula, contemplating our murky demise.

Shula, our beautiful seal-point Balinese with Tim's intense blue eyes (proving paternity, I often said), could surely be counted on whenever cowering was called for. We had always explained her skittishness away with "Well, we got her for her looks." I maintained that Shula's beauty was more of a curse than a blessing, as if she knew she could get by in life just being stunning, rather than bothering to develop a personality. (Or maybe it was I who was being catty, remembering how I envied all the gorgeous cheerleaders in high school.) In any event, Shula's a cat only a mother could love.

She didn't get that way just because best friends Morty and Miles constantly ganged up on her (Morty because he could, Miles because he just wanted to gum her a little). No, from the moment we rescued Shula from under an acquaintance's double-wide and she buried her head in my lap for the entire ride home, she's proved herself a neurotic victim. Before our bus trip, all our friends (well, at least the ones who had actually ever seen her) asked with incredulity, "You're not taking Shula, are you?" We felt she could be just as miserable on the bus as she was off it. You gotta be tough to survive in our dysfunctional little furry family.

Morty, of course, had no problem at all in the "be tough" department. Nothing fazed him. If Tim wanted to vacuum, he had to move that cat. Unlike Shula, Morty was never shy about anything, especially his own presence. Upon entering a room (including the bedroom while we slept), he'd let out a series of loud MEOWs, as if he were not a mere mutt of uncertain parentage rescued from the pound, but royalty being hugely inconvenienced by having to announce his own entrance. Whenever Tim wanted affection from me, he'd learned to say, "Pretend I'm Morty." He was not alone. Everyone in the house considered me Morty's bitch, for, as in a prison yard (which, in effect, our house had become for our indoor cats), if Morty saw Shula in my lap, he calmly caught her eye, causing her to immediately skulk away, terrified. He would then resume whatever he was doing; he didn't particularly want me at that moment. He just wanted the other inmates to know: That's *my* bitch.

Although I adore my poodle, Miles has always made it clear to me why I am a cat person; he's just so darn happy—including first thing in the morning. (I am much more in tune with felines, whose initial inclination on being awakened is not to snap to with a "Well, well! What fascinating activity is in store for us, today?" but reluctantly relinquish somnolence with an even more snarky version of what has always been my own personal battle cry: "What do you want from me?") As a result, Miles blithely follows Tim everywhere. Clearly my husband is a deity in the poodle universe. I guess I'd be that happy too, even first thing in the morning, if I knew I got to sniff God's butt all day.

As I turned off the bedroom lights (the better for Shula and I to cower), lightning struck. I remembered the large extension cord plugging the bus into an outside outlet, allowing us the electricity to run our air-conditioning, lights, appliances, computer, etc. Might we be electrocuted before we were even submerged? It seemed as if Sunnydale's Hellmouth (yet another favorite teen drama—*Buffy the Vampire Slayer*) had opened a franchise in Van Buren, Arkansas, trying to reclaim a lost member to the fold— our very own Hellbus. Unto every generation, a pathetic Princess who listens to her husband's idiotic plan is born. *Oh, Buffy, where are you when I need you?*

Meanwhile, Tim was facing a near-death experience of his own, as Frances was racing him in her Lincoln Town Car over narrow, winding, backcountry roads, hitting 70 mph to get to Cousin JT's house. On arrival, Tim found Cousin JT covered in sweat, struggling for breath, wearing only his briefs and an open bathrobe, sitting in his favorite recliner, swearing to anyone who would listen, "I'll be OK if I can just set a spell."

Living in the land of chiggers evidently makes you tough.

Of course, Cousin JT proved no match for Tim's patented

powers of persuasion, although fortunately in this case, Tim used those powers for good, rather than evil. JT agreed to go to the hospital and just in time; with two punctured lungs, four broken ribs, and a broken clavicle, he ended up spending three weeks in the ICU.

But first, they had to get him there. With Bob at the wheel, trying to both speed down the highway yet slow down for bumps (because they caused JT to gasp for breath as though each one would be his last), they started to take the exit for the nearest hospital, when JT got even more agitated, explaining "that place" had done him wrong when his wife had been a patient there a few years before. As he so eloquently put it, given the circumstances, "I—GASP!—won't—GASP!—go there!" Not wanting to agitate him even more, Bob swerved back onto the freeway for an additional fifteen-minute drive to the next, more acceptable facility.

Tim told Bob to pull in where it said, "EMERGENCY VEHICLES ONLY," assuring his father that this was, indeed, an emergency. He then instructed Bob to remain in the car with Cousin JT, so that Tim himself could do the talking. As Tim leapt from the car, he knew he didn't have much time to convey the gravity of the situation and rehearsed all the medical jargon he was going to use: how an elderly white male had suffered blunt-force trauma to his abdomen and chest and appeared to have a pneumothorax. Tim burst through the emergency room doors and wound up face to face with the triage nurse. She glanced at him wearily and he could see behind her the waiting room teeming with people who had upset stomachs and colds. He looked back at the woman, assumed his best "I'm a doctor" stance, and blurted out, "Cousin JT's been run'd over by the tractor!"

Her eyes got wide as hubcaps, for he had unknowingly spoken exactly the right language to get her attention.

"Nooooo!" she cried.

"Yeeeees!" he answered. She grabbed a gurney and an attendant, and they all raced to the car.

Later that day, as we drove into town for a quick errand, Tim tried to explain to his father the folly of asking a psychiatrist to make a house call during a medical emergency and broke out his best Dr. McCoy: "Damn it, Bob! I'm a psychiatrist, not a real doctor!" Something told me Bob had never seen a *Star Trek* episode. On the other hand, Bob did know the correct, non-MapQuest route out of town, and since we were leaving in a few days, he showed us how to go. Unfortunately, there was construction, considerably narrowing the two-lane road. Worse, it had large, concrete masses on either side, which Tim helpfully informed me were "Jersey barriers." Naming them didn't ease my apprehension.

"Are you sure we'll fit?" I kept asking Tim. Yes, yes, he kept trying to reassure me.

"But look how little room there is! What if you hit a—"

Finally, he interrupted with an exasperated "Maybe we can get Bob and Frances to drive you to the highway."

"Maybe we can get Bob and Frances to drive me to the airport," I retorted under my breath.

Our last night, Bob and Frances took us a few miles away to the home of Joanne and Jay. There, most Wednesday nights for the last decade, Jay and his friend Don played bluegrass. Jay, a distinguished-looking seventy-year-old, strummed a guitar and mandolin. Don, a handsome, slightly younger, lanky man with a ready, knee-slapping grin (unless he had an instrument in his hand, when he compensated for the lack of knee slapping with an even larger grin), played the guitar and banjo.

We all sat out on the deck with another neighbor couple and Joanne and Jay's two-year-old Chihuahua, Troubles, running back and forth between each of us, begging for a lap. It was obvious Troubles was female, as I'd seen this sort of grass-is-always-greener attitude often in my practice among young human women: As soon as Troubles got the lap she professed to want, she'd decide there was better lap to be had and demand to get off. Tim and I each held her many a time, knowing full well there'd be hell to pay when we got back to the bus, in the form of accusatory looks from our own animals when they figured out we'd been cheating on them.

Although during our entire visit thus far I could not understand why anyone would want to live in Van Buren, that night I found myself charmed. As we sat out on the deck, surrounded by tall, graceful trees, night fell and hummingbirds gave way to fireflies. A deer and her fawn lingered at the edge of the yard. But it was not until I was enveloped by the easy company of longtime friends that I could understand how people might want to settle here. While Tim and I enjoyed going out with other couples, it was all too often something we'd have to "schedule." It was almost as if by doing so, we were sacrificing something else—although what it was, exactly, was never clear. Our lives were so crammed with demands on our time that something we should have found pleasurable became almost another burden. I never got that sense from anyone in Van Buren.

Jay and Don played a few tunes, then let their fingers rest while everyone chatted a spell, then played some more. Don laughed at times while he strummed, presumably because he'd made a mistake, although I never did catch one. As Bob told him, "Don, if you didn't laugh, no one would know you'd hit the wrong note!" During one of their breaks, Jay talked about a cow he had with some muscle disease that made him smell real bad. Don offered that it wouldn't bother him, because he couldn't smell: His nerves had been cut during a dental surgery years before. "But," he went on with that ready grin, "there's a guy at work who can't taste or smell, so I figure I'm ahead of the game."

He came to playing late in life: At age thirty, he simply felt the call, found a teacher, and discovered he had a gift. Unfortunately, we didn't get to hear enough of that wonderful sound, as Don had to leave early to be up at 3:30 the next morning for his shift at the manufacturing plant. It seems that even more than that gift, his true talent is to understand what's important in his life; although by selling it he could make what he earns in a year at the factory, he refuses to part with his banjo because he has never heard another with as good a tone. Out of all my possessions, I could not think of one I held as dear.

As we got ready for bed that night, Tim and I talked about how much we enjoyed the evening. He remarked that it was a throwback to a simpler time, when people depended on each other for entertainment, rather than technology. I wondered which is simpler, really: relying on radio, Internet, and TV for social glue or on ourselves and each other, on our own imaginations and talents to delight and ultimately bind us together. I had been so focused on the change in lifestyle thrust *on* me by this trip, that I didn't even consider it might actually be causing changes *in* me. We hadn't even started the official journey yet, and already I was encountering ideas and experiences that were putting a chink in my designer armor of dearly held beliefs.

Surely, if I'd had even an inkling that it might cause me to change in any way, I would have protested this whole bus thing far more vigorously.

Yet, as I looked at my husband, brushing his teeth and humming one of Don's tunes, I couldn't help but think that maybe, *maybe* Tim had the right idea all along. That, perhaps, poking my head out beyond my own door once in a while might open me up to experiences that could never be as rich when passively observed in my pajamas, sitting in my favorite chair in front of the TV. Tim had, in a variety of ways, been trying to point that out for years, but just hearing the words never convinced me. Then, even more surprisingly, Tim commented that through sharing bluegrass in the woods, he got a glimpse into how I experience life, living in the moment (OK, so it's usually an indoor moment) instead of worrying about tomorrow or planning what it should bring. We realized that night, that while reveling in our differences is fun, perhaps, even after all these years, we each had something to learn from the other.

The rest of the summer was a blur of packing up the house, readying it for our renters, and putting whatever belongings we were not taking in storage. Vanture kept the bus for a while, working the bugs out—minor details like getting the door to lock, fixing the broken stereo cabinet, inducing both the lying bitch not to lie and Peter to fix the TV.

When a girl finds herself forced to live in a bus for a year, the least she can do is throw a fabulous going away party. Besides, one must always look for occasions to wear one's boa.

We and the Vanture guys invited all our friends and neighbors as well as everyone who worked on the bus. We got plenty of snacks and even more plentiful booze (these were mostly our friends, after all). Chris and John surprised us with what I think was the sweetest, albeit shortest-lasting gift we've ever received:

a case of our own "vintage" wines complete with a picture of our bus on the label.

Tim and I were busy greeting guests at the entrance to Vanture's warehouse when one of our friends came over and, a bit timidly, asked to see the bus. It was clearly visible in an adjacent garage bay, but Tim gamely shrugged and took him over for a private tour. It was only when he got to the passenger's side that Tim realized what the fellow's hesitation had been: There was a line. A long one. By then, 125 people had showed up to the party. What I found even more astounding than the sheer volume of people was that every single one of them wanted to get into the very bus that I couldn't wait to get out of.

The same friends who initially told me how crazy I was about the whole bus thing were now actually trying to be supportive in the face of the fiasco our meltdown cruise had been. There were variations of "I'm sure you'll get used to it" and "All the bugs are certainly worked out by now," sprinkled with "What an adventure!" But, seeing my hands shake and my lips quiver whenever the words "bus," "road," or, for that matter, "hi there!" were uttered, they would usually resort to leaning in close and urging, sotto voce, "Get Tim to hypnotize you."

For some reason, our neighbor Jackie seemed to share my bus phobia, even though I've never seen anything larger than a perfectly respectable van parked in front of her house. When I related my fear of overpasses, rather than try to reassure me as everyone else had, Jackie instead exclaimed, "Oh, no! Of course there's less room than the signs say! When they pave the highways, they don't take away the asphalt that's already there. They *add* to it!" I gave her a wide-eyed look and asked, "Did Bob make you live on a bus, too?" Of course, her husband never had, but Jackie's Australian, so maybe that explains something.

Chris and John had their own rock band and played occasional gigs around town. A month before the meltdown cruise, when I was not yet feeling homicidal toward my spouse about the whole thing of bus, I asked if they'd be willing to back me up if I sang a song as a surprise for Tim. They were thrilled to do something nice for my husband (he still had that effect on people), and got Kirby and Manny from their shop to play keyboard and drums, respectively. John's adorable eighteen-year-old daughter, Katie, sang backup. We practiced a couple of times and it all went well, but still, I had never sung in front of anyone before.

Chris, as lead guitarist, had arranged that when his band warmed up, he'd bring Tim and me over to say a few words to the crowd. Tim started with a hysterical monologue about building the bus and then learning to operate it, in which he thanked his driving instructor, Robin, for her gentle ways. He explained, "If I did a turn properly, she'd say, 'Nice turn. You wound up in the lane in the right position'; if I screwed up a turn, she'd say, 'Good entrance into that turn'; and if we nearly hit a lamppost, she'd say, 'Nice application of the turn signal.' "

When Tim finished, Chris handed me the microphone, and as we'd agreed, I pretended to be terribly nervous speaking in front of all those people. I hemmed and hawed so convincingly that I clearly had Tim fooled. (He told me later he started getting really anxious for me, until he remembered, "Wait a minute. My wife, shy?") Even Chris, who had been in on it all along, felt compelled to step in front of me and helpfully comment, "Just say it like I'm the only one here." *Nice ad lib, Chris. Now get out of my spotlight.*

When I determined I had made the audience so uncomfortable that no matter how I sang, it would be a relief compared to what they already endured, I grabbed the mike, turned to the band, and commanded in my best gravelly voice, "Join in anytime, boys."

To the tune of the Pointer Sisters' version of Bruce Spring-steen's "Fire":

I'm riding in your bus.
You turn on the radio.
You're pulling me close.
I scream, "EYES ON THE ROAD."
I say I don't like it,
But you know I'm a liar.
'Cause when you brake . . .
Oooooh, squeal of tires.

Late at night,
You're drivin' us home.
I say, "Park in a Wal-Mart,"
But you're in the zone.
I say I don't love bus life,
But you know I'm a liar.
'Cause when you brake . . .
Oooooh, squeal of tires.

It had a hold on you right from the start.
How could I compete with that Series 60 tart?
Live in it a year?
I said I'd never agree,
Until those four magic words . . .
In-motion satellite TV.

Ralph Kramden and Otto.
And now my Tim.
My new motto
Is "Leave the driving to him."

My words say, "HOLY SHIT WHAT HAVE WE DONE?"
But my words, they're lies.
'Cause when you brake . . .
Oooooh, squeal of tires.

Oooooh, squeal of tires.
Hot bumper over tires.
Aluminum wheels on tires.
New lug nuts with tires.
Skid marks from tires.
I like the way you're drivin' now . . . tires.
Take me home to tires.

I told friends who missed the show they could "catch it soon
at a Wal-Mart near you."

Toward the end of the evening we wrapped the "Name Our
Bus Contest." We had put up a bulletin board with small squares
of paper, explaining that whoever wanted to enter should write
down their brilliant idea for a bus name on one side and their
own on the other, tacking the bus name side up (we didn't want
the judges to be unduly influenced). After a couple of hours, Tim
and I took the bulletin board down and conferred in the Vanture
conference room. Names like "Boris" and "Fred" were quickly
discarded. We also disqualified "Paradocs," as too many people
would share the prize. Personally, I liked "Crosswalk Killer," but
Tim, who within nanoseconds of thinking up the idea for the
contest had decreed himself head judge, demurred.

It came down to my friend Sheryl's "Wheels of Justice" (Tim's
last name—Justice, not Wheels) and the eventual winner, "Princess Lines," by our friend Jane Ann, a woman who, although she
had worked with Tim for years at the hospital, obviously knows
his wife quite well. The prize? To christen the bus, of course. As

Tim put it when he announced the winner to the crowd, "Christening is obviously a Christian activity and in trying to be sensitive to my wife's Jewish heritage, I decided to be culturally aware and use Mogen David wine, or as we liked to call it when I was growing up, Mad Dog Twenty/Twenty."

After a first unsuccessful attempt (*oh, Lord, please not an omen*), Jane Ann was able to break the bottle on the front bumper. As the fortified wine ate slowly into the cement floor, Manny stared forlornly at the spot just christened and sighed, "I'm gonna have to fix that Monday."

Finally, we (OK, mainly Tim) were ready to take off for the year.

I shed many tears.

(At least I still had some left.)

Chapter Four

MOUNT POODLE

Headwater High

2 parts vodka
2 part Tuaca
2 parts lemonade
squeeze lemon

Mix ingredients in shaker. Sugar rim to delineate target. Plant feet firmly on ground, aim, and pour into glass with a high, arching, perfect stream. When you think you've finished, shake out every last drop. Feel immense relief. Don't forget to put back lid.

We had already been on a whirlwind tour, driving across nine states during the three weeks of our meltdown cruise. Now, Friday the 13th (I wasn't superstitious—yet) of August 2004, our year was to officially start. We had very few concrete plans, other than to spend Labor Day weekend with a friend of Tim's in Minneapolis, head to the Northeast for fall colors, and then stay warm in the South for the winter. After that, we thought we would travel up the West Coast before spending the following summer in Alaska. But for now, we were embarking on our first "real" trip, the official start of our yearlong full-timing it in our Prevost.

Tim could tell that even the few weeks just spent at home had done nothing to dim the memories of our meltdown cruise. (Perhaps it was my recently developed—albeit no less unfortunate for being new—facial tic.) Then there was my sanguine response when he asked if, rather than hook the Jeep up at home, I could just follow him.

"To South Dakota? Sure."

"No," he dashed my hopes with a snort, "just to the gas station. It'll be easier to hook up after we get diesel."

In spite of my apprehension about moving again (or, perhaps due to what shrinks call "counterphobic behavior," because of it), I launched into the pre-takeoff routine that had become automatic on our meltdown cruise. And although we'd never spoken about how to divvy up our respective roles, as usual, we didn't have to: Tim checked the mechanical systems (if we had been at a campground, he would also have unhooked our power, water, and sewer lines), while I played flight attendant and ensured that all the overhead (and other) bins were in their stowed and locked positions, going through each of our three "cabins" and giving every door an authoritative tap. There were quite a few bins to check and I planned on talking to my union rep about overtime.

Two days before we left, Tim parked the bus in front of our house to give us a chance to pack it with all our clothes, food, outdoor furniture (lawn chairs, table), pet supplies and provisions, maintenance equipment for any possible breakdowns, computers (laptops, printer), linens, and, it seemed, every other of our worldly possessions that we could not possibly live without for a year. Thankfully, the bus had a lot of closet and storage space in the living areas, and there was even more underneath in the bays, although two of the three were taken up with the heating/cooling systems, fresh, gray, and black water tanks, and generator.

Upon entering the bus, my buddy seat was immediately to the left, custom-made double-wide, to accommodate both the bus butt I planned on growing (I intended for my husband to learn that living one's dream could have its nightmarish aspects) as well as one or two cats sitting up front with me. Across the aisle was Tim's driver seat and behind that, a coat closet. Above the windshield was storage for all the stereo/TV equipment, and just adjacent, folded up and hidden precariously (or so it seemed to me) in the ceiling over my seat, was our 42-inch flat-panel plasma TV. A coffee table that could extend into a dining table was behind the buddy seat, with a reclining sofa on the other side. Behind the sofa was a desk (which housed the satellite Internet system) and behind that, a breakfast bar, which delineated the start of the kitchen.

For two non-cooks, that kitchen (not even counting the Blue Bahia granite) was a slight bit of overkill: side-by-side refrigerator/freezer, dishwasher drawer, combination microwave convection oven, sink, pullout pantries, pullout cutting boards, wine rack, appliance garage, and HAL, the all-in-one washer-dryer unit. Further back, a stainless steel pocket door separated the kitchen from the bathroom, which included a toilet, the twelve-hundred-dollar over-the-counter (and over-the-top) glass sink whose faucet was mounted on a stainless steel tile backsplash, and, finally, a fairly large shower (to accommodate one human washing one standard poodle), also done in stainless steel tile.

Both the sink area and shower boasted matching inlaid strips of colorful glass in blues, greens, and mauves. (The bathroom was so striking, in fact, that when I first saw it, all I could do was exclaim "Oh my God!" over and over again. The tile guy was still there, finishing up his work. I learned only later that he was upset at my outburst because he hadn't realized I was actually happy. What a poor, poor fellow, to not know what it means when a woman screams, "Oh my God!") Another pocket door led to the bedroom, with its queen-size bed over storage drawers, cabinets above, second TV, bookcase, closet, and nightstands.

All in all, just the very bare bones of what a Princess needed to survive a year on the road. How all of this was made to fit comfortably in a 102-inch-wide, 40-foot-long space (as measured on the *outside*) was truly a testament to Vanture's work.

In a fitting precursor to the paucity of planning we intended for the rest of the year, the choice of South Dakota as our first stop was dictated largely by my lifelong desire (why, I haven't a clue) to see Mount Rushmore. We found, however, that the majesty of that mountain lies in stark contrast to the road leading up to it, which impressed solely due to its vast array of kitschy Americana ("World's largest catfish!" "World's largest tin family!" "51-foot Teddy Roosevelt!"). Although we were somewhat horrified at first (Reptile Gardens! National Presidential Wax Museum! Cosmos Mystery Area!), after a while, the constant bombardment of the absurd could not help but win us over, a sort of paean to freewheeling, audacious, good old American free enterprise. We finally succumbed to a mutual weakness for crazy rides that I hoped was not a portent of disaster for the whole bus thing (I could already envision my epitaph: *She Left the Driving to Him*) when we joyfully flung ourselves down the two-thousand-foot

President's Alpine Slide upon whose parallel tracks it is absolutely forbidden to race.

Tim won.

Of course, no trip to this area could be considered complete without the obligatory put-your-head-in-a-poster-cutout-of-Mount-Rushmore-and-pretend-you're-a-president that seems to be on every street corner. In our case, it was Tim—lifting all sixty pounds of poodle, who, as always, followed our lead without hesitation, sticking his trusting, furry neck through the hole that had been the head of our first president. I swear that dog could sense the significance of the occasion, for rather than his perpetual, openmouthed, tongue-trailing grin, he shut his muzzle, got a faraway look in his eyes, and managed to appear pensive just as I snapped a picture. Perhaps he was pondering the senseless waste of Washington chopping down a perfectly good tree to lift one's leg on.

While Mount Rushmore itself did not disappoint, what we enjoyed most about our time in the land of "Great Faces, Great Places" was taking day trips in the Jeep. This started a pattern repeated throughout the year in which we'd pack a cooler with drinks, snacks, another bag with treats and water for the dog, toss it all (along with said dog himself) into the backseat and head off to explore.

Miles had always preferred riding in back, even when only one of us was in the car. We think it stemmed from his puppyhood when, for the first six months of his life, he belonged to a Boulder macrobiotic chiropractor who fed him brown rice. When the guy decided he wanted a "heartier" dog to take backcountry snow hiking with the two huskies he already owned, we jumped at the chance to snatch Miles from his bony little fingers. That very first day, Miles leapt into the back of our car (the huskies, being huskier, undoubtedly always won the front seat) and never looked back. As we absconded with our new son, feeling like we'd just orchestrated a daring rescue, I shouted at the fellow's upright skeletal remains, "Your dogs are carnivores! Deal with it!"

It was also in South Dakota we discovered our TV was finally working (although still not terribly reliably). Normally, this would have been cause for celebration or, at the very least, watching the evening news shows, but Tim and I had gotten used to not having the tube on during dinnertime. We still had happy hour outside our rig, sitting on our lounge chairs and watching the sunset with Miles. Then we'd go in, turn on the stereo (which was now working just fine), and listen to music while we ate and talked. If one of "our" songs came on, we'd even get up and dance a little, space permitting. We liked this new tradition so well, in fact, that we made it permanent and never once turned the television on during dinnertime again.

It never occurred to me that South Dakota was part of the Old West. Even after living away from New York for a quarter century, I suppose I still viewed the country like that old *New Yorker* cartoon, with The City at the center of the universe and everywhere else, well . . . everywhere else. True, Colorado considers itself part of the West, but obviously its citizens haven't looked at a map lately; one can't get much more smack-dab in the middle of the country. And while there are several historic "Western" buildings sprinkled about, there seems to be just as much of a Southwest feel (something I understand even less, geographically speaking), with many homes sporting saltillo floors, mission tile roofs, and the inexplicably ubiquitous (and even more inexplicable that they exist in the first place) purple coyotes.

Tim, a native Nevadan, always considered himself a Westerner, not that I had ever seen much evidence of "the West" in Reno, either. Now, as we traveled throughout South Dakota, Tim explained that for him, "Western" didn't necessarily mean how a place looked, or even where it was, but more how it felt. To be Western was to adhere to a "live and let live" attitude, to believe that an individual had to make it or fail on his or her own. Finally, it also meant possessing a fierce love of the out-of-doors. (No wonder I didn't have a clue.)

I guess not being Western myself (and perhaps even more relevant, belonging to the Eastern mall-worshipping crowd), I had never considered "the West" to connote anything other than a certain landscape or architectural style.

So it was in South Dakota (which, technically, is even less west than Colorado, but OK, I'm trying to go with this whole state-of-mind thing) I finally understood what it felt like to be in a place that was Western. Funny that it didn't feel foreign at all. It's as if the ethos of the Old West is so quintessentially American that no matter where one is originally from (and even for a first/second-generation daughter like myself), it seems like a shared history. As corny as it sounds (maybe some of the fifty-one-foot Teddy Roosevelt was rubbing off on me—down, Teddy! Down!), it feels like coming home.

Thus, I got a thrill strolling through downtown Deadwood (about forty miles northwest of Rapid City), a former mining camp during the last, great gold rush in the continental U.S., and getting a taste of the Old West, especially when wandering into the saloon where Wild Bill Hickok was gunned down. He, perhaps, epitomized the "live and let live" attitude better than anyone (although it could be argued that in his case it was more "live and make die").

Wild Bill learned his legendary shooting skills growing up on his father's farm, a stop along the Underground Railroad in the 1840s. There, his natural ability with a gun proved useful in protecting escaping slaves. Later, working as a stagecoach driver, he killed a grizzly bear with a bowie knife, furthering his already growing reputation as a fearless, "wild" fighter.

As a town constable, he pioneered "posting": tacking to a tree the names of men he planned to "shoot on sight" the next day. Most thus notified skedaddled out of town right quick. He was later a scout for the U.S. Army during the Civil War and then a U.S. marshal. Between jobs, he supported himself as a professional gambler, and a dispute over cards resulted in the first ever recorded quick draw. Hickok won. After losing positions as sheriff and marshal due to overzealous killings, he returned to his gambling life for good. But his luck couldn't last: He was shot in the back of the head at a saloon in Deadwood at the age of thirty-nine while playing poker, after his preferred—and safer—seat in the corner was already taken. (His last cards, pairs of eights and aces, are now referred to as a "dead man's hand.") The assailant, seeking revenge about yet another poker-related slight, was later hanged.

Of course, tourism's tentacles attempt to heighten any "authentic" experience anywhere, only serving to ultimately dilute it. (Here, taking the form of life-sized, albeit rather ragged dolls sitting at a poker table, representing Hickok et al. at the time of the murder.) Neither of us minded so much in South Dakota.

In Keystone, in fact, just a few miles from Mount Rushmore, we stopped to have lunch on the veranda of the historic Ruby House Restaurant. Although it was a lovely day and the food was quite good, the best part turned out to be listening to the barker next door entice passersby to the "cowboy comedy blah blah" show. Soon, he was joined by tough, authentic-looking, ten-gallon-hatted actors who shot blanks into the air, cracking their whips while occasionally accosting children with "I'm your new babysitter, kid." It seemed that this old mining town's latest inhabitants were carrying on the sense of humor established by their forebears: When gold was discovered here at the turn of the century, several miners named claims after their wives. One of the richest thus called his "The Holy Terror."

Tim and I could certainly relate; he knew exactly what he'd name a mine, if he ever had one. Before we left, I programmed my cell phone with various ringtones, assigning unique ones to people in my contact list, so I'd know who was calling before I ever looked at the phone. Thus, one place I worked for (and didn't particularly like) rang Darth Vader's theme. A contractor friend was "Men at Work." Tim was quite pleased with his, the first few notes of Beethoven's Fifth Symphony (supposed to signify fate knocking on one's door). Since he wasn't interested in having ringtones on his phone, I only assigned one—for me. Whenever I called him, the familiar music chimed out and people would invariably smile.

"Isn't that *The Nutcracker?*" they'd ask, sugarplum memories dancing in their heads.

"Yup," Tim replied. "My wife: the Nutcracker." Pretty darn good name for a mine, too.

Badlands National Park more than lived up to its name, its barren landscape whittled by millennia of winds and water into serrated peaks and canyons of sediment, sandstone, and volcanic ash. There are many hikes in the park which would appeal to anyone who enjoys surroundings that are largely treeless, grassless, and waterless. Perhaps it's because my ancient ancestors wandered in the desert for forty years that I tend to avoid those vistas like the plague.

What I did enjoy was our visit to nearby Wall Drug Store. I wouldn't be surprised if the local constabulary used ability to point in its direction (rather than to one's own nose) as a sobriety check, for there are more signs indicating the way than there is bad land in Badlands. Wall Drug, in the town of Wall (taking its name from the Badlands wall—a narrow, sixty-mile-long spine of buttes), started out in the early 1930s as a barely surviving pharmacy in a barely surviving town. After the proprietor's wife got the inspired idea to put signs on the highway offering free ice water during the summer, travelers flocked to the place, buying ice cream and other supplies to last them until Yellowstone or the not yet completed Mount Rushmore.

Since then, although the free ice water tradition remains (there's now also free coffee. That, plus the five-cent donuts, meant Tim was on overdrive by the time we left the store, making me thankful he was only driving the Jeep), much has been added, including statues of a gorilla, giant rabbit, jackalope, bison, and T. rex. Tim and I thought we'd just stop in for a quick bite of their famous buffalo burgers, but ended up spending a few hours reading the many old, laminated articles about the place on the walls of Wall, hung along with historic photographs and thousands of new ones: The store gives out free "Wall Drug" signs to anyone who asks and people have taken pictures of them in all sorts of far-flung places, from the Moscow airport to the South Pole. We also couldn't help (along with hordes of visiting children) pretending to ride the various "animals," although we resisted singing with the life-sized animated Cowboy Quartette. Wall is simply more pure Americana at its glorious, corny best.

At nine dollars per person, I was skeptical about touring the

Crazy Horse Memorial. That much money to see yet another gargantuan mountain carving, this one not even finished? Besides, you can view the thing from the road. I still don't know why we actually paid the admission and entered, but we were glad we did, because the monument itself isn't even the half of it: The Crazy Horse Memorial is less about what will eventually become the largest sculpture in the world and more about one man's single-minded determination and willingness to sacrifice his life for what even he acknowledged was a small step toward righting a wrong.

After Boston-born artist Korczak Ziolkowski won first prize for his sculpture at the 1939 World's Fair, the Lakota chiefs, seeing all the ruckus in their backyard at Mount Rushmore, invited him to the Black Hills to carve a memorial to their long dead warrior Crazy Horse.

"My fellow chiefs and I would like the white man to know the red man has great heroes, too," Chief Henry Standing Bear wrote the sculptor.

Crazy Horse, an inspiration to Native American tribes all over the country, resorted to war only when treaty after treaty was broken by the government. His singular desire became for his people to live free, without depending on the white man's promises or having to seek permission to live as they chose. He never signed a peace treaty, was instrumental in Custer's defeat at Little Bighorn, and in 1877, was fatally stabbed in the back by an American soldier while under a flag of truce.

Undoubtedly, the artist, who was born exactly thirty years to the day after Crazy Horse died, felt a kinship with the great leader. For Korczak's fierce independence was also born of mistreatment by those who were charged with looking after him: Orphaned before he could talk, he grew up in a series of foster homes where he was badly abused. He never took a formal art, architecture, or engineering lesson in his life and only started work on the memorial in 1947, after volunteering for service in World War II. Then, much like the man he would spend the rest of his days honoring, Korczak began a lifelong pattern of eschewing government money by turning down a State Department commission to create war memorials in Europe. Instead, he settled in the Black Hills and, while living in a tent, began to tackle the six-hundred-foot mountain.

He not only had to sink a well and build a log cabin to live in, but also construct roads and a 741-step staircase to the top of the summit. In a grainy old film clip in the Visitors Center, an elderly, but still wiry, heavily bearded Korczak looks intently into the camera and tells the story of how, in the early years, he had to crank the temperamental air compressor at the bottom of the mountain (which powered his drills at the top), climb all those steps, and get as much work done as possible before having to head back down to crank it up all over again. During the span of several decades, he broke many bones, endured three back operations, developed arthritis, had a massive heart attack, and underwent bypass surgery. Still, he labored on the memorial until his death in 1982 at age seventy-four. Korczak always understood that his undertaking was too much for one man and one lifetime: He left three books of detailed plans and scale models for others to continue his dream. When completed, all four presidential heads on Mount Rushmore will be able to fit into Crazy Horse's head alone.

His wife and seven of their ten children vowed to continue, and they have—all with private donations, as Korczak had determined never to take government money for the work, refused to draw a salary, and twice turned down ten million dollars in federal funding. His family continues the project, which will absolutely, positively, and unequivocally be completed sometime this millennium. Although only Crazy Horse's face is finished, one can still make out the general shape of the warrior, sitting on his horse, pointing off to the distance in answer to the derisive question once asked him by a white man: "Where are your lands, now?"

"My lands are where my dead lie buried," he replied.

I was surprised to be so moved by what, on the surface, seems like such a small gesture. When one looks at the enormous task still ahead, it's easy to be skeptical about the wisdom of the entire undertaking. But after hearing the whole story, I realized how unfair it was to judge Korczak solely by what was visible on a mountain. Much more than a sculpture, his legacy is that of a man who stuck to his beliefs in the face of overwhelming hardships, willingly dedicating his life to the pursuit of helping a people regain their dignity, just as he had regained his. I tried to put myself in that selfless situation and sadly concluded I wouldn't have made it past my first visit to the mountain and the realization that not only would there be no room service, but nary even a room.

Korczak's influence on me didn't end at his mountain; back at the campground, as Tim washed our windshield, the elderly woman next door asked if she could pay him to do hers—right then—while her even more elderly husband, who insisted on washing it himself, was at the store. Of course, Project Nerd jumped at the chance. And of course, superheroes never accept payment for their work. As I watched Tim trot over to her RV, I thought of the memorial and realized that while most of us can't tackle something that huge on behalf of someone else (and while I've never washed a vehicle in my life), there are smaller kindnesses to be done, so small, in fact, that though they may seem insignificant to the doer, one never knows what the value might be for the person on the receiving end.

In that spirit, I e-mailed an old friend of my late uncle, who had known him all the way back to his vaudeville days. After George died the previous year, Jerry and I hadn't kept in touch. But he e-mailed back the very next day to say how much he appreciated hearing from me, that it had been a welcome break from dealing with his wife's illness, something I didn't even know about. Jerry's pleasure at my small gesture pleased and surprised me immensely, and as I got a taste of what Tim must feel with much more regularity, I recalled once remarking to an acquaintance that my husband was a much better person than I. She somehow immediately assumed I was lacking in self-esteem. (I *said* she was only an acquaintance.)

"Don't say that!" she snapped. I tried to explain that I was simply stating a fact, a fact I felt no qualms about whatsoever. Tim's being so kind and thoughtful, not only to others but especially to me, always made me secretly feel like I was getting the better deal in our relationship. Now I was starting to see that it wasn't about any "deal." I was witnessing firsthand the pleasure my husband derives from helping people. Taking a deep breath, I resolved to be more like Tim and try some of this kindness-to-others thing he's always been so keen on, as I wondered if perhaps, at least in this one small way, I shouldn't necessarily leave the driving to him. (While I had gone into psychiatry in the first place to help people—and I like to think over the years I have—after so long in the "helping professions" it was easy to feel tapped out, unlike my husband, who seems to possess a bottomless reservoir of altruism, at least when he's not hatching evil plans involving me.)

My skepticism never wavered, however, when we joined the thousands of visitors a year to the Corn Palace, an auditorium in Mitchell, South Dakota. Alas, it is not actually made of corn, but rather simply decorated with it—bushels and bushels and bushels of it—with the occasional oats and prairie grass thrown in, in an utterly misguided attempt to break the monotony. As Tim observed, it was doubtful anyone could get away with saying they made an Ice Palace in this neck of the woods by hosing down a Holiday Inn in January and calling it good. So what in the world is up with the Corn Palace? Voicing our perplexity as to why people would visit the thing, we were told, "It changes every year! If you come back, you'll never see the same mural again!" We assured the earnest fellow this would not be an issue for us. Adding insult to injury, we tried to salvage the drive out by wandering around, stalking various eateries, but in the township surrounding this supposed Palace of Corn, we could not score even one measly cob.

It was almost Labor Day by the time we left for the Midwest and our next stop, Minnesota. I had assumed the whole "Land of a Thousand Lakes" moniker was hyperbole, but ended up concluding that, rather, it was quite the understatement. Exploring the northern part of the state in Park Rapids and Walker Lake, we found the scenery was so picturesque and peaceful, that while sitting waterside in shirtsleeves at a cute outdoor restaurant, eating fish 'n' chips made with fresh walleye, seeking shade under a large, colorful umbrella, it was hard to imagine the weather would soon turn as harsh as anywhere in the country.

We headed to Itasca State Park and the headwaters of the Mississippi, where Tim wanted me to take a particular picture of him. It was a guy thing, he explained: He knew we would eventually reach New Orleans, where the Mississippi River ends, and thought it would be "neat" if he, er . . . pretended to go to the head at the headwaters, then, in a manner of speaking, appeared to follow his own trail all the way to the end. Of course, he wanted a record of both auspicious occasions. A diptych of disposal, if you will. I thought it was a grand idea, as for years I had collected photographs of various animals relieving themselves for a bathroom picture book I eventually wanted to publish, *Porcelain Inspirations*.

Now I was thrilled to get a chance to turn the tables on my sneaky husband, for unbeknownst to him, Tim had just signed up to be the only human entry in my future tome. This would not be the first picture I had taken on our bus trip intended for that particular book. The second day of our meltdown cruise, on Highway 80, a few hours from the Nevada–Utah border, we had, as always when driving to Reno, passed through Battle Mountain. I was fascinated with the town, largely because it epitomized what I saw as the idiocy of the Western custom to brand their peaks, no matter how peak-ed. I never saw this phenomenon in the East, but out west it seemed that any town with even a pimple of a hill felt the compulsion to slap a large letter on it. Why? Did they fear the mount would wander into a rival town's pasture? In any event, I had Tim stop our rig on the side of the road, determined that Battle Mountain, Nevada, would provide the cover shot for my eventual masterpiece, *Porcelain Inspirations*, as it had not one but two letters on its crusty, brown lump—BM.

Still, Tim should have known better than to aid and abet my photo fetish, given our last foray into snapshot scatology. Several years before when we were in Yellowstone National Park, we stopped by the side of the road near a herd of bison and even closer to a horde of European tourists. As we scanned the former, me with camera in hand, Tim, ever helpful, exclaimed, "Look! Over there!" I immediately followed his gaze and zoomed in on a rather large specimen, catching the deposit in midair, making for an excellent shot. The tourists, also alerted by Tim's triumphant call, murmured and strained, trying to figure out what fantastic sight awaited them. When they did . . . gasps. Then utter silence. *Hmm. I thought Europeans were supposed to be less prudish than Americans.* I just laughed it off. Tim was mortified.

So here at the headwaters he stood, back to me, on a log that stretched across the river. He planted his feet, strategically placed his hands, and turned his head to the camera, as if surprised at being caught. Just as I snapped the picture, he truly was: A family rounded the corner and stopped in their tracks, not realizing Tim was pretending—not that that would have been much better. I just laughed it off. Tim was mortified.

We scurried away only to run into yet another historical character who tested my cynicism: Mary Gibbs, the first female park commissioner in America, who, in 1903, stood up to a logging company that had built an illegal dam, intending to flood part of the forest for its sluice. A crew even threatened to shoot anyone who touched the levers that opened it. This slight but scrappy twenty-four-year-old took her job (which she assumed upon the death of her father) seriously. After politely, but to no avail, asking the brawny men to stop their activities, she came back with a constable and a warrant in hand. Again, the loggers, holding rifles, offered to make good on their threat. The constable backed down, but not Miss Gibbs. She stared right at them and declared, "I will put my hand there, and you will not shoot it off either." She did, they didn't and even more: Impressed by her bravery and determination, they opened it themselves. (She couldn't have, anyway, as it took the strength of six men.)

Hearing her story, I couldn't help marveling that while I'd do just about anything to avoid the outdoors (I had once, after all, when tired of craning my neck to view a meteor shower, announced, "I'm going inside to watch it on CNN"), this woman had risked her life for it. *Maybe I should see what all the fuss is about.*

Tim, always willing to take advantage of my temporary losses of reason, unhooked our bikes from the back of the Jeep and actually got me to take several rides. Normally, I'm not one to exert myself if I can help it. Although I've worked out almost every morning for years, I find doing it so abhorrent that I pretty much avoid moving around any more than absolutely necessary the rest of the day. (I once bought a pedometer to measure how many steps I took in a twenty-four-hour period. Then I tried to break my record. For most people, this would involve walking more.)

Tim always thought it strange that while part of my workout included ten minutes on the treadmill at the highest incline, whenever we'd have to walk up the hill to get to our house, I'd whine and make him tow me. (That, of course, didn't count the times I simply refused and asked him to go home, get the car, and drive thirty seconds to fetch me. *If jumping horses can balk at the Olympics when there's a gold medal at stake, why can't I?*) He didn't seem to understand that working out while watching some reality TV show took my mind off the exertion part. He actually thought it more interesting to be outside. Not only that, but that *the outside itself* would make me enjoy the exertion—like it has magical properties or something. (I always assumed my consort had at least twenty IQ points on me, but statements like those really make a Princess wonder.)

Yet as the wide, paved lanes stretched for mile upon stunning mile through forests, skirting still, glimmering bodies of water large and small, they beckoned, just too inviting, even for me. We hardly saw another soul while we pedaled and I marveled how that could be possible with scenery so striking, not to mention exertion so flat and therefore relatively effortless. After all, if I could appreciate how pleasant these excursions were . . . *Maybe these Minnesotans aren't as hardy as they're cracked up to be.*

Of course I had to take a break from nature for the duty every Princess must perform once in her lifetime—the pilgrimage to Mecca, which in my kingdom is known as the Mall of America.

Roaming it was a workout all in itself—the highest form, in fact, as it combined the truly great indoors with . . . shopping! Tim, however, was a bit put off by the crowds and dowdiness of it all (neither of which I noticed). While I bought some blouses, he headed over to Ikea, a place he'd heard tell of, but never actually been in. Once inside and fully grasping what it was all about, his Project Nerd sensibilities became highly offended at the notion of giving people the false sense of his sacrosanct, do-it-yourself ethos, when all they were really doing was connecting the dots.

In Minneapolis, we visited one of Tim's friends from residency, the always hip, always happenin', and ever-single Dave. Yep, that Dave—Tim's shill on our first date. His latest girlfriend was lovely, of course. They all are, but we've learned through the years not to get too attached.

Tim had always envied Dave: He was movie-star (rather than psychiatrist) handsome, knew hordes of interesting people, and was always dating some woman more fabulous than the last. He seemed to lead a charmed existence, one in which he searched for—and found—experiences and relationships that only got progressively bigger and better. He appeared to live life to the absolute fullest, only to then constantly top himself. Tim, on the other hand, always felt ill-equipped to go out into the world with anything approaching Dave's sophistication and gregariousness.

Now, for the first time, Tim's envy of Dave changed, even

though Dave had not; Tim realized that at this point in his own life, it was important to be happy with where he was. Although Dave still seemed perfectly content, Tim understood that if he had been the one constantly striving to experience more, he would have been left with less—specifically, without the long-term relationship he had cherished for so many years.

With this new insight, Tim started questioning not only how he defined happiness and the way he thought he should go about achieving it, but even his assumptions about midlife itself. He could now see that the key for successfully navigating through this stage in life was to appreciate how he grew and what he acquired from the youthful experiences he did have, to learn to appreciate what he'd become and develop it further, rather than panicking, always searching for something new. *Great. Couldn't he have figured this out before upending my life with the bus thing?*

Our last night, Cap'n Dave took us out on his boat on Lake Minnetonka and invited a few friends along, one of whom, we discovered, had lived through my worst nightmare: having the top of his converted bus sheered off by a low underpass. It happened twenty years ago when, as a late-blooming hippie, Scott packed wife and kids up in a converted school bus and drove to Mexico, where they were having a grand old time. They did think it strange, however, that other Americans they met would often remark, "It's too bad you haven't had some hardship here. Then you'd really get to see how wonderful the people are." Well, the moment his bus rammed into that bridge, creating flying projectiles of all the belongings they'd stowed on top, hordes of people came running up. At first, Scott tried to fend them off, thinking they wanted to scavenge his stuff, but it soon became apparent they only wanted to help.

So Scott, in what I'm sure felt to him like closing a karmic circle, gave me the same admonition: "I hope you have some hardship on your trip." *Right. Any more hardship and I won't be around to close the karmic loop on the next idiot wife going along when her husband lives his muy loco dream.* Still, maybe because I'd been so touched by the accounts of other Midwesterners' fierce determination against all odds, I found Scott's story (and perhaps the fact that he was still around to tell it) strangely reassuring.

After Labor Day, we scrambled farther east. I'd been tracking the fall colors on the Internet and we didn't have long. Months before, just because I knew it would tickle Tim, I'd submitted our rig to *Bus Conversions* magazine, and I had to admit, it gave even me a thrill when we were informed we'd made the upcoming centerfold. Yes, I had graduated from a fancy-schmancy Ivy League school, then medical school, and was a triple-boarded psychiatrist, but I could now count among my greatest accomplishments fulfilling a lifelong ambition to be a Miss September. Tim, of course, ordered about a dozen copies and sent nearly as many off to family and friends. He had truly become, in *Bus Conversions* magazine's highly technical term for those who love their buses, a "busnut." And I suppose that made me, the wife lugged along on busnut adventures, nothing more than a lugnut.

Shortly after our magazines arrived, cementing our celebrity status, we were driving down the highway when Tim saw a converted bus coming from the opposite direction.

"That's a . . . a . . ." he stuttered, straining to remember what type it was. I, of course, couldn't have cared less and would rather he concentrate on driving.

"It's a bus, honey," I stated with as much patience as I could muster.

"What do you mean by that?" he demanded, as offended as I would have been had he referred to my prized beaded Fendi evening purse as a handbag.

"What I meant was, who cares what kind it is?" I asked with an edge in my voice, willing him to focus on the road.

"That's no way for a Miss September to talk," he chastised, shaking his head. "And the month of your reign isn't even over yet."

No, but the year of our bus trip might soon be.

Chapter Five

MOOSELESS IN MAINE AND OTHER HAIRY NEW ENGLAND TAILS

Elusive Moose

1½ parts Godiva liqueur
1¼ parts crème de cacao
½ part vanilla vodka (or 1 part raspberry liqueur if tracking moose in forest or ½ part crème de banana if tracking moose in jungle)
2½ parts cream

Mix ingredients in shaker, expel into glass. Squeeze chocolate syrup on rim. Plop in a chocolate bonbon to allow for satisfying splash. Wipe.

We made our way to the East Coast, planning to chase the fall colors as south as they took us. Although we stopped along our route (most notably in Ohio, on Lake Erie, for equally spectacular sunsets and roller coasters), there were many days, for hours on end, when we (OK, Tim) did nothing but drive. I found that I actually liked just sitting, perched up high on the buddy seat, with Shula—who seemed to be cowering ever so slightly less—in my lap.

I've always prided myself on being a supreme multitasker: While working, I can talk to a doctor about one case while writing up my review on the last, while flipping through my appointment book deciding when to schedule haircuts—mine *and* poodle's—while having a cable news show on in the background. I like to keep busy, provided I can remain sedentary, of course. I know that left to my own devices, I tend to . . . rot. I force my brain to stay active just as I have to force myself to exercise.

A friend once dragged me to a yoga class.

"You'll love it!" Susan, one of the most gorgeous women I've ever known, exclaimed. *I guess if it works for her.* Then, "It really clears your mind!" *Great. If my mind were any clearer, I'd be dead.* But I went. I figured living in Boulder meant I had already putatively signed up for yoga, anyway. Boulderites are just so darn fit, some kind of exercise must be required in the city charter for citizenship. Hopefully, if I got yoga out of the way, they'd let slide that I never hiked, skied, or, for that matter, left the house much. (At the farmers' market, Tim swears he once saw the result of what occurs when Boulder's penchant for political correctness collides with its extremist attitude toward health: eggs labeled "vegetarian fed, cage free and voluntary.")

Anyway, I really gave yoga a chance. Really, I did. Two classes. I just couldn't take it anymore. I was bored. Deathly so. Besides, what was the point in putting that much effort into doing something just to think about nothing, when I was already so adept at thinking about nothing without making any effort at all?

That's why on the bus I was surprised to discover how much I loved just sitting up front with Tim. He always tried to explain the lure, the Zen (as he called it) of driving. I could never understand it. To me, driving was simply a means to an end. All that stuff about how "it's the journey and not the destination" seemed to be nothing more than one big rationalization people used when they didn't like where they got.

But sitting up front with Tim, talking or not, I started to see the appeal: no pressure, no hurry, no expectations. Just *being*; sitting, getting lost in the scenery flying by. Of course, sometimes we couldn't help being pulled back into reality, such as when a navigational issue reared its ugly head.

By now, we had divvied up the duties on board with military efficiency. When the bus was in motion, Tim was captain. I was his yeoman and if he wanted a drink or a snack, I'd hut to and get it for him—no sense in having the driver distracted by a growling stomach or parched throat. Of course, I might also take the opportunity to fix my own favorite snack: counter egg. Taking a hard-boiled egg out of the fridge, I'd crack it on the Blue Bahia, remove the shell, sprinkle salt on the counter, roll the egg in it, and voilà! Counter egg. After all, why bother with a plate when an egg already comes so perfectly complete in its own handy container?

This habit never seemed to bother Tim when I did it at home. Maybe it was the larger counter and, thus, more efficient (and less obvious) salt dispersal. Whatever the reason, I found it completely unnecessary when, on the bus, he started threatening to spray Bitter Apple (a dog repellent) on the Blue Bahia. He was horrified I was too lazy to take out a plate. *He thinks that's lazy?* Lazy is the time, working at a new hospital, I gave myself food poisoning by heating up lunch on the windshield of my car (parked out in the scorching summer sun), because I didn't want to bother looking for a microwave. *That's* lazy. (Yeah, I know. As a doctor, I should have realized. But in my defense, since it sure felt like no living thing could survive in the inside of my car, I assumed it got hot enough. Besides, I don't recall thermodynamics even being covered in Physics for Non-Majors. As Tim later explained in painstaking and excruciating detail: The amount of calories of sun energy available to warm my meal was offset by heat loss, since the container wasn't insulated and therefore did not reach sufficient . . . well, you get the idea.)

In any event, when the bus stopped, our roles changed a wee bit, reverting to their more natural state; Tim did the laundry and dishes, was free to tackle any Project Nerd duties as he saw fit, and also took on all quartermaster responsibilities, keeping our bays fully stocked. Just in case the magnitude of his assignments appears one-sided, it's important to note that I was still doing some insurance reviews, and when mobile, I took on the additional task of bursar, dolling out the money whenever we hit . . . er, encountered a toll booth. ("Can't you drive the bus in straighter so they don't see we're towing a car? It's two dollars an axle!") Lastly, and most unfortunately for us both, I had also been pressed into service as navigator.

"Why in the world would you want me to navigate?" I had asked. "I have no sense of direction and I can't read a map."

"True," Tim sighed. "But who else is going to do it? Miles?" We both glanced at the poodle, considering. Even the fact that he was happily, if sloppily, gumming Morty's head didn't seem to completely disqualify him. And truly, Miles seemed to enjoy chores as much as his father. Whenever Project Nerd tackled his outside tasks, Project Poodle could be counted on to trot close behind, veering off to accomplish his own important work (cornering rocks, barking at them, and when sufficiently vanquished, moving them around with his paws and mouth), achieving a success rate that rivaled his father's. Still, as far as navigation was concerned, although it was close, we knew there was really no other way. With Tim the designated driver in perpetuity, I simply had to be navigator. Lord help us.

Of course, our fancy bus was equipped with a GPS. And of course Peter, the electronic wiz who installed it, did the same bang-up job of explaining it as he did getting the TV (and just about everything else) to work.

"Just put the CD in and you're all set!" Peter assured us, handing me the GPS in its box. After much procrastination, I finally took the thing out once we'd left familiar Colorado. The designers of such an amazing gadget might think they're cunning, but I'm cunninger; I quickly discovered the disc was larger than the device.

"Look!" I exclaimed to Tim, indignant, as I slapped the CD to metal. "There's no way to get this in there!" Being even less technologically inclined than his wife, Tim just shook his head.

It had taken me a few hundred miles to realize that the CD was meant to be installed on my computer and from there, I could transfer the maps to the GPS. Still, we hadn't realized there was another, even more crucial step: programming. In our ignorance, we decided to test the GPS one day when we were driving the Jeep.

"How do you think we tell it where we want to go?" I queried the Captain. He shook his head again. Then I got a brilliant idea. I was hankering for some onion rings, and jokingly (OK, half jokingly) commanded it, "Find Wendy's." Just then, a male voice intoned, "In . . . fifty . . . feet . . . turn . . . left." We looked at each other, then at the road in wonder. Sure enough, there, fifty feet ahead, on the left, was a Wendy's.

"Find frozen custard!" I demanded. Nothing. *What a worthless, piece of . . .* By the time we left Minneapolis, we not only figured out how to use it (and that the Wendy's thing had been a bit of a fluke) but also learned to rely on Map Breath (as we started calling it) except, of course, when there was new construction.

Despite my poor math skills, my nonexistent sense of direction, and my total inability to read a map, I might have had the occasional navigational success if I weren't also, as Tim put it, "concrete as a sidewalk." Like the time in Ohio when I tried to leave a Target and was stumped at the door. The sign on it said "ENTER ONLY," then on the next line, "DO NOT ENTER." *Enter only, do not enter? What the hell does that mean?* I tried to get through the door several times, but couldn't. I might be there still had I not noticed an elderly blue-haired lady hobbling by with a walker, effortlessly exiting through the door next to mine. I ensured that no one was looking, then quickly slipped out behind her. Back on the bus, I expressed my outrage to Tim.

"If it said 'ENTRANCE ONLY, DO NOT ENTER,' that might make sense."

"You were exiting, sweetie."

"Yes, but I was entering the little alcove thingy to exit."

"Whatever you say, dear." I caught the grateful look he threw the GPS's way. Sometimes, I feel like what used to be termed an idiot savant—without the savant part.

When we left East Harbor State Park in Lakeside, Ohio, we thought we had finally worked the bugs out of our GPS system and decided to give it the ultimate test: Could it guide us directly to the Wal-Mart at 5555 Porter Road in Niagara Falls, New York, where we planned to spend the night?

We agreed we would follow the GPS's instructions to the letter, no matter what Mr. Rand McNally said. (He's a little anal for my tastes, anyway. Sometimes, too many lines on a map are just plain confusing.) I programmed the GPS and all seemed to be going well, until just after we left Buffalo. We were traveling north on 290. The GPS offered no instructions, neither on its screen nor in its haughty female voice, even though it seemed obvious to me and Rand that we would soon take 190 north to Niagara Falls.

"I don't know, sweetie," I began. "I don't understand what she wants us to do. If we keep going on this road, we'll end up back in Buffalo. I think we need to take 190." As I studied the map, our route seemed even more certain. Soon, there would be no turning back. Not for a forty-foot Prevost dragging a Jeep.

"You're sure, Number Two?" he asked.

"Aye, Number One. 190. I just don't get what she thinks we should do." When we came to the point of no return, though, it became clear; 190 split off from 290 to the right. Tim easily made the adjustment. Still, in past such situations, Map Breath had instructed, "Bear right." This time, she was silent.

"She screwed up," I said.

"No," Tim mused. "It must be the map program she got that malfunctioned." I shot him a sideways glance. Then I recalled I had programmed Map Breath myself with a man's voice, specifically to keep the Lying Bitch company, hoping the promise of some libidinal satisfaction might get her to start telling the truth about our tanks. Somewhere in Michigan, it seemed, Map Breath had undergone a sex change. And I hadn't been the one to perform the procedure.

Tim, who struggled to even turn a computer on, later admitted he'd somehow managed to stumble his way through Map Breath's menu to change the voice function.

"It just feels more natural to have a woman telling me what to do," he explained.

When we finally pulled into Chez Sam, Map Breath intoned in that smug way she has, "Destination." I retorted, "Oh, so now you have something to say." But Tim was quick to point out, and rather excitedly, I might add, "She did get us here. Exactly to our destination!" Now I finally understood what was going on.

"Why do you always take her side?" I demanded.

"What are you talking about?" he replied. But I could sense the truth under his flimsy protestation.

"I bet if you had to choose, you'd leave me to have her on this trip!" I sputtered.

"I'm not even attracted to her," he insisted. "Although, if I did leave you, you'd never be able to find me," he snickered. I was not amused.

"Why do you always listen to her and not me?" I queried, quite reasonably, I thought.

"I guess that is hard to explain, what with your stellar navigational skills." OK, I deserved that. Only a few hours earlier, Tim had me consult Rand to see how far we were from Buffalo. Reading all those little numbers along all the superfluous squiggly lines was blinding. Instead, I found the distance scale and determined that fifteen miles was about the size of a knuckle. Five knuckles later, I offered, quite satisfied with myself, "OK. Five times fifteen is seventy-five. But it's really a little less than a knuckle length, so . . . we could be anywhere from forty to seventy-five miles from Buffalo." Tim rolled his eyes. Just then I spotted the "Mileage Between Cities" chart at the top of the page. Why hadn't Rand made this more obvious? Like I was supposed to figure out that buried in all this map stuff was actual useful information. (Sometimes I think Rand is just showing off. No one likes a braggart, buster!)

"Oops!" I chuckled.

"How much more is it?" he sighed.

"Actually, we're only twenty-two miles away. Guess knuckles aren't the best way to measure."

"Apparently not yours," the Captain muttered under his breath.

We overnighted at Wal-Mart, joining the familiar circle of rigs around its perimeter. As usual, ours was the last one left in the morning. Although we'd both seen Niagara Falls before, we couldn't resist another look. This time, we got to see it at night, illuminated with different-colored lights every ten minutes. I found the display tacky, but Mr. Outdoorsy actually liked it. Still, as we stood among many other couples, all holding hands (some of whom should have instead been on their cell phones arranging rooms), Tim commented that while he could appreciate the Falls' beauty, he couldn't really see what the big romance was. *I bet he'd rather be here with her.*

"If Map Breath's so great, why don't you try getting *her* to live in a bus with you for a year?" I challenged.

"Uh . . . that's what she's doing, honey." *Oh, yeah.*

I got over it quickly. Really, I did. Only, every now and then, upon making a wrong turn, I still delighted in Map Breath's befuddlement, as I watched the question mark linger on her screen while she recalculated her tight, little, metallic ass off.

For the rest of our time in upstate New York, we stayed at a rustic campground in Ithaca, where I went to college at Cornell. During my three and a half years there (a multitasker, even then), I'd never appreciated the bell tower, visible throughout much of campus. It seemed like just another measure of how overwhelmed I was in my pre-med studies, chiming in hourly, counting down the dings to my grade point average with every dong. Even though I passed it daily, I never took the time to make it to the top.

Now Tim and I climbed the 161 steps to the chimesmasters' room. Since 1868, this unique instrument (which at twenty-one bells is one of the largest and most frequently played chimes in the world) has been given voice by students who compete annually for the honor of grabbing and stomping on a console of wooden levers with their hands and feet—*Attack of the Mensa Ninja Nerds,* if you will. Between the climbing and the chiming, it's no wonder one chimesmaster received physical education credit for her efforts. The students were happy to answer any questions and even played requests, although "Stairway to Heaven" was not in their repertoire. Frankly, after all that exertion, followed by a stunning 360-degree view of the campus, Ithaca, and Cayuga Lake, it was hard to concentrate on the music.

Gasping for breath aside, I did feel rewarded for finally reaching the top, in the form of extra credit for my psyche: Although part of my clinical work had been helping patients understand that they could never go back and relive, I was now learning the value that different choices could make going forward in life; choices not unlike taking a year off for an adventure, rather than staying on the same unfulfilling course. A futuristic do-over, if you will.

Getting to the top of the bell tower reaffirmed for me that Tim and I *were* making new choices about how to live our lives. And whether it was finding time for that climb (even in Donald Pliner leather loafers) or putting our careers on hold, we were doing things differently than we had in the past, giving us hope that the lessons learned on the road about what was truly valuable might just stick.

As Tim followed me up the narrow stairwell, he playfully pinched my butt with every step, a pleasant (and painful—in a black-and-blue sort of way) reminder that all I had yearned for as a student twenty-five years before had come true, even if I hadn't taken the time to notice it until now: I was happy. At twenty years old, had I articulated what I thought I needed in life, I would probably have said a big house, a successful husband, and a great career. Yet all I really needed for true happiness was the homeless, unemployed bus driver right behind me, pinching my butt every step of the way.

I love this area of the country, the Finger Lakes, although I never really got the whole "Finger" part. I mean, if you look at a map, there are actually eleven of them, even though only seven are commonly admitted into the fingerhood. Who has seven or, for that matter, eleven fingers? Perhaps the area was once struck by a radioactive meteor, leading early cartographers to accurately reflect, through honorary nomenclature, the supplemental digits on their subsequent mutated generations. Or perhaps these communities, smug in their abundant natural beauty, are giving the finger(s) to the rest of the state? Whatever the rationale, I heart New York's Finger Lakes.

Remembering how much we loved biking around the flat trails of the lakes in Minnesota, it was not difficult for Tim to persuade me to take a few rides here too, something I also never did while in college. Near Cornell, we found a delightful, easy, two-mile bike trail along Cayuga Lake and, as we rode, were treated to the quintessential Ivy experience—watching the crew team as we paralleled the student rowers. (Now, that's exertion.)

Of course, we also took the Jeep on several day trips throughout the region for ice cream and wine tastings, passing waterfall after waterfall along the way. (They don't say "Ithaca is gorges" for nothin'.) When we entered the Neutral Zone in the town of Romulus (between Cayuga and Seneca lakes), I couldn't help asking some of the natives if they called themselves Romulans (as Tim tried to pretend he didn't know me). It was as if *I* were the alien. Next time, I'll wear my Spock ears; then maybe they'll understand what I'm talking about.

We headed to Bar Harbor, Maine, and while my phobia about the bus careening still surfaced, it was an actual crash that caught me by surprise; that of my computer. (Peter had installed a program I finally ran for the first time which was supposed to "clean it all up," since, of course, it was my practically brand new computer's fault that the satellite Internet wasn't working properly.) Out of the Bangor yellow pages, Brian to the rescue. We soon learned that he was much more than just another computer geek; this obsessive, chocoholic (rows of neatly stacked peanut butter cups in his office were a dead giveaway, even with my, by now, dusty diagnostic skills), number-three-ranked-in–New England water-skier, regaled us with the trials and tribulations of following his passion while living in that frigid clime. I certainly admired his tenacity, but despite the lure of multiple outfits (including different weight wet and dry suits, albeit all in black), I couldn't help wonder if there was a leaky valve in his tank.

Although water-skiing, especially in the freezing cold, was not what I would choose to do, meeting Brian certainly brought home what had been somewhat of an alien concept in our household: the importance of pursuing what one loves. I couldn't help wonder if we were being attracted to certain people on the road for a reason (which in turn made me wonder if I'd lived in karma-crazed Boulder way too long). For after only a month on the road without any career at all, not to mention discovering histories of characters and meeting actual people like Brian, Tim started dreaming about a part-time private practice, taking on only the types of cases he enjoys. And in a long overdue nod to his inner Project Nerd, he also pondered spending the rest of his time working with his hands, renovating old houses.

Ever since Vanture started our bus conversion and we became friendly with the guys in the shop, Tim had been envious of the owner. Chris said he didn't understand people who got up in the morning and complained about their jobs. He woke up every day looking forward to what he had to do. As Tim started thinking about his work life in a new way, he reminded me of what Chris told him.

"That's how I want to be," he said.

Although I lamented being the only woman I knew married to a white-collar man with blue-collar aspirations, it thrilled me that Tim might actually start taking better care of himself. And it turned out my husband was not the only one contemplating new ways of relating to the world: In exquisite Maine, anticipating some lovely photographic opportunities (I had found, unfortunately, that the artistic possibilities of my new hobby—nature photography—were rather limited indoors, no matter how hard I tried), I actually suggested a (short) hike.

It wasn't hard to get hooked, as long as we were walking in Acadia National Park. Even though we had a perfectly nice view of the ocean from our campsite (I suppose it's not really that I hate nature, just that I prefer experiencing it through a window—unless I have a camera in hand—which, I guess, is still kind of like experiencing it through a window, just a much smaller one), almost every day we'd head out with Miles for the park. There were so many varied "hikes," ranging from short strolls for me to long, arduous climbs for Tim, that I'd sling my camera over my shoulder and actually have a smile on my face while lacing up my shoes. We even spent a day at the beach, where some certifiable people—and believe me, I've certified patients for less—were actually swimming.

Maine was Miles's first taste of ocean—literally. As he cavorted on the shore, running away from the waves (although poodles are, by nature, water retrievers, ours has always eschewed getting himself wet), he could not resist taking a drink. SNORT. Poor poodle. Throughout the rest of the year, he always repeated this mistake at the ocean, never able to grasp the concept of salt water.

One day, we got to talking to an elderly park ranger. He and his wife had spent most of their lives traveling the country, working in one national park after another. While I still could not ever imagine that for myself, for the first time, I could understand the appeal for other people of doing so: living what you love, every day, rather than living with what you love (like—and Lord help me for saying this—shoes). I wasn't anywhere near there yet (and wasn't at all sure I wanted to be), but now I could at least see what the attraction was for others.

The ranger boasted that the sunsets on Cadillac Mountain were the best of any national park, including Denali in Alaska, where he'd also spent some time. Hearing the word "mountain," I figured I was out of luck and the only way I'd get to see the sunset was if I could convince Tim to take my camera. But, turns out, you can drive right up to the top, then make your way on foot over an expanse of flat rocks to find a spot and await the multihued extravaganza. That evening, as we sat and watched the waning daylight sweep over the ridges, pools of water, and ocean, creating an otherworldly landscape, I could almost imagine what it must be like taking a moonwalk, but without having to endure the rigorous training, the nauseating G's, the tragically disco-inspired space suits, or the diapers.

We also spent several pleasant afternoons wandering around the town of Bar Harbor. After years of shellfish drought (although not kosher since childhood, I still can't bring myself to eat the stuff), Tim insisted we go to lobster pounds for all of our evening meals. (He even sampled lobster ice cream at a local confectionary. The verdict: "Tastes like vanilla," which, I guess, is the chicken of the dessert world.) I couldn't even force myself to try a bite of the no longer forbidden, if still-foreboding, crustacean. It's not a religious thing; I just can't understand the appeal of having my dinner stare at me while I dismember it. As my late Uncle George might have said, "With all that pounding, no wonder I always have a haddock." *BaRUMbum!*

Most of these places pounding lobsters were decidedly no-frills, so much so that I wondered why they didn't make us pull in our own traps. At least they all had ocean views.

Our idyllic time in Maine lulled us into believing that all was right in our own little bus world. Tim actually allowed himself some pleasant musings about the fact that we hadn't had any disasters recently. Up until then, he worried every time he started the bus that something would go wrong, but now he was feeling his confidence rise. He realized, looking back on all our adversities, that they had been learning experiences which only left him more secure in his busing abilities. For the first time, as he gazed at the limitless ocean view we were about to leave, he felt he knew our rig well and could handle anything.

He felt one with the bus.

Tim and I completed our departure preparations while the pets completed theirs. Somehow, Miles and Morty always seemed to know when we were about to pull up stakes. They arranged themselves on the love seat, sitting together expectantly. (Miles with an expression seeming to say, as always, "Oh, my! What adventure shall we have next?" Morty with one that was more "This better be worth waking up for, assholes.") Shula, it seemed, remained in denial, so I scooped her up from the bed and sat with her on the buddy seat. Tim turned the ignition key. Nothing.

The battery was dead. He immediately realized how ridiculous the whole "one with the bus" thing had been, especially given that we were backed into a campsite with no easy access to the engine compartment. Although we called AAA, the mechanic who arrived informed us very apologetically (he was a Mainer, after all) that he could not give us the 24-volt jump we needed. What's a Project Nerd to do? Like any superhero in crisis, he must return to the very source of his power: in this case, Sears—specifically, the Craftsman tool department.

"Do you want me to look up the address for Sears on the Internet?" I asked, trying to be helpful.

"Nah," PN replied, gazing off into the distance, with an almost imperceptible nod. "I can find it."

Of course he could. Maps were for mere mortals. Bat signals for wusses. My superhero husband comes fully equipped with his very own homing device. I don't know how he does it, and for once, he can't really explain it to me. It seems he's just hardwired to home in on home improvement stores—kind of like salmon spawning. (Although if that's what's going on at Sears, Tim'll find he has a lot more in common with those fish—it'll be the end of his life cycle, too.)

Tim bought a 12-volt battery charger (sadly, that was all Sears had, proving the old adage "You can't go home again"). It took over twenty-four hours to charge the bus. Unfortunately, our gray water tank was full; we had planned to go to the dump station on our way out of the RV park. So that night, under cover of darkness, we surreptitiously and illegally drained our gray water into the New England countryside before it overflowed our tanks, in what we later termed the Midnight Dump of Tim's Bus Rear.

As much as I'd grown to love Maine, I was a bit put off by just how darn *nice* people are in this state. When someone smiles at you in New York, it could be benign, it could be malicious, or it could be just plain crazy, with about an equal likelihood of any of the above. We New Yorkers have therefore mastered the art of looking through people, as if the entire city consists of urban ghosts. Doing that seemed a bit creepy in the Pine Tree State, so I forced myself to smile back. It's actually not that bad.

Those Mainers are not only genuinely friendly, they also like to *do* things: Brian offered to deliver the computer to me (over an hour drive) after his repairs took longer than expected. The AAA mechanic returned on his own, just to see if the spare battery Tim bought did the trick. With all the niceties abounding, I feared I'd lose my mind in a state full of Tims. I felt especially panicked when I sneezed in a bar of locals and they all said, "Bless you." Try that in New York City, where instead, the next day, patrons would be scanning the paper for my obituary in the hopes they could snag a cheap apartment.

Since we had an extra day or two we hadn't planned on (we hoped no more, as the weather forecast indicated the imminent arrival of the season's first snow), we took a suggestion from Brian and drove the Jeep northwest to the nearly 75,000 acre Moosehead Lake. It was a three-hour drive, and by the time we got there, we were ready for lunch. We happened upon a cozy place in Greenville, The Black Frog, with good food and an even better menu. With entrées and descriptions such as "Mooseballs: Unquestionably the tenderest cut of the moose. Sautéed or broiled to perfection and graced with our own special sauce. Requires 48 hour advance notice and 25% deposit . . . $1,495.00." Or "Blooming Onion: The kitchen hates making this. Irritate them and order it anyway." Or "The Misteak on the Lake: Either a great steak sandwich or this restaurant."

Afterwards, we grabbed some homemade ice cream across the street, liberated Miles from the car, and sat on a bench by the lake to watch the seaplanes land and take flight. Thus sustained, we took a chance in the wilds and drove for about a hundred miles on a logging road Rand marked "private" and which didn't even register on Map Breath. It was quite rough and gravelly at times, with many places to veer off for four-wheeling and moose watching, although despite all the posted signs about moose crossings and "high impact" moose areas, Tim and I were apparently the only people ever to have been to Moosehead Lake and not encounter one of the beasts.

About halfway along, we crossed the Appalachian Trail at Mount Katahdin in Baxter State Park, near where hikers of the 2,160-mile footpath finish up in the fall. Sheryl (the same friend who came in second naming our bus) hiked part of the trail years ago. Her lifelong dream is to finish it (I apparently not only have lunatic patients, but lunatic friends as well) and she had told me the hikers always appreciated some "trail magic" (i.e., unexpected bits of good luck like food or a lift). With Miles in the back, we didn't have room for the latter (and truly, the hikers were rather ripe), but I did hand out a couple of my low-carb snack bars. They were taken gratefully, only reinforcing to me how truly miserable the whole hiking thing is.

We managed to get out of Maine just in time to avoid the snow, but caught considerable precipitation in the form of rain when we stayed just off Cape Cod, Massachusetts. The RV park there had a Jacuzzi, and after partaking, we hung our bathing suits on a line over the foot of the bed. I awoke the next morning with my feet soaking wet. I nudged Tim. Could it be the bathing suits? He sleepily said yes, but even in my foggy state I realized that if we'd both worn size 20, there was no way a bathing suit could hold that much water. Our bus was leaking.

It rained for two days straight. Our bus kept leaking. Tim donned his best Project Nerd water-repellent rain gear, retrieved the brand-new Holy Grail of ladders he'd stowed in the bay ("What's wrong with your old ladder?" "On the bus, I need a ladder to do more than one thing." "I didn't know ladders did more than one thing." "It's a stepladder *and* an extension ladder." *I see.* A veritable Swiss Army knife of ladders, if you will), and draped heavy plastic over the bus. He wasn't the only superhero in the park doing so, although surely, none of them sported accoutrements as spiffy. When the weather finally cleared, PN of course went even further, using super-duper caulk recommended by Chris to fill in all the cracks, applied with a brand-new caulk gun. Then he cleaned all the water spots on the inside of the bus with the industrial fabric cleaner he also got at the local Home Depot. (There always seemed to be one of these near an RV park, probably because lots of PNs, wings clipped by their wives, use various rigs as their alternate modes of transportation.)

It was also in Massachusetts that I rediscovered Friendly's. As kids, we used to go to Friendly's for ice-cream treats, and for really special occasions, we'd preface our desserts with one of their fabulous burgers. Being an East Coast thing, Tim had never heard of it until I squealed with delight when we happened by a Friendly's in our Jeep. I hadn't thought about the place in years.

"We have to go! We have to go!" I exclaimed, channeling my inner twelve-year-old as I bounced in my seat. Tim dutifully drove us back for dinner that night.

I remembered not only the food but the service, which strives to live up to the restaurant's name. To every single one of my change orders (fried onions *and* a slab of raw onion on my burger, no bacon, no bun, low-carb chocolate in my milkshake, ranch dressing with my onion rings, and don't forget the steak sauce), the waitress whooped an enthusiastic "NO PROBLEM!" As a kid, to have an adult hang on your every word and treat every request as gospel was kinda nice. As a bus phobic, to hear a "NO

PROBLEM!" in a situation where I could really be assured there was none was kinda liberating.

But the next Friendly's we tried near Boston (yep, I was on a roll reliving the highlights of my childhood, just as Tim was on a roll sleeping on the couch because he couldn't stand the reek of onions in our bed) seemed to lack the same . . . Friendly-ness. When I gave my by now usual order, there was not a "NO PROBLEM!" to be heard. Instead, the waitress practically sneered, "The woman likes her condiments." Hadn't she been trained that sarcasm is not particularly friendly?

Then, my order complete, I was treated to a "She's a veritable condiment queen!" I consoled myself with the fact that at least she was giving me a promotion of sorts from Princess. Tim, who always rolls his eyes at my dining requests (and who takes great pride in following *his* order with "and I'll have it exactly as it is on the menu"), was trying not to let his soda shoot through his nostrils after my Heinzien coronation. Then, unfortunately for us all, I noticed my ice tea glass said "Free Refills." You must understand that at Friendly's, freverything is freenamed. The onion rings are "fronions," the shakes, "fribbles," and so on. So I asked the fraitress, "How come the drinks aren't called freefills?" She shot me a strange look, finally got it, and narrowed her eyes in a manner that was anything but friendly.

"Freefills. Cute. I'll let management know. One more thing for them to throw at us."

That was the last time we dined at Friendly's.

In early October, we dipped into New Hampshire, mainly to climb to the 6,200-foot summit of Mount Washington (by car, of course). As we waited on line just before the entrance, I leapt out of the Jeep to take pictures of a pretty stream that perfectly reflected the hues of the surrounding trees awash in the colors of fall. The air was warm but with that crisp hint of winter to come, layering the moment with a familiar wish that things could stay just as they were. I thought of how lucky we were to be able to do this, to experience and see all we had thus far, and I realized I owed it all to Tim.

I rushed back to the Jeep to tell him just that, with the caveat that if he ever repeated it, I'd disavow all knowledge of the statement and never say anything nice to him again. As this was only too easy for him to believe, he never did mention it, although I could often tell, as we shared similar moments of contentment in our travels, he was remembering nonetheless.

The view from the summit was stunning, but it was cold up there. Real cold. No wonder its observatory clocked a world record wind gust—231 mph—in 1934. Tim suggested I put rocks in my pockets. But I just held on to him the entire time we were outside, especially after noticing one of the buildings had giant chains securing its roof to the ground.

We traveled on to Vermont, where, near Montpelier, we encountered equally glorious leaf and local color, as we ran into a fellow busing couple. The wife was a sixty-year-old Jimmy Buffett fanatic and self-proclaimed Parrot Head whose dream had come true when she won a costume contest and got to dance onstage with her idol. I recognized a fellow Princess immediately (they were, indeed, from Long Island), in spite of her traveling incognito, masked by this seemingly strange fixation.

"I have so much fun. I'm high on life. I don't need drugs as long as I have Jimmy Buffett!" she proclaimed. I was dubious, but her boundless energy and optimism won me over. I immediately bought a Jimmy Buffett CD and even made "Margaritaville" one of my ringtones.

It was not unusual for us to meet lots of people in the RV parks. Well, mainly Tim met them, of course. He was the one who walked Miles every morning, and sixty-pound standard poodles are great conversation starters.

"What kind of dog is that?"

"He's a poodle."

"THAT'S a poodle?"

In any event, when I ventured out, Tim would introduce me to anyone he'd already met. I noticed he was introducing me as Doreen *Orion*, to indicate my last name was different than his, Justice, and I realized he did it in deference to what he imagined were my feminist sensibilities.

"Sweetie, do you know why I didn't change my name when we got married?" I asked. He thought about it a moment, then answered, "No. I guess I don't."

"It just seemed like a royal pain to have to change my name on my driver's license, my Social Security card, and all my diplomas. It's fine with me if people think I'm Doreen Justice."

"I should have known," he laughed.

Of course, there were times he regretted introducing me at all. For if we lingered to talk, the inevitable round of "What do you do for a living?" started. When people find out we're psychiatrists, it always amazes me how many come up with the same lame question, all imagining we've never heard it before.

"So, you've been analyzing me this whole time?" It's at this point that Tim cringes and tries to slink away. He knows what's coming.

"Why?" I sweetly inquire. "If I were a proctologist, do you think I'd want to look up your butt?"

It was while in New England we realized we were not the only ones on the bus who seemed changed by the journey thus far. Shula had acquired balls—specifically, Morty's. Now she was the one who growled and spit when *he* got too close to *her*. She'd even taken a swipe or two at both of her brothers. While it was my belief that a life in motion was making her irritable (for Shula, was living on the bus akin to being perennially transported in a giant cat carrier to the vet?), Tim theorized she was simply emboldened by the newfound knowledge that if she could survive this, she could survive anything. Obviously, as two shrinks, we realized we were expressing our feelings about my bus phobia through her.

And why not? Good-natured, ready-for-anything Miles took after his father. Cranky old-Jewish-man Morty was clearly my son. No wonder Shula always seemed left out. Maybe it was, indeed, feeling she finally had something in common with one parent—her mother—that was bringing her out of her shell. Too bad she picked the wrong parent.

Rather than taking her on, Morty simply walked away from Shula's outbursts. Perhaps he was mellowing, along with his father. As for Miles, he still believed the entire world existed to lavish praise and affection on him, a notion only reinforced by our travels.

Chapter Six

SOUTHBOUND IN THE FIRE LANE

Fire in the Hole

2½ parts Bacardi 151
1½ parts orange curacao
squeeze lemon

*Hold lit match in one hand, shaker in other. Bring together
until hair catches fire. Make note to use only 80 proof rum
next time.*

By mid-October, we were headed to New York City to
my parents' place in Queens. Since there was simply
nowhere to park, we had to de-bus and ditch our rig at a storage facility in New Jersey. Then we gathered up the pets and a
few belongings in the Jeep and settled into the Orions' spare
bedroom.

Tim had a lot to learn when he married into a Jewish family,
and his education began the day of our wedding. We included

Jewish traditions in our ceremony and I don't think he really understood what he was getting into when he signed the ketubah (wedding contract), written in Hebrew.

"What's it say?" he whispered to me.

"Oh, you know . . ." I explained with all the nonchalance I could muster. "Just that we'll be good to each other . . . that sort of thing. It's an ancient document. All couples getting married have to have one." I watched intently as he signed his name after mine. It was only a few weeks before he realized his mistake.

"Oh, honey! Tim!" I sang out sweetly. Already suited up in steel-toed boots, Carhartt pants, and work shirt, he bounded down the stairs, thrust his hands on his hips, took a wide stance, and nodded his head.

"Project Man at your service, ma'am." (I suppose here I should fess up: We had always referred to his alter ego as "Project Man," until the day he showed up in thick prescription safety goggles. It was at that point I christened him "Project Nerd.") I gave him a sardonic look from the couch.

"Oh, sorry," I said, scanning the windows. "Hope I didn't blow your cover." Then, "Can you please move some furniture? I want to see what the armoire will look like over—"

"I'll do it later," he assured me. "Right now I'm in the middle of—"

"Oh, but sweetie," I interrupted, batting my lashes, "it says in the ketubah you're supposed to do what I ask, when I ask it." To his astonished look, I just shrugged and pointed out, "You signed it." (Years ago, I learned a much simpler tactic that any woman of any religion can use: If there was something I merely needed him to read, I just put it on our computer and labeled the file "My Hot Lesbian Fantasies." Worked every time.)

During our nearly fifteen years together, Tim got to be well versed in Jewish cultural issues, although one time in New York, he had a rather rude awakening when my father confided a secret to him.

My dad is a retired college professor but had been a journey-man cabinetmaker earlier in life. During my childhood, he even made all the furniture in our house. Whenever we visited, Tim tried to get Henry to show him some tricks of the trade, but soon learned that my laissez-faire attitude to . . . well, life had to come from somewhere. For example, when Tim queried how to make a cabinet joint perfectly tight so it had no gaps, my father responded, with a wave of his hand, "Ach. Just use a little *schmear*." Tim eventually understood this particular use of the Yiddish word for "spread" to be indicative of wood putty.

My father's attitude resonates through every fiber of his being, even down to his vocal cords. Born in Austria, he fled in 1939 during his teens, emigrated to Israel, and served in the British Army in World War II, so his accent is rather indescribable and, I've been told, rather unintelligible. The first time they met, Tim found Henry barely comprehensible, prompting him to pull me aside and say, "You didn't tell me your father had an accent." To which I asked, "What accent?" My mother, born in this country to two Jewish immigrants from a Russian *shtetl* (a small Jewish village formerly found throughout Eastern Europe), is a speech pathologist and also a retired college professor. She even wrote a best-selling textbook, *Pronouncing American English*. Her meth-ods may be the gold standard, but they haven't managed to crack my dad's cords. She thinks he's just being stubborn. As my fa-ther's daughter, I assure her he's not; stubborn is too much of an effort.

A few years back, after my parents moved to New York City and my dad could no longer have a woodworking shop at home, he rented a space in a not-so-great neighborhood to pursue his hobby. One day, as he left the place, he was mugged at knifepoint and thrown to the ground. We happened to be visiting shortly afterwards and my father confided what happened to Tim, admonishing him, "Don't tell my wife or daughter." He was afraid we would make him give up his rental. The next time we visited, after my father had already relinquished the space, the subject of crime in the city came up. He chimed in, "I was mugged," and proceeded to tell us the story. My mother demanded, "Why didn't you tell me?" as she shot him a look Jewish wives have perfected ever since Zipporah reproached Moses, "What? All this wandering for only nine commandments?" (Obviously, her nagging was quite effective.) My dad just shrugged his shoulders, absolving himself of all responsibility.

"Tim knew," he said. Now it was Tim's turn to face both Orion women's wrath.

"Why didn't you tell us?" we demanded. His defense—"Henry told me not to tell anyone"—only deepened the hole my father had dug for him.

Now, secure in the knowledge I could rely on my husband to be an information sieve, we settled in for a couple of weeks. Although Tim loves New York City, his alter ego loves my parents' apartment in Queens even more. There's just so much for a Project Nerd to do, as while my mother can come up with a multitude of chores, my father insists on taking his retirement literally. So whenever we visit, she makes a list for Tim, who inevitably finds ways to tweak it just a bit.

On this particular visit, my mother wanted Tim to rearrange some furniture in the living room and repair broken grout in the master shower. Instead, Tim took her shopping for new furniture, including an entertainment center and TV, regrouted all the tile in the shower and tub, installed a new vanity, fixed a leaky toilet, and repaired a door that wouldn't shut. Then he made a list for our next trip. Maybe it's her Depression-era mentality, but while

Gertrude likes the thought of having things look nicer, she has a hard time following through to get them that way. She needs someone to push her, and Tim is only too happy to do it. And with the whole bus thing, it was nice to see Tim was finally starting to push himself to get more from life, too.

It was just as well that Tim helped my mom shop for furniture: To say our house where I grew up in Great Neck, Long Island, was the laughingstock of the neighborhood would be like saying Kiss's costumes are only slightly over the top. Of course, one could argue that the band is only expressing its own style. So were my parents; a style I call Shtetl Gothic. It wasn't just the orange Formica countertops in the kitchen (which were a perfect accompaniment to the orange Formica panels in the dark brown cabinets) or the massive black Formica dining table with its even more massive antiqued red wooden chairs. That's *antiqued*, as opposed to antique. You know, the stuff that has black, skid mark–like streaks running through it to simulate class, without any actual danger of achieving it.

My parents had so perfected their unique style with the furniture my father had constructed from scratch, they soon branched out, becoming equally adept at taking established, venerated old designs and making them their own. Perhaps that's what they were thinking the day they added vertical strips of wood, antiqued red, to the black shutters of our formally elegant, white-columned colonial.

The neighbors never (openly, anyway) complained about any of my parents' "improvements"—that is, until the day a few of them came over to cajole Henry into mowing the lawn. Style (or lack of it) was one thing, but knee-high weeds in the suburbs were quite another. My father always maintained he liked the "natural" look. But when pressed, it became obvious he had simply started rehearsing for retirement decades early. Why bother mowing the lawn when you just have to keep doing it over and over again? No wonder that in my lazier moments, Tim calls me "Henrietta." Then he ponders how in the world he ended up married to an old Jewish man.

Of course, I'm no stranger myself to stylistic misfortunes, as I'd had long hair since I was in single digits. Shortly after we arrived in the city, in the spirit of the year of trying new things, I wrangled an appointment (did I mention I'm a Miss September?) with a stylist, Nick Arrojo, from my favorite reality TV makeover show, *What Not to Wear*. I knew he'd want to cut it all off, and he did, although he seemed rather surprised I didn't protest. (I was rather surprised I didn't cry.) Tim came, not only because he wanted to meet a celebrity, but to record the moment for posterity.

Nick went along with good humor, even pointing to the growing pile on the floor, saying, "There, that's the picture!" I must admit I was a bit taken aback when this former working-class Brit gave me a lesson in royal behavior: As he cut, rather than pin pieces of coif out of the way himself, he had a young woman employee hold my hair back for him. However he did it, I was thrilled with the result and couldn't help wonder why it always seemed to take me so long to come around to good ideas—traveling around the country in a bus, notwithstanding.

Having a couple of stationary weeks also gave me some time to reflect about how our bus trip seemed to have brought out my "inner Doug."

My beloved cousin Doug, whom I am closer to than any other human being save my husband, has always been terrified of flying. So terrified, in fact, he once took a Greyhound bus from New York to Mexico City, just to avoid a flight.

Years back, we both had to be at a family function across the country. Since I refused to travel by bus (ah, the good old days) he reluctantly, and only after the promise of prodigious drug samples, acquiesced to accompanying me via airplane. It was a delightful four-hour trip—for me—as I tormented him by periodically clutching the armrests, exclaiming, "Did you hear that?" and shooting him dramatic, panicked looks.

If only Doug could see me now, on the bus. Terrified on the bus. And although we've laughed many times over the years about that flight, when I saw him in New York City, I apologized profusely. His graceful commiseration about my current mode of travel meant a lot to me. It also taught me that while cruelty can be fun for a few moments, compassion has a much longer shelf life. (Not that Doug is immune from the taunting gene, mind you—he is my first cousin, after all. In fact, when Colorado was having a particularly horrendous winter, he couldn't resist e-mailing me: "I see that you just had another blizzard. Did Tim tell you about it?")

And there is something to be said for gentle ribbing. I'm the only one in our entire family, including his parents and siblings, who has ever been allowed to see Doug's apartment. It's a mess, even by my slothful standards. Tim and I always tease him that gay men are supposed to naturally migrate toward interior design and cleanliness. On this trip, we were even able to hold up a specific example: The gay couple who rented our house moved in on a Wednesday and had a dinner party on Friday. Not only was there not a single box in sight, but the place was immaculate and looked much better than it had—ever.

Doug moved into his apartment in 1997 and still threatens to clean the bathroom. To his credit, though, he said he was postponing replacing the carpet until his sick cat passed away. Well, Shayna has been RIP for the last four years, but her copious vomit stains remain, an immemorial memorial testament to Doug's disdain for cleanliness.

From New York, we gave my mother a ride to her favorite weekend getaway, Atlantic City, New Jersey. I was reluctant to acquiesce to this, Tim's latest harebrained scheme, because my mother is not the calmest person in the world. I figured if *I* was afraid to ride in the bus, I'd probably end up having to medicate her, and since treating family members is strictly forbidden by the AMA, would lose my medical license, to boot.

Yet, sitting next to me in the buddy seat, she turned and said, with the widest smile I'd ever seen on her face, "I don't know why this makes you so nervous. It's terrific!" I was put to shame. *If this woman can ride in the bus unafraid, so can I.* I vowed when the year ended, I would investigate a potential cure for millions of phobics: hanging out with an even worse phobic.

While in Atlantic City, I introduced my mother to the concept of fruity martinis. She became as smitten as I. We quickly discovered a restaurant with an impressive menu of the tasty treats, parked ourselves at the bar, and endeavored to become fast friends with Ted, the resident mixologist.

Ted had been a bartender in town for twenty-six years. While he was very helpful pointing out some favorites on the menu, I think he was mostly relieved assuming a middle-aged woman and her mother, chaperoned by their bus driver, were unlikely to raise much of a ruckus. And indeed, after we'd had a few, *he* seemed to loosen up even more than we had and started lamenting about "kids these days." He told us he'd carded a girl who had just turned eighteen. She strode up to the bar and informed him she wanted a "Sex on a Pool Table." He asked if she knew what was in it. She did not. Neither did he. As he related his tale, Ted shook his head in disgust.

"I told her I could make a Sex on the Beach, but Sex on a Pool

Table?" He sighed and shook his head again, repeating, "Kids these days." Then Tim, who was making his way through Ted's formidable list of microbrewed beers, discovered the bar bet, vis-à-vis my mother. He wagered Ted that he couldn't guess Gertrude's age within ten years. Ted was off by nearly twenty. Tim got a free beer and started perusing the joint for his next patsy. My mother, initially taken aback at being treated as an object of gambling, in the end wound up quite pleased with the grudging compliments all around.

After a spate of gaming and all-you-can-eat buffets (which we referred to as barfatoriums), Tim and I were ready to hit the road again. On our way out of town, we dropped my mother off at the Greyhound terminal. After she assured Tim the bus ride home couldn't possibly be as wonderful as the one down, we continued south.

With my mother sitting in the buddy seat next to me, Shula had been left to fend for herself and find her own spot while the bus was moving. She must not have appreciated it, because as soon as we dropped Gertrude off, Shula leapt up next to me, without my having to go get her. From that point on, whenever Tim started the ignition, that cat raced up front to take her rightful place before anyone else could steal it.

As always, we got varied responses from tollbooth operators along the way, from "What a beautiful cat!" (Shula) to "Are you towing a vehicle?" Tim had perfected his reply: "No, that guy's been following me too close for the last hundred miles." But on the Jersey Turnpike, we got a rather unique query: "Is this Tom Jones's tour bus?" Pleased at being taken for a professional, Tim reluctantly informed the woman it was not and questioned her in turn. Apparently, Mr. Jones was performing in Atlantic City soon and she already had her tickets.

"Get his latest album, sista!" she exhorted me. "You'll love it!" I did. And do.

At our next RV park, near Silver Spring, Maryland, we had our only parking mishap of the year. Normally, whenever we arrived at our site, if we had to back in (rather than pull through), Tim unhooked the Jeep, I drove it out of the way, then ran back to guide him into the spot (wearing secure shoes). Although Peter had finally installed the backup camera after our meltdown cruise, it wasn't working, of course. Still, my hand signals had become more professional (well, at least less frenzied) and we had developed a system whereby we usually completed the maneuver flawlessly. But this time it was already dark and neither of us noticed a post sticking two feet up from the ground. Backing into the spot, we dented one of the baggage doors on the side of the bus.

It was easy for me to shrug off, but Tim felt terrible. I assumed this was simply a blow to his male ego; backing shit up is supposed to be manly stuff, after all. It took me a while to understand the full extent of his humiliation. Tim's childhood was spent in old, run-down homes. Nothing was ever new and whenever something inevitably broke, his parents had to find the cheapest way to repair it, if it could be repaired at all.

The first time he took me to Reno, we passed a parking lot and he observed, "That's where I grew up." In a dilapidated house built in 1903 and never renovated, Tim lived on that spot until his family moved out when he was thirteen. When they left, they took their parlor furnaces, the only way to heat the place. A few years later, another even poorer family moved in and fashioned a makeshift fireplace to keep warm. That winter, the house burned to the ground and the family lost three of its children. Tim still remembers the shame he felt when, pointing the place out to a friend, the kid asked incredulously (and with a touch of pity in his voice), "Oh my God, you grew up there?"

We stayed in Maryland mainly so I could meet a host of e-mail and phone friends I'd had for years, through one of the insurance companies I worked for based there. It was an odd experience, finally putting faces to the voices I thought I knew so well, and it made me wonder how I came across to people myself. One of the longtime care managers, Flo, who always seemed to call to review a case during my morning workout, chided me regularly for my exertions.

"I ain't got no time for exercise! My ten kids keep me too busy," she'd laugh. When I got to her cubicle, I stopped dead in my tracks. I was expecting Jabba the Social Worker, but Flo was absolutely gorgeous—and svelte.

"How do you stay so thin having ten kids?" I blurted out. She laughed again.

"Oh, I've only got three. They just feel like ten." Seeing Flo made me realize how other people who've never actually viewed me probably view me. To them, I must seem a typical shut-in, that is, someone dressed in fashion from the decade in which she last had contact with society. I simply could not abide that thought. *Maybe I do need to get out more—or at least say I do.*

When I met another of my e-mail/phone buddies, I immediately felt cheated: All those years without knowing I had a much younger friend with dreadlocks. Yet if I had seen her in a coffee shop in Boulder, I would have thought I had nothing in common with one still in her twenties and so hip.

This left me wondering how I became so narrow. As a physician, I was trained to gather information and make judgments about people, but now I wondered if perhaps that training hadn't served me terribly well. (Do medical schools give refunds?) What else was I missing by being blinded by the belief that I had all the facts? How many other dreadlocked or punk or gothic (and I do love those pointy-toed, lace-up boots) young women, or old ones, all of whom populate Boulder in droves, had I never even considered getting to know?

Then we went out to dinner with Scott and his wife. He had quit the company a few years before but still kept in touch. I figured him for a latter-day hippie type. While we were working together, he called me "Dude," until I unfortunately joked, "That's Dr. Dudette, to you"—unfortunately because that's what he started calling me. This time, I was not mistaken.

There were Dudes and Dudettes all around during dinner at the Baltimore harbor, and after our meal, the four of us strolled the waterfront. I'd lived in the city for a summer, nearly twenty-five years before, when I dated a true Baltimoron—but that's another story. The harbor was just starting to be renovated at the time, and now I enjoyed seeing the finished product, particularly with a couple of locals. Tim, on the other hand, was fascinated by the row houses. We mused that if we lived there, on scrub day, when the neighborhood women scoured the white marble steps on their hands and knees, Tim, joining them, could get some good cleaning tips.

Finally, we went over to my cousin Jane's (Doug's sister's) house in Chevy Chase. As Tim related stories of our journey (omitting all the mishaps—she is, after all, a government attorney specializing in safety issues), it was evident Jane could not comprehend how we seemed to be having so much fun. Hearing about it all, I realized with a start that we were, indeed.

We traveled south through Virginia, staying at a campground that, in our RV guidebook, boasted a lake and a view. I really should have known by now not to trust those park descriptions or even their names, for that matter, for the industry seemed rife with false advertising: The idyllic-sounding Whispering Pines RV Park had been more like Deafening Rail Yard. Then there was Vista View RV Resort—the view was of the town dump, and as for the resort part, let's just say the amenities included a mossy swimming hole and a Tuff Shed with an air hockey table.

So at this particular place in Staunton, Virginia, the "lake" we got to "view" was a duck pond, at best, with pretty mangy-looking birds, to boot—certainly unworthy of any l'orange sauce. At least the campground was close to Shenandoah National Park, where the 105-mile Skyline Drive provided spectacular scenic overlooks and walking trails. Tim even got me out of the Jeep for a stroll or two. We spied a marker for the Appalachian Trail (a capital "A" with a vertical line perpendicular to the horizontal one of the letter, to make it look like an arrow) and marveled at how far hikers had to go from here to where we had seen the end near Moosehead Lake in Maine.

Once out of the park, we kept passing signs for the "Natural Bridge," so decided to investigate. It's actually a geological formation (yeah, Tim loved it), a creek which carved out a gorge through a mountain of limestone, forming a 215-foot-high arch. Its span is so wide that Highway 11 passes right over it. Because it was known in the eighteenth and nineteenth centuries as one of the Seven Natural Wonders of the Modern World, it, along with Niagara Falls, drew hordes of visitors from as far away as Europe. Just for thrills, the braver amongst them were lowered over the edge in a hexagonal steel cage while a violinist played.

Look, those people didn't have TV back then.

We did find it compelling enough, though, to crane our necks and use binoculars to see where, in 1750, a young George Washington was said to have carved his initials partway up the arch when he was surveying the site for Lord Fairfax. (Quite the environmentalist, the father of our country. He takes an axe to a cherry tree and tags a previously pristine ancient rock formation. Nice going, George!)

Near Charlottesville, Virginia, Monticello became for Tim a highlight of our trip, granting him a presidential pardon, if not ultimate victory, in our years of Thermostat Wars. For it was there, on the tour of the third president's grand abode, we learned of Jefferson's "fire point," i.e., the temperature at which he was willing to light a fire: 55 degrees. As I scowled, my normally reserved husband high-fived the startled tour guide and exclaimed, "Jefferson's my man!"

Monticello showcases many of the prolific inventor's creations. Our favorite had to be the Great Clock in the grand entrance hall, which spanned the length of the room, powered by sets of cannonball-like weights descending on either side of the door, where vertically, from top to bottom, the days of the week are listed. Jefferson ran out of space, so he had a hole built in the floor; thus, Saturday is in the basement. The Founding Father equivalent of *schmear*.

Leaving Virginia, we got a lesson in being neighborly when we parked overnight at a Wal-Mart near Richmond. A sixtyish woman walking her Labrador mix stopped by the bus. She was "camping" too, in her van, she said.

"So do you all stay at Wal-Marts all the time?" When we demurred, she reassured us, "Well, don't worry. Everyone stays here." She was right. By the time we got to bed, six more large rigs were parked nearby in our own prefab' and fully fabulous neighborhood. The next morning, as we returned from some shopping, we could hear the rumble of our generator all the way across the parking lot.

"I can see why campgrounds don't allow people to run those things," I said, then wondered aloud why we couldn't hear anyone else's, as the morning had quite a chill. Tim explained they could all use their rigs' batteries for heat and added pointedly, "They don't have their Internet satellite, surround sound stereo, dishwasher, and washing machine running."

"Oh," I replied. "I guess they're roughing it."

He shook his head.

"Don't you find it funny we're living in a luxury home at the Wal-Mart?"

I thought about it for a bit, then had to admit, "No, not really." I suppose once I got used to the idea of living on a bus, then actually lived on a bus, nothing else in my world could appear terribly askew. Just the night before, we had seen a Wal-Mart employee returning carts to the store, dressed as an Elvis impersonator. Even his reflective vest didn't seem all that out of place.

As we left the state, I consulted Rand and wondered why Virginia is Virginia and not East Virginia. We had, after all, gone through West Virginia to get to Virginia and were now headed to its southern neighbors North and South Carolina. And we'd already been to North and South Dakota, so it seemed confusing that Virginia is just Virginia. Tim sighed while I prattled on about this (apparently only to me) fascinating paradox. I guess now he knows how I feel when he ruminates about things mechanical.

In Cape Hatteras, North Carolina, we discovered even more about being good neighbors from a little-known story of the brave souls instrumental in helping the Wright brothers take flight. That part of the coast has seen so many shipwrecks—over six hundred since the sixteenth century—it's known as the "Graveyard of the Atlantic." The reasons for the shipwrecks have something to do with the collision of opposing currents and the propensity for hurricanes, as well as navigational challenges, but since I'm not Tim, it was enough for me to understand it's a treacherous spot for mariners. Rescuers trying to save sailors' lives as well as salvage ships have a long tradition here. After Wilbur and Orville set up shop in Kill Devil Hills, whenever they needed manpower to help launch, they'd hang a red scarf and those good neighbors (as if they didn't have enough to do already) would come on over to help.

Although it's not like I was hanging out waiting to save lives or anything, I had always been unwilling to help Project Nerd with his home improvement schemes, no matter how much he said he needed me. Of course, he always managed to rope me in anyway—sometimes quite literally. I really don't think I can be blamed for my lack of support, considering that his propositions ranged from the merely ill-advised to the decidedly deranged, if not potentially deadly—for us both.

There was the time a big boulder fell near our driveway. Note I said "near." It was actually just *beyond* a portion of the road we used. In other words, that boulder could have stayed where it was for millennia and we would not have been inconvenienced in any way. A normal husband would use the phone to have it removed. Project Nerd (why, oh, why can't I be like a typical superhero's wife—blissfully ignorant of my husband's true identity?), in an effort to "save the association some money," dug a pit just off the road, then used a come-along attached to his truck, which was in turn attached to a strap around the boulder. This, he assured me, would "scoot" said boulder into the pit.

Unfortunately, since I had always absolutely refused to drive his monstrosity of a truck (some large black thing from the 1970s which Tim insisted on referring to as a "classic," and which, the one time I did drive it, was so wide, I couldn't tell where I was in the road and bent one of his precious wheels on a highway divider), he did, while I "steered" the boulder with a lever. I learned very quickly that boulders don't "scoot." Perhaps even more importantly, they don't "steer" very well, either.

He once made me help him move a two-hundred-pound TV. After all, why do it when there happened to be several burly construction guys at our house who could easily have pitched in to lift the thing? Oh, no. Much better to wait until he's alone with his pip-squeak wife. So, using a piano dolly (PN keeps several in his super-secret lair, which mere mortals refer to as a "garage"), he employed stacked scraps of lumber (he's got a lot of that squirreled away, too) to fashion "steps" upon which we (and I dearly wish I could put "we" in quotes here) walked the TV down to the dolly, wheeled it to its new spot, then reversed the process. After that incident, I strongly suspected the "nerd" part of his alter ego enjoyed the challenge of figuring out how to get these crazy things done even more than the "project" part liked doing them. But, even so. Why should I suffer?

Unfortunately for him, the time I finally decided I'd had enough almost proved his kryptonitian undoing.

PN was cleaning the gutters on our house two stories up when his ladder slipped. Not wearing his cape that day (I guess he didn't have enough laundry for a red load), he couldn't simply fly away to safety and was left dangling, hanging on to the gutter with one hand, one foot perched precariously on a lone rung. He used his other hand to bang on the window. I ignored him. After all, I was used to tuning out all the noise around the house whenever Tim's alter ego was about, and this time was no exception. Until the incessant screaming began.

"I'M FALLING," and the like. Obviously, this was not at all accurate, as one glance out the window proved him to be nearly stationary. "I'm going to fall" would have been more precise. Grammar Nerd, he's not.

As I ran to his aid, I couldn't help wondering why my resourceful husband didn't figure out how not to fall all by himself. I was certain, using the knowledge he'd gleaned from his precious Physics for Majors class, that some equation about mass, gravity, and density (of his brain, perhaps) would come to him eventually. After all, my glance out the window already confirmed he had just figured out a way to stop time. Is it really any wonder I never wanted to be a sidekick? For even more justification, I need only recall Toto, Robin, and Kato. Their outfits are so pathetic.

After I steadied the ladder, I treated Tim to my usual lament when he got himself into project-inspired fixes and needed me to bail him out.

"Why can't you just call some guy friend?" It took me a long time to understand why he couldn't. His close male friends, men he'd known since college and residency, lived over a thousand miles away. Calling some neighbor we barely knew, or even a colleague at the hospital, would only reinforce that due to the demands of his work life, he hadn't made close connections with men locally. It was something he missed but always put on the back burner, thinking there would be time later. It seemed later arrived while we were on the road. For even though the connections were brief, he socialized a lot more, especially in the RV parks where making the rounds with the dog might include stopping to admire someone else's rig. As a result, if the bus needed some tinkering, he gladly accepted the help of a campground neighbor who wandered by. This made him realize even more how much he'd missed the whole male camaraderie thing, and he swore he'd do better when we got home.

Of course, after getting help with some home improvement project, Tim figured he'd be inviting the guy out for a beer. On Cape Hatteras, he wouldn't have to, as there was always the Brew Thru—a drive-through beer place. This is no drive-up, fast-food window, but a store you actually drive through the middle of. A clerk then takes your order, then runs around and pulls out bottles while you sit in your car, marveling at the convenience of it all. Finally, an acceptable way to combine two of my husband's favorite pastimes: driving and beer. If only there'd been a heavy machinery shop out back, he could've had a trifecta.

We traveled to the interior of the state, where we stayed at one of the most unusual campgrounds we've ever been in (and one that, for once, lived up to its name): Rolling View State Recreation Area, about a half hour east of Durham. While a lovely setting on a lake might be expected in a state park, what was different here was that such a bucolic atmosphere could be found smack-dab in the middle of an urban area. The only issue we had with the place is that the gates close at 6 p.m., so campers returning in their tow vehicles have to park outside, then walk about a mile to their rigs in absolute pitch darkness. We learned to bring a flashlight.

Just west of Durham, in Hillsborough, North Carolina, we stumbled across the Burwell School Historic Site. There, in 1837, in a nondescript, white clapboard house, Anna Burwell, wife of the local pastor, opened one of the earliest female academies. This trailblazing woman (who undoubtedly never had the notion to just sit around in her pajamas and, if she did, would not have found doing so appealing in the least) came up with a full curriculum of literature, history, and language all on her own, educating two hundred students over two decades. She was even an early proponent of physical exercise, making her young charges dance indoors when the weather was too inclement to go outside. At one time, the Burwells' modest four-room abode was home to more than sixty people, arguably the most extraordinary of whom was a young slave, Elizabeth Hobbes Keckly.

Even after enduring harsh beatings at the hands of the pastor, Keckly was not beaten down. She eventually bought her own freedom and traveled north, where, as an accomplished seamstress, she made dresses for wives of prominent politicians, including Mary Todd Lincoln, who would later refer to Keckly as "my best friend." Perhaps Keckly's greatest achievement was not even made on her own behalf; dismayed by the press's treatment of her beloved Mrs. Lincoln, she wrote an eloquent book about their relationship, intending nothing more than to defend the First Lady to the public. That book, however, in which she details her life as a slave, has become an important historical document, valued by many for so much more than she originally intended.

As we poked around in the backyard, we saw a small, extremely sturdy building that seemed to have weathered the years better than any other on the property. Now we understand what is so impressive about a "brick shit house."

Keckly's story couldn't help but drive home how insignificant our trials and tribulations on the bus had been, even as we still struggled to fix Peter's many mistakes. Up to this point, we had gone nearly four months without a reliable TV signal, an unimaginable hardship at the start of our trip. Now we no longer cared. Still, it became somewhat of a badge of honor to systematically purge our home sweet bus home of all things Peter. So, after having some parts shipped our way, Tim climbed up on the roof. (Let it be noted I wanted to end that sentence right there, but Tim insisted I add the words "with the azimuth motor.") He actually would have finished that particular project quickly if he had not also taken the opportunity to grasp the three-foot plastic dome covering the satellite dish, thrust it in the air over his head, and, silhouetted by the sun, proclaim, "LET THERE BE TELEVISION!"

People in the park were undoubtedly confused as to whether they were seeing some sort of Bus God or just a superhero with too much time on his hands.

Once he came back to earth, we stared at the screen open-mouthed and, as mindless commercials played, realized how much television is like crack. I could feel my IQ drop a few points, but was powerless to tear myself away.

"Look!" Tim marveled. "They got movin' images and everythin'!" I tried to rise, but was rooted to the reclining love seat. I cursed its plush leather pillows, specifically designed to maximize viewing pleasure. Then I realized I was still holding the remote. *If I can just get my index finger to move.*

"Must . . . stop . . . picture . . . machine . . ." I somehow managed to press the "off" button. The spell broken, we turned toward each other.

"That was one bad relapse, man," I lamented. Tim agreed. In a direct contradiction to everything our training had taught us about addiction, we vowed to severely ration TV and found it's not so difficult when there is so much around us to actually experience and when viewing becomes a choice, not the avenue of least resistance after a long, hard day at work.

As if to help our resolve, the motor on the TV lowering device soon burned out due to Peter's poor design. About a week after we had it replaced, I noticed a wisp of smoke coming from the ceiling. Tim stood directly under it.

"Did you light a match?" I asked. It wasn't as stupid a question of a nonsmoker as one would think, for only a few days before, seeing a tick on Miles, Tim had done just that. Now, though, he just said no and resumed his tinkering with the dashboard. The wisp grew less wispy and more fanned out. I must have had the same perplexed expression on my face as the first caveman who had ever achieved . . .

"FIRE!" I screamed. OK, so I've been known to exaggerate. I guess that's why Tim shot me an incredulous look. But when he followed my gaze upward, he saw it, too. He sprang into action, pushing the button that should lower the TV. Nothing happened. As the smoke grew, I started opening windows.

"Where's the fire extinguisher?" I coughed. Although I had never seen it, I rightly assumed Project Nerd's alter, alter ego, Mr. Safety, had installed one. (In fact, as I should have known and later discovered, he actually had installed two, one at either end of the bus.) Tim ran to the kitchen, grabbed it from a cabinet, and pulled the safety ring as he leapt over the coffee table. He let 'er rip . . . right in his face. Perhaps without his usual superhero accoutrement of safety goggles, he couldn't see where he was aiming the thing. He quickly righted it, just as a flame lapped out overhead.

It was over in a few seconds. (The cleanup took hours.) Then Tim manually lowered the TV, a laborious process involving a flexible extension on his electric drill which, he painstakingly and in excruciating detail explained, made it work like a Dremel tool. (I suppose I should say here what a Dremel tool is, but I don't know because I was really not in the mood.) Miraculously, there was no damage, just the burned wire. I didn't even care about that. All I could think was how fortunate we were this happened while we were home. Strangely, I didn't even contemplate the potential damage to the bus. *Everything is replaceable*, I realized. Except, if we'd been out, Miles, Morty, and Shula would have been toast.

What is happening to me? "Everything is replaceable" was hardly a thought becoming a Princess, but it was my only thought. While I adore my pets, after a lifetime of rampant and, yes, even resplendent consumerism, I would have expected to have given some of my belongings, certainly at least my shoes, a second thought. But I really didn't care.

Everything is replaceable.

Well, at least I haven't gone so completely insane as to think this occasion doesn't call for a commemorative martini. And a lovely shade of orangey-red it was. I called this newest nectar Fire in the Hole. It was a toss-up between naming it that or Dumb Luck, which I realized was what we, two Yuppies with no experience with busing, epitomized. We were so dumb, in fact, we didn't even know what we didn't know. In one searing flash, the fire brought home how much we needed to learn on this trip.

Chapter Seven

LORDY, MIZ SCARLETT!
I DON'T KNOW NOTHIN'
'BOUT DRIVIN' NO BUSES!

Pelican Pucker

1 part rum
2 parts Midori
splash pineapple juice
splat sweet 'n' sour
squirt lime

Sugar rim to lower pucker factor. Mix ingredients in shaker.
Let 'er rip.

Throughout the fall as we traveled deeper into the South, I reminded Tim of his pledge to me at the very start of our journey, exacted in a feeble attempt to salvage *something* from the bus thing: we would not see snow the entire trip. Sensing that after all we'd been through, even a temperature drop on a sunny day might sever my already tenuous commitment to the rest of the year, Tim not only did his best to live up to his promise, but even suggested a two-week sojourn on the South Carolina coast. (We skipped Kentucky because winter was setting in. The only other continental state we didn't hit all year was Rhode Island. We just kinda missed it.)

Once settled in Myrtle Beach in an RV park right on the ocean, we took daily strolls on the shore, amidst a frenzy of activity. Everyone, and I mean *everyone*, was trolling for fish: seagulls dive-bombing the water with a splash; sandpipers, like cockroaches on stilts, scurrying out of the way of crashing waves; porpoises, as if members of a synchronized swim team, going for the grouper instead of the gold; pelicans gliding over the water, bodies still until they spied their prey or took a few beats of their wings.

The pelicans were my favorite, and as I scanned the water for them, I reluctantly had to acknowledge that I'd developed a fondness for something in the "great" outdoors. They just looked so unlikely to get airborne and, once flying, even more unlikely to stay that way. I positively squealed with delight when they landed, feet thrust forward, neck pulled back, wings raised and flapping wildly, as if anticipating some horrible crash. It doesn't take a Freud to figure out that I identified with the poor birds; as a bus phobic, I could easily (and quite gratefully) disembark anytime. What could a bird that's afraid of landing do?

It was especially strange that I enjoyed watching the pelicans, as I'd never been particularly fond of birds. In fact, there was at least one time when I was positively terrified of them.

During some house construction which included replacing our roof, there was a period of time in which the gables were open. This was apparently taken as an open invitation to a couple of unwanted guests. I discovered them one Saturday when I walked into the living room: two huge, angry, menacing, avian creatures (which Tim later identified as "sparrows") flying about, flinging themselves against the windows in an effort to get out of the house. I seriously considered flinging myself against the windows, too. I really don't know why they upset me so. Maybe it was because I feared my world was turning upside down: This was a clear violation of the uneasy truce I'd maintained with the out-of-doors my entire life. If Mother Nature now saw fit to nullify our agreement by violating my personal space, what other horrors might she wreak on me? Gardening?

My first impulse was to scream. I have always believed in following one's gut and this was certainly no time to be changing philosophies. I indulged my instincts with gusto and for quite a prolonged period of time. Tim was working in the hospital and there was no one else within earshot—even with my pipes. If a Princess screams in her castle and no one is around to hear her, did she really scream at all? Uncertain of the answer to that one, I called my husband. He happened to be in a small assessment room, doing an initial evaluation on an adolescent, and answered his phone.

"Hi. I'm just finishing up with a patient. Can I call you right—?"

"THERE ARE BIRDS IN THE HOUSE!" My screams reverberated through the receiver and into their tiny space. I didn't think I could get any more upset—or any louder—until Miles, Morty, and Shula (who had to pick this moment in her life to become brave) ambled in to see what all the ruckus was about. Needless to say, they hardly shared my aversion to the creatures. The thought of watching the birds ripped to shreds before my eyes made me feel faint—unfortunately, I didn't.

"NO! NO! GET AWAY!" I screamed at the pets. As I ran around trying to shoo them into the bedroom while keeping my distance from the birds, I became hysterical. OK, even more hysterical. Now I was screaming *and* crying. Tim tried his best to calm me.

"Sweetie. Sweetie. SWEETIE." It wasn't helping. Finally, he said in exasperation, "Sweetie, the young man I'm interviewing wants to know how come *he's* the one in the psychiatric hospital." That did it. Once I started laughing through my tears, I was able to corral the pets into the bedroom. After several pleading calls to a rather astonished Animal Control ("You said you need us to get a couple of birds out of your house? Not bears. Not bats. Birds?"), I joined Miles, Morty, and Shula, locked myself in the bedroom, and awaited the intruders' subsequent removal.

So, on Myrtle Beach, as I marveled at the pelicans, Tim marveled at my marveling. Then we both marveled at the people; they fished from shore, or in tiny boats just offshore, or in larger boats farther out. Some even fished way up on the beach, but not for food: Men (always, men) with metal detectors combed the sand for coins. How those things work, exactly, is slightly beyond the scope of this memoir and well beyond the interest of its author, but I'm certainly not the first to observe that these devices inherently attract metal and repel women.

Since watching the pelicans required walking on the beach, I did so, willingly, only reinforcing my long-standing objection to hiking (at least before discovering how much I could distract myself with a camera): Beach, flat. Hiking, uphill. I'd always believed the government should install escalators in the mountains of national parks, making them not only accessible to the handicapped, but also to lazy sloths like me. The environmentalist objection could easily be quelled by having the moving stairs be solar powered. And by thus widening the parks' appeal, more funding would surely follow, further placating any nature-loving sensibilities. I think I'll write my congressman.

In truth, on those rare occasions I hiked in a forest (usually once a year, just to remind Tim why he didn't want me to go more often), I was always bored by the sameness of it all. Yes, a forest is pretty. But at walking speed, the scenery just doesn't change that much minute to minute. Worse, when the aim of the trek is to get to the top of some peak, or the edge of some lake, why all those hours of mind-numbing exertion for a few minutes' view? I'd be much happier (as would my companions, I'm sure) if someone would just send me a postcard. But by the ocean, where walking was largely flat, the fresh air really *was* different from the air inside (unless you work in a Morton's factory, but that's another issue). And the scenery—the movement of the waves—was ever changing, the underlying sea life incapable of doing you harm unless you're foolhardy enough to venture in. No need to wear bells, slap on DEET, or carry rocks. (To scare a mountain lion, you're supposed to throw a rock, right? But you're not supposed to look small—or, in other words, bend down to pick up a rock. Explain *that*, outdoors nuts.)

I always assumed I got my nature-loving ways from my father. When Henry first saw the Grand Canyon, he was heard to remark, "Eh. It's just a big *loch* [a hole]." *You got it, Dad.*

Myrtle Beach also astounded us by the plethora of swimsuit shops on almost every block. How many people, after all, decide to vacation in a beach community but forget to bring their swimsuits? Evidently, nearly everyone. And, as Tim observed, judging from the number of topless bars, apparently a lot of them are men who forget to bring their wives, as well.

Then there's another plethora—of pancake houses (which really didn't seem to jibe with the swimsuit shops at all). Within a two-mile stretch, we passed: Pancake House; Plantation House of; Pan American Pancake and Omelets; IHOP; International Omelets and Pancake House; Denny's, House of; Farmhouse; Grandma's Kitchen; Country Kitchen; and Mammy's Kitchen.

The names of the swimsuit shops were not much better. In the same two-mile stretch, we passed: One Whales (clearly owned by someone with no business sense); Five Star Discount Beachwears; an Empire USA; two Wings (a silly name for a decidedly gravity-bound activity); an Eagles Outlet; two Atlantis Beachwears; four Pacific Beachwears and two Pacific Superstores (someone with my sense of direction must have named those); two Bargain Beachwears; a plain old Beachwear; and Tim's (and, I'm sure, every man's) favorite, the Tantalizing Twins.

We had only planned to stay a week in Myrtle Beach but extended it to two, taking our long daily (or more) walks by the shore, holding hands and alternating with each other for who got to take the poodle's leash. In between strolls, we set up beach chairs on the sand and settled in with books. Although always a voracious reader myself (when I found the time), I'd never actually seen Tim sit and read before (unless it was an instruction manual and then only on the sly). In fact, I'd never seen him just . . . sit. But, looking up from my novel, there was no mistaking it. He was simply staring out at the waves.

"Whatcha thinkin'?" I finally asked.

"Nothin'," he said. There could not have been a more perfect response.

It had been weeks since nearly being burned to a crisp and I was feeling more and more comfortable on the bus. This terrified me. It's one thing to gain an intellectual understanding that the trappings of one's former life were just that. It's quite another to actually feel that way. For a time, to compensate, I made it a point to cling even tighter to relics of my prior life, taking

the concept of "everything is replaceable" to new heights by ac-
quiring more to replace. I therefore reasoned that an afternoon
at Tommy Bahama's would surely make me feel an even greater
connection to all things beach.

Meandering through the fabulous Myrtle Beach outlet mall,
I found myself truly taken up into the spirit of the surf, buying
mounds of beachwear, not only at Tommy's, but at various other
stores. Back at the bus, I engaged in a futile effort to cram the
purchases into my measly allotment of closet space. Tim had already left with Miles (after an afternoon at a mall, he was itching
to get outside) and waited for me by the shore. I sat back on the
floor in frustration, bags scattered about. *I'd rather be out on the
beach, too.* Then a nagging thought. And no matter how hard
I tried to push it aside, there it was. *I don't need beach clothes to
feel . . . well, beachy.* I got Tim to drive me back the very next
day (I was taking this Leave the Driving to Him thing quite
literally, even if it only involved the Jeep) to return every last
purchase.

It was around this time that a new alter ego of Tim's was
born. It shouldn't be surprising that my husband is a gentleman.
Even after all these years, he scrambles to open doors for me. He
always walks on the outside, near the street. He always drives
when we're together (well, OK, maybe that's just Mr. Safety's bid
for self-preservation), but he also won't let me carry anything.
So now, on Myrtle Beach, he of course insisted on bringing
both beach chairs to the sand. He also toted any water or snacks
we might want on our long walks. Whenever I tried to bring
something along (even my camera) he'd take it from me until I
needed it. So, one day, I found some pretty seashells in the sand
and decided to collect a few. I had no pockets. Tim did.

"Oh, Tim! Sherpa Tim!" I sang out. He had to laugh. If the

hiking boot fits, after all. As he put the shells in his pocket, he gave me a kiss.

"As long as I'm a Sherpa with benefits," he said.

We met another busing couple in the RV park. They were from Virginia and the husband was recently semi-retired from his job as an actual city bus driver. The wife still ran a computer lab in a high school and . . . was a bus phobic! She swore she had never been in one before, that it all began six weeks ago when they started taking trips. She recited the all-too-familiar litany: Hates sitting up front hearing everything rumble behind her. Hates the overpasses, always asks if they'll fit. Hates the curve of exit ramps, always announces their speed limit. Her husband just ignored her as Tim did me.

While the menfolk compared engine sizes, the womenfolk compared coping strategies: They had wooden venetian blinds on their windows and she made sure they were rolled up before they headed out, to reduce the clacking sound. I shared with her my method of putting socks on the martini and wine glasses in the wine rack to reduce the clinking sound. (I left out where the socks came from: i.e., if the driver gave me enough warning of our departure so I could retrieve them from a drawer in the bedroom, or if he didn't, when I was forced to simply reach across the aisle to the laundry bin perched over HAL, giving new meaning to the phrase "dirty martini.") We then went on to debate the relative horrors of clacking versus clinking and called it a draw.

I must admit, I felt quite superior (after all, married to a professional bus driver and *still* phobic?) until she informed me that like mine, her seat had no armrests. But she got her husband to

install an oh-shit handle to clutch. *Why didn't I think of that?* I
had to concede, even though I was Miss September, I had just
been trumped by Bus Phobic of the Year.

We tore ourselves away from the beach for a few days here and
there to take some day trips in the Jeep. We've never really been
architecture buffs, but we'd never lived in a place known for historic homes, either. Much more than the buildings themselves,
however, we found we enjoyed hearing the stories of people who
had lived in them so long ago.

At the Mann-Simons Cottage, we learned that Celia Mann,
born into slavery in Charleston in 1799, managed to gain her
freedom, then walk all the way to Columbia, where she bought
the cottage and supported herself as a midwife. Her descendants
continued to live in the home for over a century. Her story of
sacrifice and struggle was quite a contrast to the opulence and
privilege of the Nathaniel Russell House; while in France, a gov-
ernor's wife had a piano crafted for the house, with the explicit
instructions that it be missing one octave in order to fit in her
stateroom for the shipboard journey back.

Just before we left Myrtle Beach, we ran into a man at a restaurant who shares a last name with Tim (our reservations either
happened to be for the same time, or if you're a Boulderite, this
was meant to be). On his rare visits to his father, Tim was always
under the impression that half the state of Arkansas were cousins, but this man (who knows his genealogy), really seemed to
be, however distant.

After dinner, as we sat together over dessert and coffee, Tim
learned more about his origins than he had ever known, and
realized that like me, he'd been missing out because of assumptions. He never took an interest in the Arkansas side of his family before, largely because as a child, he'd gotten the distinct
impression they were something to be embarrassed about. His

father didn't talk about his kin and never took Tim to visit them. Then, as an adult, shortly after our marriage and years after his father moved back there from Reno, Tim went to Arkansas for the first time. On that trip, Bob took him to see an elderly lady. Tim had a vague feeling of familiarity, but couldn't quite place it. After settin' a brief spell, they left and Bob informed him, "That was your grandma's twin."

Tim hadn't known his grandmother had a sister, let alone a twin.

But now, hearing that his ancestors were spear-carriers for William the Conqueror, how a later relation, a major in the British Army, deserted to support the Revolution, and how several more recent ones intermarried with the Hatfields, Tim realized it wasn't really important what the history was, just that his family—like every family—has one.

With apologies to Margaret Mitchell (and my long-suffering husband) I just could not help but constantly cry, "Lordy, Miz Scarlett! I don't know nothin' 'bout drivin' no buses" the entire time we were in Atlanta, Georgia. Maybe I shouldn't have read *Gone with the Wind* three times that summer of seventh grade. Tim, of course, had only seen the movie, dragged by a college girlfriend. He recalled that while they were in line, he couldn't figure out why everyone else brought seat cushions. When the lights went on after two hours of film viewing, he thought, "Well, that's kind of a weird way to end the movie, but oh well," and started to leave until his girlfriend set him straight—it was only intermission. No wonder he winced and rubbed his butt every time I did my Prissy imitation.

As a diehard *GWTW* fan, I was particularly taken with the

Cyclorama and its Rhett Butler surprise. The Atlanta Cyclorama bills itself as the longest-running show in the United States, on display since 1893. At 42 feet high and 358 feet around, it's basically a huge cylinder of art (the largest oil painting in the world) depicting the Battle of Atlanta, which slowly revolves around its audience for nineteen minutes. (I, of course, ensured seating was involved before going in.) What makes it a "show" is the accompanying music, narration, and foreground figures. The artists who worked on the Cyclorama were all specialists: i.e., one might just do the sky; another, horses; still another, faces, etc. Apparently, cycloramas used to be quite popular, commissioned by the victors of various wars (Civil, Franco-Prussian, and the like) and there are still almost twenty active ones in the world today. Atlanta's was originally commissioned by Union General John "Blackjack" Logan, then a senator, as a sort of campaign poster for his vice-presidential bid. He never got to use it; he died two days before it was completed.

The surprise Rhett connection: When Clark Gable came to see Atlanta's Cyclorama during the *GWTW* premiere in 1939, he informed the mayor that no painting of the city could possibly be complete without Rhett Butler. The mayor obliged, having him added to the foreground—as a dead Yankee.

We worked up quite an appetite with all this revolving, so headed for The Varsity. Rather than dine in our car at this, the world's largest drive-in restaurant, we opted to take our delectable burgers to a table inside for our feast. We'd often found that the hip burger place in most towns is a hole-in-the-wall. Not here. Serving 16,000 people a day (double if there's a Georgia Tech home game), the historic Varsity (it opened in 1928), with its soaring ceilings and expansive dining areas, is kind of the Versailles of burger joints.

Of course, the city of Atlanta is forever tied to the Reverend

Dr. Martin Luther King, Jr. But when we visited the Center for
Nonviolent Social Change, we wished we hadn't. Rather than
a stirring testament to the man and his life's work, the buildings
and grounds (which, judging by some old pictures, had once pos-
sessed a reserved dignity) were run-down and worse, practically
empty—except for some Hare Krishnas singing and drumming
with a lack of energy that appeared to mirror their surroundings.
We found out later that the center was in a bit of limbo, with the
King children and his widow (who has since passed) deciding if
they should relinquish control and turn it over to the National
Park Service, which could then rejuvenate the place, both inside
and out.

On a five-hour round-trip drive in our Jeep to Scottsboro, Ala-
bama, we passed through Chattanooga, Tennessee, and spied a
sign for the Chattanooga Choo Choo. We just had to take the
exit and see what this was all about. It's actually a Holiday Inn
where, in addition to the regular hotel, guests can stay in train
cars out back. Tim cringed once again when I couldn't resist
asking the bellhops, "Pardon me, boys. Is that the Chattanooga
Choo Choo?" Their blank looks indicated that either they'd
heard it too many times before or never at all. *Maybe I should
introduce them to the Romulans in the Finger Lakes.*

Why were we headed for Scottsboro? Fine. I'll admit it: the
famed Unclaimed Baggage Center, where airlines send luggage
left unclaimed after ninety days. I do a lot of shopping at used-
clothing stores, but even I had to admit it was kind of creepy
sorting through all these things that were never voluntarily relinquished. It was easy to see that some of it probably meant a
lot to the owners, who might, even now, be wondering what

ever happened to their stuff. I felt a little better going through the books and CDs, which seemed less personal, but there wasn't much there. Of course, back at the clothing racks, I managed to quash my discomfort long enough to find just a couple of items (a Tahari blazer and J. Crew jean jacket, for all fellow Princesses out there who need to know. Although if you've been missing either after a flight taken long ago—never mind).

The people-watching was even better than the actual shopping. Tim, as always, was a good sport, and after quickly realizing he wasn't going to find anything in the place (apparently men who were 40 Long with a thirty-two-inch waist did not lose their bags), wandered around, then kept me company while I waited in the extremely long line to pay for my purchases. (One might think the Unclaimed Baggage Center's checkout was going for too much authenticity by attempting to re-create an airport check-in.) Two guys in camouflage garb passed in front of us.

"They don't want to be seen in this place," Tim whispered. Just as I succeeded in stifling my laughter, another man sauntered by holding a couple of hockey sticks. (How in the world do you lose a hockey stick on an airplane?) Tim, feigning enthusiasm, oohed and aahed.

"Wow! They've got hockey sticks!" he exclaimed. It seemed the young couple standing in front of us could also see the absurdity of it all. When the woman showed her husband the dickie she planned to purchase, he screwed up his face and asked, "What is that, a shirt for your boobs?"

During our time in Atlanta, we stayed at an RV park in nearby Marietta that felt hidden in plain sight; set among tall trees just off a busy highway and behind a strip mall with a car dealership, it was still surprisingly quiet. We could almost fool ourselves into thinking we were out in the countryside. So we decided to really go for it at our next stop, Savannah.

There we stayed at one of the loveliest campgrounds of the entire year, at a state park on Skidaway Island. Although it was forty minutes from town, the drive was well worth it. Our huge spot overhung with Spanish moss in the sprawling park was a treat. But there was no sense in taking this roughing-it stuff too far and we still managed to maneuver the bus so that both our satellite TV and Internet worked.

There were days we never left Skidaway, instead exploring the many biking trails through the swamps. For the first time, I could understand the pull of camping, being out in nature without the usual trappings, as there was so much else to do. (OK, so maybe I had my usual trappings like TV, Internet, microwave, queen-size bed, etc., just not in *their* usual trappings of a house.) This feeling quickly subsided, however, with the arrival of our new neighbor. He came in a beat-up van, pitched a tent, and promptly got drunk by 10 a.m. This was repeated on each subsequent day (without the arriving and the pitching parts). Actually, he could easily have been drunk well before ten, but since that was when I woke up, I had no way of knowing. Every time he saw us, he'd say he wanted a tour of our rig, as he planned to build a bus from scratch someday and knew we had "sompin' special." We just smiled and demurred with as vague excuses as we could muster.

After a few days, some female relative came by. Loud arguing ensued. We imagined she was doing an intervention. The next morning, he was gone. For his sake, I hoped he was on his way to Betty Ford. But I couldn't help remembering what Dee Brown (Chris of Vanture's brother and a retired railroad engineer) said to help me feel better about the journey we were about to undertake: Dee much preferred living on the road in a rig versus staying stationary in a house. As he pointed out, in a house, if you don't like your neighbors, you're stuck. In a rig, you just move. I could see now he had a point.

In Savannah itself, we walked. A lot. Architecturally speaking, it's one of the best-preserved cities in America and walking allowed us the time to take it all in at the pace it was meant to be appreciated. Still, armed with the Visitors Bureau's map and guide, it was a lot of walking. An awful lot. Walking that was interrupted only by touring a few of the historic mansions, which, in turn, involved interrupted walking. We did so much walking, in fact, that I started sitting on anything handy—a bench, a stoop, a fence rail—every time we paused, however briefly, to admire a house. It wasn't that I was perpetually tired. Most of the times I sat I wasn't even tired at all. I did it, as I proclaimed to Tim, to "prophylactically rest." He rolled his eyes and the next time I sat, said, oh so empathetically, "One of your rubber rests, eh?"

We walked to the Andrew Low House, considered one of the great Federal-style homes in the country and where Juliette Low founded the Girl Scouts. Not knowing what constitutes Federal style, I couldn't really judge, other than to say I sure wouldn't be averse to living there. We then ambled by a century-old Presbyterian church whose bell has three methods of pealing: one arm strikes the hour for the clock, one strikes inside for funerals, and another clapper rings for weddings. Our guide sheet pointed out that Woodrow Wilson was married there, and I couldn't help thinking that if ole Woody had been a practical joker, he might have slipped the pealer two bits to strike the funeral bell during his wedding ceremony.

We continued our stroll past where General Sherman stayed during his March to the Sea. The wealthy cotton merchant who put him up hoped the general would in turn not burn Savannah and perhaps also allow him to keep his crop. While Sherman didn't burn the town (instead offering it to President Lincoln as a Christmas present in a famous telegram), he did take the cotton, prompting the merchant, a Mr. Green, to see red and send the general a rent bill. Sherman paid. The Green-Meldrim House, then, is a fine example not only of Gothic Revival but of genteel chutzpah.

Off Telfair Square, we saw a fine example of genteel wrath: When Mary Telfair bequeathed her mansion to become the Telfair Academy of Arts and Sciences, she specified that no liquor of any kind ever be served there. This request was honored for years until champagne hit the menu at an art reception, during which a portion of the ceiling inexplicably hit the floor. Thereafter, spirits have been served (and placated) in a tent in the square.

We also visited Mickve Israel, the third-oldest synagogue in the U.S. and only one of two in the world built in a Gothic style. Used to more traditional temples, we found it almost disorienting to wander under the pointed arches and flying buttresses, gazing up at the ribbed, vaulted ceilings. Then, our docent, Leo, an incredibly warm, sharper-than-I'll-ever-be ninety-year-old, wove his own story of sailing from Heidelberg to America as a young man fleeing persecution into those of the earliest congregants. They included Civil War heroes and a widowed tavern owner who gave her proceeds to the Union. Hearing the familiar history (my father's and his immediate family, as well as my mother's parents, had also fled persecution from other parts of Europe), I felt more grounded.

Of course we took Miles with us as we walked. And apparently, we were not the only ones to enjoy hoofing it through the city with our pooch: Troup Square has a Victorian cast-iron drinking fountain—for dogs.

For me, though, what most epitomized our trip to Savannah, and perhaps the entire genteel South, was my visit to Joseph's

Salon. Look, I can't help it; I'm shallow that way. (What do you want from me?) Still, bear with me here, for Joseph has coiffed the ladies of Savannah for years in the downstairs of his lovely townhouse and I've never had my hair done in such a graceful atmosphere by such a master craftsman. As the scissors flew in his hands, the "darlin"s and "suga"s were flyin' out of his mouth and back at him again by the waiting female throng.

Tim was to pick me up and we were going directly to a fancy dinner in this oh-so-foodie town. Ever the Southern Gentleman, Joseph offered to let me change upstairs in his bathroom, so that I'd be more comfortable. *Sigh.* If I were a rich woman, I'd fly to Joseph's every six weeks to get my hair done. I'd had a cut or two since Nick in New York and was beginning to despair of my hair ever looking that good again. But Joseph somehow managed to transform the helmet head my hair had become into a stylish bob that allowed my natural wave to flourish. (Funny how during my long-haired childhood, I had taken great pains to straighten it with giant curlers, bobby-pin wraps, and other tortures to tresses only adolescents would put themselves through. Why is it that at any age hair seems to be the great equalizer among women? Although almost every one of us wants to be tall and thin, it seems pretty universal that those with straight hair prefer curly and vice versa.) Dinner that night was one of the best we'd ever had, at the chic 45 South. The food was out of this world—as was the bill. We tried not to ruin the evening by realizing it had just cost us a tank of diesel.

Throughout the South, we stopped at sights rich with the history of the Civil War and the struggle for civil rights. But it was always while poking around old homes and plantations that we got a more personal view of the inhabitants of long ago. Out-side Savannah, the meaning of the word "genteel" was further brought home to me not by a person of yore, but by yet another ninety-year-old docent, this one named Dody, who, directing us along the garden path of a mansion, commented with a wave of her hand, "Walk this way. There are herons in those trees with no regard for anyone." It would have been worth being the ob-ject of heron disregard just to hear her say that line. Sadly, I had to admit that if I were the guide, the most genteel word out of my Yankee lips would likely have been "doo-doo."

Although I promptly vowed to use less profanity, I could not be blamed for falling off the well-bred wagon as we left our Skid-away Island campground. Tim was lamenting the tightness of his belt (what they say about Southern cooking is all too true) and tried to loosen it while driving on the wide, deserted street. I went wild-eyed, grabbing at his waist to do it for him. He would have none of it.

"There's no one on the road. Take the wheel," he commanded. Before I could scream, "Are you insane?" his hands were on his belt. Mine did, indeed, fly to the wheel. Unencumbered by stric-ture—or, apparently, morals—Tim purred like Shula after a good neck scratch.

"Told you I'd get you to drive the bus," he said. I started to pro-test that it wasn't really driving, but thought better of it: After all, if I convinced him I was right, I'd undoubtedly really be driv-ing the thing before long. To this day, Tim still can't understand why I didn't enjoy my brief time at the wheel.

I suppose that interlude only proves there are limits to living in and trying to understand each other's worlds. For Tim, nir-vana is being at the helm of some powerful engine. For me, it's riding on that engine in first class. Unlike me, Tim has a hard time being pampered. It took him years to agree to ride in a taxi.

Being driven, especially paying someone for the privilege, just wasn't right. While he was growing up, his family did everything themselves—they had to. And they took a certain pride in that. Once Tim had the means to hire stuff out, he still viewed doing so as a weakness. Gradually, through living with me, he's come around—on some things (as if he has a choice).

I was actually glad cooking was not one of them and that Tim became discontented with allowing others to prepare our food (like the Colonel or Ronald or that guy dressed as a giant pickle). Although we'd gone to plenty of restaurants on our travels, now that he had the time, Tim swore we were done with TV dinners. Of course, when my husband decided he was going to learn to cook, he not only bought cookbooks, but books on the science of food. And, of course, I teased him—until I started tasting his creations. Then I shut up. Fast. As usual, if Tim set out to do something, he did it well.

Even though he loved cooking in our upscale, if tiny, bus kitchen, being a guy, he still liked to grill outside. His usual pre- amble: "Me go light fire. Me go burn shit." Whether indoors or out, we'd pick some music for Tim to cook to, mix up some mar- tinis for me to watch him with, and take some breaks here and there to dance. The whole process of food preparation—buying fresh ingredients, chopping, sautéing, baking, broiling, and boil- ing—rather than just removing from freezer and microwaving, greatly enhanced the entire experience (even for me just watch- ing him). And not only for our taste buds, but for the whole social aspect of what is commonly known as a "meal." I guess we hadn't really understood what the word meant. Perhaps most astounding of all was that we didn't have to rely on Stouffer's to pick a side dish. We could do it ourselves—maybe even two! What a concept.

The bus had other restorative effects on our domestic equilibrium, for finally, after years of capitulation to my slovenly ways, Tim was able to enjoy a certain measure of tidiness as we were forced to regularly straighten up. It's not just that our house had never been neat; we had stopped aspiring to neat long ago. Livable would have been an improvement.

During my internship on a psychiatry ward at a VA hospital, the attending once took her students on a tour of patients' rooms. That woman could diagnose with uncanny accuracy, just by observing the state of the allotted living spaces on her ward. When she commented, "That's a schizophrenic bed," we could instantly see what she meant: The sheets were askew with clothes, toiletries, even food in the mix, seemingly ground into the white cotton linens, a blur of no longer discrete things with their own shapes and boundaries. I often imagined that attending, standing in the entryway of our home, shaking her head and sighing, "That's a schizophrenic house."

It wasn't that I actually enjoyed living in a rank Dairy Queen Blizzard, it was just that tidying up seemed like such a tremendous waste of time, given that the law of entropy dictated that things tend to disorder themselves naturally. (Poor Tim. Figures that would be the only lesson that stuck from Physics for Non-Majors.) And it wasn't only large items that were subject to my twisted thermodynamic logic, but smaller, seemingly insignificant particles, as well. For example, what is the point of putting toilet paper on the holder? It's not like it lasts for a year or anything. Pretty soon, you've got to put on another one. Why not, then, just leave the new rolls somewhere handy, like the top of the tank? For years, Tim had been trying in vain to wait me out, but with each new roll, he eventually succumbed and put it on the holder himself. By then, though, the paper was almost half gone, so to my way of thinking, his feeble attempt to keep the dispenser gainfully employed became even more pointless.

By definition, living on a bus meant having to keep the place neat: Whenever we pulled up stakes, we had to stow everything that had been left out so nothing would lie in wait as potential projectiles. Dishes, silverware, newspapers, books all had to be put away. For the first time in our lives together, we were creating the sort of environment Tim had craved since we started cohabitating.

Sometime after our initial date that wasn't supposed to be a date, I went over to Tim's bachelor pad. I thought I was in a model home. I simply could not believe anyone actually lived there. Was he fooling me again? The carpet looked like it had been raked. There were coffee-table books neatly stacked—on the coffee table! The kitchen counters were bare. If he'd had a dog, I swear the dog bed would have had pillows with a mint bone on top. I was afraid to touch anything. Surely it was all a cardboard façade. Now I was living in a model of sorts myself, and even more unbelievably, a mobile one.

While Miles's bed still had no pillows or mint, Morty certainly didn't care. Both cats slept on the bed with us every night (and Shula stayed there most of the days we were not on the road), with Morty shifting to the "dog" bed once we got up in the morning. This led Tim to often remark, "Isn't that nice of Miles to let Morty sleep on his bed?" *Right.* Like his brother, I don't think Miles ever quite grasped the concept of "dog" bed, either. Or, perhaps just like his father, Miles was all about simple pleasures: It was enough in life to have a bowl of food and a small, quiet place to himself, surrounded by people who loved him. Why ask for anything more?

They could teach me a lot.

Chapter Eight

MY FAVORITE WINE HAS ALWAYS BEEN "I WANNA GO TO FLOOOORIDA!"

Secession Swizzle

4 parts vodka
3 parts guava juice
1½ parts raspberry liqueur
squeeze fresh lemon

Mix ingredients in shaker. While sipping, draw your own flag and come up with catchy country name. Drink. Repeat until total surrender to unseen invaders or cold hard floor.

It was time for an oil change.

For normal folk, this would not be anything of note. But I'd had plenty of experience with oil changes or, more accurately, with Tim doing them. Yes, Tim. Oil changes are too mundane (theoretically) and therefore well beneath Project Nerd.

My husband seems to have an oil change curse. Although the explanations of what go wrong vary, the one constant is that they are always completely unintelligible to me: The oil pan plug stripped after being tightened improperly by the last person who changed the oil, necessitating a trip to the hardware store—oh, horrors!—to buy a special socket (whatever that is) for his socket wrench (ditto) to grip the stripped nut (hey, I'm not making this stuff up). Of course, my husband was never that mythical "last person," who, it turns out, was second only to me in nincompoopery, since I had insisted on buying a service plan in the first place and then had the gall to actually take advantage of it. No wonder we always had to have multiple cars; Tim needed one he wasn't working on for the inevitable hardware store trip to get a part for the one he was.

Other famed Halliburtonian fiascos included the time the oil filter was on too tight (same "last person"), requiring Tim to shove a screwdriver through it, providing leverage to pry the filter off. Then there was the time he actually got to the point of pouring the new oil in, but forgot to fasten the oil pan plug first (no other "last person" here, I'm afraid), running a few quarts out onto the garage floor. This led to hours upon hours of sopping up the black muck with sawdust. (He keeps a trash barrel full of the stuff for just such absorbent-requiring emergencies. By way of explanation, I'll just quote him: "Everyone with a garage has some absorbent around." *I see.*)

So, when Tim announced that after nearly ten thousand miles we were due, I could hardly be blamed for shuddering. Changing the oil on a bus? We could all drown! But then he informed me he wasn't going to be doing it himself.

"Not Project Nerd?" I asked with dread. Tim shook his head.

"We're passing close to the Prevost place in Jacksonville. They should do it." Mr. Safety was rearing his lovely head. Since the repair shop could also do a full safety check and was familiar with all the lube points (whatever those are), that's where we headed.

You might think for a Princess, staying at a mechanic's shop would be worse than being locked in the deepest, darkest castle dungeon, but I was most pleasantly surprised. Not that it was beach blanket busing or anything, but with free electric hookups, level spaces, busnut neighbors, and even a grassy spot for the dog, we spent a most pleasant few days just hanging out, waiting our turn. When it came, I opted to remain on the bus while two hydraulic lifts levitated it in the shop, enjoying the sensation of being airborne until I noticed the Prevost next to ours. It had a huge gash all along the side and the front was bashed in. I called out the window to one of the mechanics and asked what had happened. Apparently, some "last person" (I was about to see Tim's point with regard to those service plans) had put a wrong tire on. It had blown out on the highway, smashing the bus into a median.

"You can get a great deal on it!" he assured me. "The guy's wife is refusing to ride in it anymore." *Indeed.* Suddenly, feeling airborne in the bus had lost its appeal.

We headed over to the Gulf Coast, and while we enjoyed the view of the water from our RV park near Fort Myers, I was less than thrilled with the owners' haphazard attitude toward government services, as evidenced by their incredulity that I actually received the package I was expecting in the mail.

Most full-timers (which we were for the year, God help us) used a mail service. We had given the USPS a change of address form to forward our mail from Boulder to a place in Pensacola. It seemed a lot of these mail-forwarding places were on the water, as not only full-time busers but boaters used them, as well. A few months back, I mistakenly made this observation to Tim, who responded with a gleam in his eye, "Living on a sailboat! That's our next adventure!" Yeah, sounds romantic, but Tim and I know nothing about boats. (God help us. Again.) Whenever we knew in advance we'd be at a certain RV park at a certain date, I called the service, gave them the address, and they forwarded whatever had accumulated. I've always been a fanatic about getting the mail. Tim says that's because as a near shut-in, it's one of my few links to the outside world. Maybe so, but then I always have to remind him that we shut-ins prefer the more politically correct term "hermit." *Geez.*

In any event, at this RV park, as in most others, mail is delivered to the office and, from there, distributed to guests via cubbyholes with site numbers on them. My incredulity came into play as this park's process of getting the mail into the cubbyholes was more miss than hit. In fact, I discovered my package, along with everyone else's mail, in a pile scattered on the floor beneath the cubbyholes. There was a time this would have made me apoplectic. But getting the mail had become less of an event for me during our bus year, maybe because it came with less regularity. Or maybe, just maybe, because I was getting out more.

From Fort Myers as a base, we drove around Sanibel and Captiva islands in the Jeep. While the beaches were lovely, we enjoyed the five-mile Wildlife Drive at J. N. "Ding" Darling National Wildlife Refuge even more. It's part of the largest undeveloped mangrove ecosystem in the U.S. and was named after the political cartoonist instrumental in blocking the sale of the land on Sanibel Island to developers. At Jay Norwood "Ding" Darling's urging, President Truman signed an executive order creating the refuge in 1945. We saw tons of birds (there are over 220 species there), including some that were apparently quite rare (judging by one woman's reaction, a red-tailed hawk is the Armani Couture of the avian world), and even an alligator or two.

I never have developed an affinity for bird-watching (except pelicans and most definitely not sparrows). I'm sure bird-watchers are very nice people—even the one I insulted in the refuge. She had the misfortune of glancing up at Tim and me as we slowly drove by the thicket she was staring into. Noting the bewilderment on my face, she mistook it for interest and shot me a triumphant glare.

"Yellow . . . crested . . . night . . . heron" was all she said, like a town crier announcing the queen's arrival to the wretched masses. Why hadn't anyone ever told me bird-watching was a competitive thing? I could actually get into this. But until then, lacking familiarity with all things avian, I felt it only fair to rely on a certain expertise of mine that my new nemesis could not possibly trump: I lifted a foot so she could see my shoe out the Jeep's window, pointing to it for effect.

"Black . . . Chanel . . . quilted . . . loafer." She narrowed her eyes at me as we passed, undoubtedly pondering the potential resplendence of her precious night heron as an evening shoe in order to rival what I apparently had done with my *Chanellium quiltus*.

In Estero, just south of Fort Myers, we wandered around the lush acres and abandoned buildings of the Koreshan State Historic Site, where, in 1894, the settlement of the Koreshan Unity Movement was founded. This religious sect seemed doomed from the beginning, due equally to its expectation of celibacy as much as its rather loopy central tenet: that the entire universe exists inside the earth rather than on the outside, as has generally been accepted by most multicelled organisms. They even set up experiments to prove their thesis and show that the horizon on the nearby beach curved upward. The last four members deeded the land to the state in 1961. These are the sort of folks who put the "od" in God.

After about a week, we headed for the other Florida coast and landed in Markham Park Campground in Sunrise. All in all, this was probably our favorite parking spot of the year, as the vast, Broward County–maintained grounds were so much more than an RV park. Even the sites themselves are palatial and could easily fit two other rigs with room to spare.

One day, Tim and I biked about a half mile from the bus to see skeet shooters at the target range. We didn't stay long, as it's not terribly exciting to watch people fire guns (unless they're firing at you, in which case excitement is the least of your worries). So we headed for the opposite side of the park to take a gander at the model airplane field. Tim was entranced. First, a little plastic plane took off from the runway. *Cute.* Then oohs and aahs from the crowd—a biplane. *Fine.* Tim turned to me and snickered.

"If these guys were real men, they'd send up a . . ." and there it was—the unmistakable roar of a jet engine. Our mouths (and every other spectator's) gaped open, watching it go through its paces. The owner even had a friend standing by with a fire extinguisher. Continuing with the theme of overkill, Tim observed how neat it would be if the skeet and airplane guys set up some joint war-game activities.

From Sunrise, it was only five miles to the world's largest outlet mall at Sawgrass Mills. Of course, Tim and I had to go. Yet, while I still enjoyed looking at all the fashion, after my experience in Myrtle Beach, I just didn't seem all that interested in possessing any.

Tim loves all things Art Deco, so he'd been looking forward to Miami, especially South Beach (or SoBe, as the southern end of the ten-mile-long barrier island of Miami Beach is called).

We spent a very pleasant couple of hours listening to the Welcome Center's audio tour, strolling around the few dozen hotels and apartment buildings, built primarily in the 1930s and designated the only Art Deco National Historic District in the country. In its Prohibition heyday, celebrities and mob bosses like Al Capone flocked to the area for free-flowing gambling and liquor. Within less than a half century, it would become a drug-infested slum. Then in 1976, the Miami Design Preservation League was founded and started restoring the original buildings to their characteristic sweeping curves and geometric shapes. I particularly liked the whimsy of Tropical Deco, buildings with ornamentation evocative of flora, fauna, and ocean liners. Tim, of course, preferred the examples of Streamline Moderne, taking a cue from more industrial and machine-inspired forms.

Afterward, we drove farther down the strip to get a better look at all the hotels. We particularly enjoyed nosing around the famous Delano, done all in white, with its interior full of fanciful Deco chairs (the one with the high-heel boot legs and arm back especially thrilled me, natch) and fur-draped settees. To truly soak it all in, we splurged at the ridiculously expensive bar (eleven dollars for a cocktail and four dollars for a not-even-eight-ounce Coke), remembering that after all, we were in Miami.

That night, we went to Little Havana and swooned over the *ropa vieja* at a local café. We asked the waiter how in the world the name "old clothes" could be applied to a dish that was so darn good. He had no idea where the moniker came from. Tim, with his cleanliness fetish, obsessed for quite a while after our meal about how he could have ingested something normally associated with donations to the Salvation Army. Then we happened upon a nightclub with a flamenco show, hosted by an MC in drag. After all, we were in Miami. It was in Spanish, and despite having taken five years of the language in junior high and high school, I was lost. Tim, who hadn't studied it any more than I had, seemed to understand quite a bit. He explained it was all our time in Tucson. *Hmm.* Perhaps another advantage of getting out more.

The northern access to the Everglades was nearby at Shark Valley, a 14.5-mile paved road we could either walk (ha!), bike (right!), or take a two-hour tram ride through for $13.95. We did none of those, but rather just strolled for about a mile, which included a couple of small loop areas. We saw plenty of birds, although most everyone, including us, was much more interested in the alligators. Perhaps "interested" isn't the right word; "keenly focused on" would be more accurate, because if you weren't careful, you could easily have tripped on one. They were all over the road—big ones, little ones, and most frightening of all, mommas with their babies. Also scattered about were signs warning people not to approach the gators, which I'm sure visitors would have adhered to if only there were signs indicating how in the world to accomplish this. What else could we do but snap pictures of each other reading those very signs as the crocodilians lay nearby?

We spent Christmas and New Year's in Key West, one of the only times we had to make campground reservations months in advance. Actually, although we should have, we didn't, instead snagging a cancellation at the last minute. It seems spending the holidays in the Keys—especially Key Weird—is insanely popular amongst the RV set.

Throughout our travels thus far, we'd scoffed at rigs, RVs and buses alike, for sporting various kitsch, from oh-too-cutesy stuffed animals clinging to the ladder in back, to lawn gnomes perched precariously on the steps, to custom wooden signs in the windshield announcing the owner's name and hometown, usually with some little logo signifying a favorite pastime, like a fishing pole, golf club, or bowling pin. Once, in a weak moment, undoubtedly after some disaster that reinforced how alone and vulnerable I felt, I made the mistake of wondering aloud if, as a token of our solidarity with other motor-homers, we should get one, too. But Tim said no, since depicting *my* favorite pastimes would entail a logo of a bed and a credit card and result in our imminent arrest for solicitation.

We had promised ourselves, therefore, that we would never stoop to such tacky displays, but then, like Ebenezer Scrooge forced to see the ghost of buses past, we had a change of heart on Christmas Eve. As we strolled in the dark amongst rigs lit up with holiday cheer from two-story, blow-up, glowing Santas, to palm trees strung with colored lights, to life-sized, nodding, fluorescent flamingos, we could not help but smile and laugh at the whimsy of it all. Then we hit upon a rig that had nothing—not even a lone blinking white light—and exclaimed in unison, "What a grinch!" Then, upon closer inspection, "Hey! That's our bus!"

In the midst of all the good cheer, even recalling our many catastrophes, we could not help but appreciate everything the bus thing had given us. We were at the one-third mark in our year, and although the time we had left seemed to stretch endlessly before us, we also understood that was not really an accurate perception. The thought of resuming our former lives in eight months' time saddened us. So, then and there, we made a vow to us and to our bus: The next time we stayed in our rig for Christmas, we'd mend our ways with our own bus bling. And more, we'd remember these days in our mobile home and with each other, and try to keep the spirit of the bus thing alive, even when stationary. We realized that despite our prejudices due to our educations, our professions, and yes, even our wardrobes, we truly were RV people—and proud of it.

Of course, some things never change, and while in the Keys, I still made my usual for the holiday dinner—reservations.

The campground itself was not actually on Key West, but on adjacent Stock Island. There had been one on Key West proper until quite recently, but it had gone condo, so to speak. Parking in the campground itself was like being crammed into a sardine can with picnic tables, albeit a very laid-back, mellow, and happy one. (But just as oily—don't these people know the dangers of tanning?) We'd never been in a park in which the amount of charm seemed inversely proportional to the amount of privacy. It would also be the most expensive place we had stayed in all year by far—a whopping seventy-five dollars per night. But since we were lucky to get any spot at all, we just forked over our dough and got over it, mon.

Walking distance from the campground was a local favorite eatery, the open-air Hogfish Bar and Grill. We were told it's more like the real Key West was before the Yuppie influx. We brought Miles. Non–animal lovers need not frequent the establishment, as the bar's gray cat (named, in typical KW, laissez-faire fashion, "Gray Cat") climbs all over the tables.

We fully intended to spend a bit of time exploring all the Keys, but once we got to KW, the laid-back attitude of the place seemed to get the best of us and we hardly left for two weeks. Not that Key Westerners are lazy. Far from it. In fact, this tiny island packs quite an impressive history of staging protests into its seven square miles—as outlandish as the protests may be.

In 1982, when the U.S. Border Patrol set up a roadblock to search vehicles for illegal immigrants and drugs at the only high-

way out of the Keys, the Key West city council complained repeatedly about the inconvenience to their citizens, as well as
the dampening effect on tourism. They had a point, for this was
the only time in U.S. history that part of the country had been
treated as foreign soil. Returning travelers were even required
to prove citizenship and subject to forced searches. Finally, the
city council and mayor reasoned that if the Feds were going to
treat the Keys as a separate country, why not become one? And
so the Conch Republic was born. Motto: "We seceded where
others failed." The mayor—er, prime minister—then declared
war on the U.S., surrendered after one minute, and immediately
requested a billion dollars in foreign aid. Although they didn't
get the money, the roadblock was soon abandoned. KW still cel-
ebrates Independence Day every April—for a week.

Then in 1995, a U.S. Army Reserve battalion had reportedly
planned to stage training exercises on KW, simulating the inva-
sion of a foreign island. Thing is, no one bothered to notify Key
West. So the mayor and city council prepared the place for an
all-out assault (which, for the Conch Republic, consists of firing water cannons and targeting folks with stale Cuban bread).
The battalion not only issued an apology the very next day, but
traded its war games for a surrender ceremony.

Then there are the unofficial embassies the Conch Republic has in such far-flung places as France and Finland. Continuing the theme, the republic also sells "passports" as souvenirs.
Some owners of the more than ten thousand passports issued
have actually used them as travel documents, gaining entry not
only into foreign countries but the U.S., as well. (According to
a *Miami Herald* story, the lead 9/11 hijacker may even have purchased one.)

Still, all this merriment is apparently not enough for some
people. When I ambled into the visitors center on Mallory Square

to get a free walking-tour map, the lady behind the counter was on the phone and obviously flustered. She kept saying "No," in progressively more exasperated tones. Finally, she ended with a roll of her eyes and a "No. I'm afraid we don't have an amusement park." She hung up, turned to me, and mustered a smile.

"How may I help you?" she offered. I couldn't resist.

"Is there an amusement park on Key West?" Her mouth dropped open and just as I was about to be treated to her choicest "no" of the day, she got the joke and laughed.

"Can you *believe* some people?" she asked. I hoped she was talking about the person on the phone and not me.

One of our favorite places in KW was the cemetery. In Boulder, we live near a historic one that's treated more like a park by the locals. People walk their dogs, play Frisbee, and even sail toy boats with their kids in a stream. It's lovingly maintained, since everyone appreciates having such quiet neighbors. So when we saw KW's cemetery listed as an "attraction" (well, it's not like they have an amusement park, is it?), we headed over.

The inscriptions on the tombstones ranged from the grateful ("God was good to me") to the downright superior ("I told you I was sick"). But most curious of all was the statue beside the grave of one Archibald John Sheldon Yates: a naked woman sitting on a rock, her hands bound behind her—a most definite beyond-the-grave example of too much information.

We did leave KW for one bright, sunny day (was there any other kind?) when we took a jaunt in our tow vehicle to feed the tarpons at Robbie's Pier, just off the road in another key, Islamorada. It was a pretty cheap thrill, very much in keeping with the whole Keys vibe, ya know? Most people got their hands all slimy, dipping them into buckets of fish provided to feed the humongous beasts, which went after their meals with the alacrity of tiny piranhas. Not me. There was no way I was going to risk getting slop on the cute little white capris I'd been dying to wear all winter. I just watched the other tourists, staying all neat and clean myself. Besides, seeing those things in their feeding frenzy was too reminiscent of the annual wedding dress sale at Boston's Filene's Basement. It's fun to watch all the shenanigans on the news, but actually participate and risk a limb? I don't think so.

We headed farther north, leaving the Keys altogether to visit an indomitable shrine to unrequited love, the Coral Castle in Homestead. We were just a tad concerned about going out of our way for yet another potentially lame stronghold as we had in South Dakota for the Corn Palace debacle, the memory of which still stung. Fortunately, that was hardly the case here.

For two decades, beginning in 1920, a five-foot-tall, hundred-pound Latvian immigrant (who'd had tuberculosis, to boot) quarried, transported, designed, and fashioned over one thousand tons of coral rock, not only using it exclusively to build his home, but for every piece of furniture, as well. This is even more impressive when you realize that some of the pieces weigh up to thirty tons. He did it all without heavy machinery, in memory of the girl who, back in the old country, jilted him the night before their wedding. To this day, no one can figure out how, with only a fourth-grade education, Edward Leedskalnin could achieve such an engineering feat.

Normally, the Coral Castle would not have interested me all that much, as lacking a mechanically inclined brain, I really couldn't fully appreciate how truly amazing the accomplishment was. But, of course, Tim could. And as we wandered around the Castle, I caught glimpses of the little boy he must have been, totally enraptured by science. Unlike during his childhood, now my husband had someone who should have been able to appreciate his passion—me. Why hadn't I? Like, ever? As I realized my horrendous, nearly two decades' long lapse, Tim's joy at sharing all the coral marvels (including a nine-ton door that swings open at the touch of a finger and a telescope designed to sight the stars) became truly infectious. Although I really didn't understand the half of it (and I *was* trying, really I was), unlike over a year ago in his den, when he painstakingly and in excruciating detail explained the inner workings of buses, this time, I didn't utter one sound of protest.

Back on Key West, we continued the tradition of not doing much, even while feeling that our days were full. We took Miles practically everywhere, as we'd never been to such a dog-friendly place, not even our own hometown. In Boulder, the canine population is said to be twice that of the people. Whenever I go to my bank's drive-through with Miles, the tellers put dog treats into the tubes along with the receipts. At Tim's favorite hardware store, McGuckin's, leashed dogs are welcome and the clerks all sport green vests whose pockets contain dog treats, distributed liberally. (This does create some problems, however, as whenever we walk Miles in the street and pass someone wearing a vest, he or she invariably startles at the giant poodle lunging toward them, nosing their clothing.)

On KW we even found a dog beach, where we discovered something about our pooch we'd never known. We'd always tried to get him to take a dip whenever we passed a body of water, be it a stream or a lake. Poodles are water retrievers, after all. He was never interested, even if we threw in a stick. At the dog beach on KW, a woman cavorting with her Labrador threw a tennis ball into the ocean, which her dog repeatedly leapt in to retrieve. Seeing us, she kept him at her side, showed Miles the ball, and tossed it into the waves.

"Oh, he doesn't like the wa—" we began. Miles jumped right

in. Then we realized: It's not that he doesn't like water, it's that he doesn't like *cold* water. *Smart dog. Takes after his mother.*

We spent New Year's Eve walking up and down Duval Street (which was closed to cars for the occasion), stopping at various bars and eateries. We'd never been to Mardi Gras, but imagined this must be the next best thing: women flashing their boobage for the privilege of getting pelted with beads by men on balconies, although somehow, Hippies Gone Wild doesn't have the same appeal as Girls Gone the same. One lass, whose self-esteem was enviable, didn't have anything to flash with at all (OK, she *was* wearing body paint). And everyone was walking with go cups (Tim's filled with beer, mine margaritas) as if the entire street were a Vegas hotel. One bar even featured a "dropping of the wench in the harbor at midnight." (She was dressed as a pirate, and judging by her steady smile, must not have had an ounce of poodle in her.) Halloween is supposed to be even wilder. *Maybe next year.*

We had a few days to recover before we were due at Disney. Key West had gotten both of us—even Tim—used to getting up at around ten every day. While this wasn't such a difference for me, feeling the paralyzing pull of the Dark Side of sleeping in (which his Pesky Protestant Work Ethic informed me was "slovenly") disgusted my husband. At home, he'd always been up by six-thirty. Of course, the night before we left the Keys, we both got so anxious about having to wake up "early" (7 a.m.) for our long drive to Disney, neither of us could sleep at all.

We're really not Disney people. I mean, Disney people don't see the Guest Relations kiosk and wonder, "Ya think they sell condoms?" Disney people don't purposely make outlandish faces on the roller coasters, just as the camera snaps a picture (my favorite: pretending to stick a finger down my throat to gag). Disney people don't scream, "Look! It's a dwarf!" every chance they get, just for the satisfaction of knowing they're in the only place on the planet they can do so and not get dirty looks. (Although Tim did insist on adding, in his best politically correct tone, "They're called little people, sweetie.")

No, we're not Disney people, but we love Disney, anyway.

We'd been to Walt Disney World a couple of times before, but always stayed at one of the hotels. This was our first time at the Fort Wilderness Campground. It was truly ironic that in every RV park thus far, no matter how many overhead obstacles—tree limbs, phone lines, high-tension wires—we had no problem maneuvering the bus around our site to get the satellite Internet working. But in the fake campground that is Fort Wilderness, Disney does such an über job of simulating roughing it that we could never lock onto the signal. It figures The World would provide no less than the most campground-like campground imaginable.

We were assigned to one of the doggie loops, costing us five extra dollars a day. *Geez. What would Goofy think?* But it was worth it, for every evening, the real parade ain't on Main Street, it's on the loop, where canines, their grief lifted after being left alone all day, lead their masters on a joyful trot. You can almost hear them sing, "Hi ho! Hi ho! It's off to poop we go!"

Miles was by now eleven years old. And while he didn't seem to be slowing down, his eyes were clouding. Tim had noticed that when he threw the ball, there were times our pooch couldn't see it very well. Disney cured all that, as just before our arrival, Tim took Miles to the groomer. Then, just off the doggie loop, Tim found a gully that seemed tailor-made for fetch (and, indeed, probably was). With the hair out of his eyes, Miles's fetching abilities were magically restored.

The poodle wasn't the only one experiencing some Disney magic, for over in the Magic Kingdom, I became entranced by a Fairy Tale Wedding, although Tim made sure to conjure up my coming down to earth. The gorgeous bride was all decked out like a princess, resplendent in her sparkling gown, complete with tiara, horse-drawn carriage, and uniformed footman. I thought it was all rather wonderful, until I heard my long-suffering husband remark, "If he wants to set her up with those kinds of expectations, he's welcome to her."

We took buses (alas, not our own) everywhere in the park. On each and every ride, Tim was like a wide-eyed little boy in a fire station as he tried to chat up the drivers, fishing for any professional secrets they might wish to bestow. He was simply in awe of their presence. There was a lot to talk about, as WDW had just purchased a passel of new buses that all turned out to have major electrical problems. So when, say, the destination sign wasn't working, the driver would have to shut down the engine and essentially reboot the entire thing. Made us appreciate our own bus even more.

And speaking of wide-eyed little boys, Tim took one of the Disney tours, "The Magic Behind Our Steam Trains." Since I'm not interested in trains and even less interested in getting up at six in the morning, he did that one on his own. The other wives must have felt the same way, as the entire group was one big gaggle of testosterone. Although Tim was fascinated by the tour, he later related that the most interesting part was watching grown men trying not to act all excited when any observer could easily tell they were positively vibrating with the wonder of "We get to see how the steam trains work!"

Since Walt Disney World is 30,500 acres—twice the size of Manhattan—the buses, trains, trams, monorails, and boats are all essential to get around. (By way of contrast, Disneyland is a mere 300 acres and could, in its entirety, fit inside WDW's Epcot Center alone.) I grew up about the time WDW was being built and I still remember longing to go throughout most of my childhood. I was never that interested in Disneyland, as The World just seemed so much more, well . . . magical.

That was the point. About a decade after Disneyland opened, Walt realized it was going to be way too confining for his dreams. He hated that cheap hotels, attractions, and billboards crept right up to his Land's borders, easily visible from within the Kingdom. It particularly galled him when he asked a father why he was leaving the park and was told that up on top of the rides, Dad could see the freeway traffic getting bad and wanted to beat it.

By the early 1960s, Walt and his team started buying up land in central Florida, a super-secret mission, referred to only as "Project X." (Maybe I should start referring to Tim as "Project N.") To achieve their objective, brother Roy set up multiple dummy corporations to buy the land, which at the time went for only about a hundred dollars an acre. People started noticing the massive purchases and speculation became rampant. Who was behind the land grab? Was it an automaker? Defense contractor? Airplane manufacturer? Finally, at Disneyland's tenth anniversary party, people got their answer.

Reporters from around the country had been invited to the festivities in Anaheim, including one from the *Orlando Sentinel*. The newspaper had 130 reporters at the time, only three of whom were female, and its editor decided just to send "one of the girls" to the party. But Emily Brevar had done her homework. During the Q&A, she pointedly asked Walt, "What are you planning to do with all the land you're buying in central

Florida?" He, of course, denied that he was building a park at all, but did so with such detailed knowledge of the area, throwing out obviously well-researched facts about the water basin and easily citing weather statistics, that his staff had to pull him off the stage. The very next day, the *Sentinel* ran with the headline "It's Disney," and land shot up to $250,000 an acre. (The names of some of the dummy corporations—like M.T. Lott Real Estate Investments—can be seen in the upper windows along WDW's Main Street.)

All that effort was in service of Walt's dream to maintain the illusion that one is truly in another world: from the lake that, as in all fairy tales, must be crossed to get to the enchanted land, to the removal of Christmas decorations in the dead of night while guests sleep (also done on Disney cruises), to the strict requirements for "cast members." They must appear in costume, but only in their areas and never with any extra accoutrements (except at MGM, where, as would be the case on a real Hollywood lot, "cast members" can walk around anywhere they like in costume, even carrying backpacks or eating lunch).

It's all so realistic, in fact, that in Frontierland, I nearly made a mistake that would have gotten me kicked out of the park forever. I guess Tim's right about how concrete I am: Trying to keep hydrated all day, then holding it while waiting an hour for a ride, I had to go to the bathroom, bad (yeah, I know it's badly, but . . .). My eyes darted about, desperate (ditto). I finally spied a couple of outhouses near a playground.

"Be right back," I said to Tim. Fortunately, he immediately grasped the situation and, within a few steps, grabbed my arm.

"Sweetie," he said, concern in his voice. "Have you had too much sun?" He then explained that the outhouses were part of the playground and not really outhouses at all. Score one (and possibly a number two) for Disney realism.

Our favorite day in the park was the one spent at Blizzard Beach. We'd never been to any water park before and now fear that all others have been ruined for us, ever after. It was simply six straight hours of exhausting fun, climbing endless stairs to the tops of various waterslides, throwing ourselves headfirst onto "toboggans" or butt-first into rafts. I had sworn for months I would not do Summit Plummet, the 120-foot, near-vertical drop, billed as "the world's tallest and fastest free-fall body slide." But Tim dragged me up the slopes of Mount Gushmore and, being the gentleman that he is, said, "Ladies first." (He told me later the only way he could be certain he'd do the slide himself was if his wife took the initial plunge, rendering him too humiliated to back down.) My decision to go ahead was fueled more by laziness than bravery; those were an awful lot of steps to retrace. So after giving Tim one of my patented "what do you want from me"s, and with a look I hoped portrayed disgust, rather than the terror I felt, I purposely didn't glance at the slide as I swung my legs over the side. The moment I slowed to a stop from 55 mph, I turned around, smiled, waved at Tim, and started the climb to do it all over again.

While we went to every park at least three times each, Blizzard Beach was the only one we didn't return to. It had just been too perfect a day.

Tim and I have always been able to play together like children. I think it's because we trust each other so completely. Yes, we have our fights, but in all the time we've been together, neither of us has ever said anything in anger to the other we regret (or that's even so memorable we remember) later. I think this allows us both to regress completely, on demand (whether the situation calls for it or, in my case, often when it does not) without any fear the other will use our behavior against us.

The only crazy ride we didn't like (and, thus, only rode once) was Tomorrowland's newest attraction, Mission Space. This G-force extravaganza just made us want to puke. The paper bags attached to every seat should have been a dead giveaway. We felt so awful after riding it, in fact, we even canceled our dinner reservations.

Quite a hardship that, since this ain't your father's Disney. The World is now a gourmand's delight. We feasted one night in Africa, taking in the fragrances emanating from the wood-burning ovens. The next night found us in Germany at an Oktoberfest complete with yodeling and oompah bands. Then we might head to Morocco, treating ourselves like caliphs, reclining on sumptuous cushions, partaking of Middle Eastern delights while being entertained by belly dancers. No wonder we each gained five pounds during our eighteen-day stay.

Although I'd heard flight attendants can be grounded for putting on weight, it was not to be for this bus attendant, as my union rep refused to budge on the matter and I was forced to leave the state with him. Even our bus itself had gained weight in Florida. When we left Colorado, it was 40,040 pounds. At the Prevost place in Jacksonville, we discovered it had packed some on, vindication of sorts for Tim, who liked referring to it as "she." Now what I viewed as her at-times temperamental attitude made sense (for surely, the development of bus phobia hadn't been all my doing): "She" was suffering from PMS (Prevost Menstrual Syndrome). How else to explain the gain other than water weight? I just hoped she didn't develop cramps.

Perhaps my bus phobia rearing its ugly headlights again could be traced to when we were in the Prevost place in Jacksonville and I saw our mutilated bus neighbor, done in by a mere two-hundred-pound tire. What appeared to trigger my tipping point (*Oh, God*) into renewed terror occurred on our way to New Orleans, at an RV park near Pensacola. We were only stopping for the night, and while I went into the office to register, a repair truck passed by. One of the gals behind the counter, in either a misguided attempt to be helpful or an utterly intentional attempt to be sadistic, proclaimed, "A refrigerator in someone's rig caught fire." To my astonished look, she was only too happy to expand on her inflammatory statement.

"Oh, yeah!" she informed me with relish. "The repair guy said it happens all the time."

"R-really?"

"Oh, yeah!" she repeated, as she added insult to injury by swiping my credit card. Then she offered, "It can even happen while you're driving down the road." I swallowed hard, signed the bill, and decided not to tell Tim. Why give the driver even more to worry about when we're barreling down the highway?

But when I got back to the bus, Tim immediately asked, "Did you see that RV pass by with all the fire damage?" My face must have gone ashen.

"Look at you!" he exclaimed with more consternation than concern. "I thought you were over the bus phobia thing." *Geez. No wonder he had patients lining up to see him with that technique.*

He should talk. By this time on our trip, Tim had developed road rage. Yes, my darling husband, who always laughed and told me to "chill" during those rare times I drove us in my car in Boulder. What suddenly seemed to be irking him now when he drove was specific to the bus.

Of course our high-tech Prevost had a highly accurate computer-aided cruise control, identical to the one truckers use. Tim therefore liked to pick a big rig going the speed he wanted to go, slip in behind him, and "trim out" the cruise control until their speeds matched. When some poor, unsuspecting soul in a car pulled out in front of him and slowed down, Tim was—horror of horrors—forced to readjust his settings.

"Oh, my. I'm sure that's quite a hardship for you," I commented with all the empathy I could muster (which, granted, wasn't terribly much) when he first told me about his new toy within a toy.

"Well, it also interrupts my daydreaming," he explained.

"You're DAYDREAMING?" I started to protest that daydreaming while controlling twenty tons of heavy machinery might not be the best idea, when a car was kind enough to illustrate his point. Tim was then kind enough to illustrate mine about his road rage.

"Idiot!" he exclaimed. "So, you only realized how slow you were going when I started to pass you, eh?" he said to the oblivious driver. I decided to leave my concerns about his daydreaming while driving for another day.

Then, as we left Pensacola, Tim was in the passing lane about to move around a slow-going truck that had a car tailgating, when the car swerved out in front of us without stepping on it. We were gaining fast. To slow down, Tim put on his Jakes, but not as much as I thought he should. We were still gaining. I was sure he was doing it purposely, to "teach the guy a lesson." But I figured the guy could get whatever schooling he needed on his own time, without a full scholarship from my husband, the Prevost Provost.

"Listen, I don't want to be a nag and I know when I tell you you're getting too close, you just lament that you could have bought a system with radar, but don't you think—"

"Why would I need a system with radar when I've got the Nag-avator?" he chuckled.

"Sweetie. Please."

"What's the matter?" he said with glee. "Afraid I'm gonna give him a chrome enema?"

Can you blame me, then, when soon afterwards, I became particularly horrified as we seemed to be mounting an assault on a low, 13'6" overpass on a road that had been quite bumpy? I was sure I could see another bump right where we'd pass under.

"Oh God, oh God," I moaned, afraid we'd hit the ceiling of the overpass. "What's our limit?"

"Thirteen," he replied, but when he stole a glance at my terror-struck face, amended it to "No, twelve-six."

"But with dolphining, we could easily hit the top!"

"Dolphining?"

"You know, dolphining . . ." I made a wavy motion with my hand, then immediately regretted inducing him to take his eyes off the road.

"Oh! You mean porpoising!" he laughed. I shot him a withering look.

"Oh, please. Dolphining, porpoising. Like you can tell me the difference between a dolphin and a porpoise."

"Well, actually I can. A dolphin is . . ." *Oh, yeah. I forgot who I was dealing with.*

Soon, though, during our worst disaster yet, my husband would do something for me I would never forget.

Chapter Nine

ELVIS HAS LEFT THE BUS

> ### Love Me Bender
>
> 2 parts passion fruit liqueur
> 2 parts champagne
> 1 part raspberry liqueur
>
> *Rest shaker on hip, gyrate, drink. If you can still recall that the love of your life is making you live on a bus, repeat.*

We arrived in New Orleans in January 2005, seven months before Hurricane Katrina.

It seems strange writing about the Big Easy now, with the hindsight that a lot of what we encountered in this most unique of American cities was lost. Having seen a great deal of the U.S. by then, we agreed that New Orleans felt the most foreign and more; strolling through the French Quarter, it was as if we were not only transported to another country, but another time.

Tim always wanted to experience Mardi Gras. I hate crowds

(well, OK, I imagine I hate crowds). So we compromised and arrived for the pre–Mardi Gras celebrations, which start a couple of weeks before and consist of parades by some of the lesser-known krewes. Although we were still lavishly pelted (I should have brought a face mask—the kids on those floats have quite the arms), I couldn't really get into the whole bead thing. I mean, why would I want to scream and beg funny-looking people to throw me some gaudy plastic doodads that wouldn't (thank God) go with a single outfit I own?

Because there were no RV parks near downtown, we stayed at one about a half hour's Jeep ride to the French Quarter. Driving there every day, we'd see several signs reading "NO Intrnl Airport." I kept wondering why this fair city would seemingly boast it had a crappy little airport that could only handle domestic flights. It took me several days to figure out "NO" was New Orleans. *Concrete as a sidewalk.*

Of course we headed to a park where the Mississippi River empties into the Gulf of Mexico, 2,320 miles from where Tim straddled the headwaters in Lake Itasca, Minnesota, nearly five months before. And, of course, I took another picture of him to complete his diptych of disposal. This time, there were plenty of people around, sitting on the grass, watching barges pass by. I was sure there was no way Tim would strike his pose. The pre–bus thing Tim would have been too uptight and self-conscious. After all, he was mortified at Itasca when that family unexpectedly rounded the bend and caught him mid–spurious stream. But, peri–bus thing Tim did not hesitate. And he was amply rewarded for his newfound brazenness as this time, even with all the people: No one noticed.

In the French Quarter, we peered inside the murky windows of the New Orleans Historic Voodoo Museum and after much hesitation ("You go in first." "No, you go in first." "I went down the slide first." "How long are you going to hold that against me?" "As long as I can") tiptoed in.

The museum was crammed into just a few small rooms, each appropriately dark and musty. Of course these days, every museum has to have interactive displays. In this case, they consisted of a couple of voodoo idols with signs telling who the idol was and what kinds of offerings it required to not vent its wrath. The interactive aspect came in as the signs helpfully imparted that the gods like candy, but if you don't have any (and not being prepared, we didn't), money would do just fine. There was even a plate conveniently situated in front of each idol. Although we'd already paid seven dollars for the admission and realized we were likely only contributing to the house collecting its voodoo vig, the place was so creepy, we ponied up the coinage anyway. No point in taking any chances.

We did learn a bit, however, about the origins of voodoo in NO. When slaves were brought to Louisiana from Africa and Haiti, they were forbidden to practice their own religions. Many were baptized into the Catholic Church. Some Catholic saints then became stand-ins for voodoo deities, worshipped as if they were gods themselves.

Next, we did a cemetery tour, and were surprised to learn that Marie Laveau's resting place is the second most visited in the U.S.; only Elvis's does better.

Not much is known about this mysterious Queen of Voodoo, and that seems to be exactly the way she wanted it. It is thought she was born in the French Quarter around 1794 to a wealthy white planter and a free Creole woman of color. Shortly after Marie married, her husband disappeared under mysterious circumstances and was presumed dead. She supported herself as a hairdresser, catering to prominent white women, all the while developing her powerful magic, mixing Roman Catholic traditions and saints with African spirits. But her true power was said to derive from the extensive network of spies she groomed among servants in wealthy households. Out of a mixture of fear and respect, they shared with her their masters' most private information. When her daughter (one of fifteen children) who bore a striking resemblance to Marie also became a voodoo priestess, the now ageless Queen seemed to travel at will, appearing in more than one place at a time. Even after she died in 1881, many claimed to still see her about town. To this day, visitors draw three X's (XXX) on the side of her tomb, hoping she'll grant them a wish.

Another tomb belonged to Bernard de Marigny, in his time known as the country's wealthiest teen. The son of a count, he inherited seven million dollars at the age of fifteen when his father died. Although along the way he lost his entire fortune gambling and died impoverished, he also named many of the city's famed streets: Music, Love, Desire (as in streetcar), and one whose name simply had to be changed, for as the area developed, four churches were ultimately built on Craps Street. (He is also credited with bringing that game to this country.)

Unfortunately, in New Orleans our waistlines continued the expansion into double-wide status they'd begun in Disney, in spite of the fact that we could not bring ourselves to try some of the more "exotic" fare. Like rabbit. We see them in our backyard. They're cute. Can't eat 'em. Deer (which I guess is called venison once it's on the plate, kind of like "cow" transforms at some point in the process to "steak," although I seem to have no problem in that department. And why, then, does chicken stay chicken?), same thing. Still, we managed. Boy, did we. (Who'da thought preparing filet mignon in a mushroom wine reduction and adding a banana could be so heavenly? I immediately requested that my personal chef come up with a similar recipe.)

By now, between the magic of Disney and voodoo, we were feeling pretty darn lucky. But, of course, neither magic could last; it had been way too long without a disaster. The drive from New Orleans to Van Buren, Arkansas, was uneventful. It was the parking that nearly did us in. The front lawn next to Bob's house had become even muddier this rainy season and, of course, the bus got stuck. It took Cousin JT and his tractor (yes, *that* Cousin JT and *that* tractor) most of a day to pull us out. I, of course, took multiple pictures of the entire process to post on my blog, prompting Tim to assert that he was going to have to get his own blog in rebuttal and call it "I Am Not an Idiot."

Tim had wanted to return to Van Buren ever since meeting his long-lost cousin in Myrtle Beach. He realized that while he now knew more about his family's roots, he still didn't know a whole lot about his father. Back on Bob's farm, they discussed what the other Justice in Myrtle had said. Bob was aware of some of the family history, and talking about it spurred him to share a bit of his own.

He revealed that when he was a kid, his own dad came to visit kin a quarter mile from where Bob lived with his mother, stayed for two weeks, and never once tried to see him.

Now Tim finally understood: We all gotta come from somewhere.

Since he was a child, Tim had struggled to make a connection to his father. Now he could only imagine Bob's struggle having no connection to his own father at all. When considered in that context, Tim realized he and Bob had actually done OK. Still, going forward, he hoped they could do better and finally softened toward the older man.

He also discovered that a couple of brothers in Bob's family had a similar relationship to what Tim had always had with one of his. One day, while Project Nerd and Project Nerd Senior (Ret.) were puttering about on the farm, Frances mentioned to me that Cousin Dana and Cousin John hadn't spoken for nearly a decade. In fact, Dana hadn't even wanted John at his funeral a couple years back. When I told Tim about it later, he was shocked.

"I didn't know it had gotten that bad," he said. "My dad never mentioned anything, even that time he and I went to see Dana and then went right over to John's."

"Yeah," I said. "But you never saw them together."

"You mean . . ." he asked, all innocent and wide-eyed, "they're the same person?" I slapped him.

Since we'd last been in Arkansas on our meltdown cruise, the Clinton library had opened in Little Rock. No matter what you think of the man, you have to admire his intellect, zeal, and energy. It's not hard to argue he accomplished a lot, whether you like what he accomplished or not. I wanted to see the building as much for the history as the edifice itself. I'd heard it was a stunning display of technology and modern architecture, although some had nevertheless likened it to a double-wide (perhaps some future prez will be fortunate enough to have his library likened to a bus) settin' on a river. Bob and Frances gamely said they'd come along, so we headed out for the over-two-hour trip in style, in Frances's Lincoln Town Car. (Men in these here parts drive the pickup trucks. Women drive the city cars.)

No one discussed politics the entire time—we all seemed to know better.

We did, though, discuss the weird nomenclature in this part of the country. As Tim and I traveled in the central U.S. through Oklahoma, Arkansas, and Tennessee, it seemed as if these states were having some sort of identity crisis, what with names of towns such as Arkola, Texarkana, and Arkadelphia. Now, when we passed Toad Suck Park outside Little Rock, we all wondered if the name reflected disgust with the amphibians or the park itself.

The Clinton library did not disappoint. Here the exhibits truly were interactive, without even one penny more exacted above *this* seven-dollar admission. Above and beyond the take on pivotal points in history, what we found most interesting were the mundane, day-to-day activities that rarely get reported. All the president's appointment books for his entire eight years are on display. It amazed us how much one human being could pack into one twenty-four-hour period, all while appearing as interested in heads of state as in Boy Scouts. No wonder, unlike almost every other little kid, I'd never wanted to be president.

Back in Van Buren, we needed a wee bit of bus repair. (One of the air bags in the suspension system had busted during the whole dolphining/porpoising thing, causing the bus to lean precipitously.) Tim found a mechanic in nearby Fort Smith (that's the big town near Van Buren. It has a Red Lobster). Bob wanted to ride along, so I stayed with Frances in the house. Tim told me later that as was her recent custom, the moment he started the ignition, Shula hustled up front in her resplendent fur, aiming for her rightful place on the buddy seat. Only this time, Bob was sitting in it. Shula stopped dead in her tracks and scrutinized him. As Tim edged the bus off the lawn, her sense of proprietorship quickly outweighed her entrenched misanthropy and she leapt up to her spot. She and Bob gave each other puzzled looks, sized each other up (he's as much of a cat person as she is a person cat), realized neither had a whole lot of choice in the matter, and settled in for the ride.

On Friday night we went "bluegrassin'," just across the Oklahoma border in tiny Roland. The sign out front of a former tire store said: "Bluegrass show-jam Friday night 7 pm until." Bob and Frances explained there'd be four invitation-only bands over three hours, none of whom were paid (although audience members were encouraged to put a dollar in the bucket by the door for electricity). The musicians did it for the practice and the joy of performing, December through April every year, until the official bluegrass season (who knew?) began and they headed out on the circuit.

My in-laws, obviously regulars, said hello to almost everyone in the small room, where we sat on folding metal chairs. Unfortunately, they also knew the ten-year-old little girl who, whenever the spirit moved her and encouraged by her relations, leapt up onstage to start clogging.

Clogging actually has origins in various parts of the world. In England, it began during the Industrial Revolution. Men in factories would tap their hard-soled shoes on the ground to the cadence of their machines, warming their feet. During breaks, they'd have competitions to see who could stomp out the best rhythms. Although there are many styles of clogging (all emphasizing beats of music with fervent foot stomping), we were apparently witnessing an entirely new breed. She sure had the fervor down. And the stomping. Actually, she was making quite the racket, just not in sync with any of the music. The girl had no rhythm.

I could only imagine how distracting it was for the musicians to essentially have a percussion section backing them up to the beat of its own drummer—one that couldn't keep time. The bands gamely referred to her as their "go-go dancer—she just keeps goin' and goin'." The folks in them there parts sure are polite. I would have thrown vegetables from Frances's garden up on that stage or, at the very least, clobbered that little girl on the head with a Dobro.

While we were staying with Bob and Frances, Aunt Virginia died. I was never able to discern if she was anybody in particular's aunt, so much as she seemed to be an aunt to everybody. I'd never met her, and although everyone said what a wonderful person she was, I really, really did not want to go to her funeral. I'd never been to an open casket one before. Of course, as a doctor, I'd seen my share of dead people, but not all prettied up. The thought was kind of freakish. (Jews don't embalm or do open caskets. We just box 'em and drop 'em.) But as one of the younger generation to attend (and therefore still able to shoulder the weight), Tim was pegged as a pallbearer. If he had to go, I had to go (so said he).

The room for the viewing at the funeral home was tiny, so even though I tried not to look at Aunt Virginia, I really had no choice. We walked in and there she was. On the one hand, it seemed so intrusive. No one likes to be looked at while he or she is sleeping, yet here was Aunt Virginia, taking her Big Sleep with everyone taking a peek. It just seemed to me that death should be more private. On the other hand, she was the proverbial elephant in the room—this was her party, she was right there, yet no one was talking to her. It's not like they were totally ignoring her, though, as everyone was heard to comment, "She sure looks purty." Well, of course she does. So does waxed fruit.

It wasn't until we were on our way home and Bob and Frances discussed how much better Aunt Virginia looked than she had in years that I understood that an open casket is a way for relatives to supplant bad memories with better ones. The realization actually made me feel more comfortable about the whole thing. *Geez. Somebody could've told me.*

On our next-to-last day in Van Buren, Frances took me to see her brother and his goat farm. There must have been a hundred goats, all bleating at the top of their lungs. (OK. Here's another one. Goat stays goat on your plate—not that I would eat it, either.) As we walked around the hill, he pointed out a few, including babies with their mothers. I was sure not to make the same mistake with the adorable creatures I'd made years before, when visiting Tim's brother Mike in Grass Valley, California. Mike had a few large pens on his property where he kept a couple of pigs, sheep, and some chickens. (OK. Last time. Pig becomes pork—at least that makes some alliterative sense; sheep becomes lamb—a kind of warped, age-reversal process that even our beauty-obsessed culture wouldn't want to emulate; then there's that chicken thing again.) For some reason, I was particularly taken with one of the pigs and asked, "What's his name?" Mike gave me a strange look.

"Ah . . . we don't name them," he said, trying to conceal his laughter.

"But how can you have a pet and not name him?" I insisted.

"Ah . . . they're not pets," Mike replied. I didn't get it until Tim took me aside later to explain. *Oh.*

As pleasant as it was to spend time with Bob and Frances, after two and a half weeks, I was itchin' to get back on the road. While I could appreciate the kinship of a rural community like Van Buren, it was all just a little too social for me. Maybe it's that I'm an only child, but I like having alone time. It would drive me crazy to have people stopping by the house every day and, even worse, expecting me to get dressed and stop by theirs. Tim, too, found himself struggling with liking the sense of community versus not having much else around but community to like. Finally, he seemed to settle it for himself as he mused, "I'd like living here if I didn't know any better."

After such a long time stationary, getting back on the road seemed unfamiliar. My usual "pre-flight" routine wasn't routine anymore. I even forgot to secure a few things before we took off and they went flying, causing a mess but no real damage. Then there was all the truck traffic on I-40. We'd never seen so many big rigs. And since the dreaded Jersey barriers lined the highway due to road work, I kept imagining that if we had to stop suddenly for, say, a moose, we would swerve right into the median and tip over—just like that bus in Jacksonville. The fact that moose had never been seen in the area (as Tim informed me) was of no comfort.

By the time our five-and-a-half-hour trip to Marion, Arkansas (just outside Memphis), was over, my hands were shaking. As soon as Tim stopped the bus in front of the campground office, rather than go out and check us in, I made myself a martini. I didn't stop to name it. Eyeing my glass, Tim asked, "Have you figured out which rehab you want me to drop you off at yet?"

I knew this entire area of the country was quite different from what I was used to. What I hadn't considered was that I'm quite different from what the people here are used to, as well. That first night, in search of provisions, we took the Jeep to a relatively upscale supermarket. I wore my usual bus winter attire, a pink velour Baby Phat tracksuit . . . and felt overdressed. Judging by the stares I got in the frozen food aisle, that sentiment—and more—was duly returned.

We went to Memphis specifically to see Graceland, something we'd both always wanted to do. We're not the only ones; it's the second most visited residence in the U.S. (The White House is number one.) The fourteen-acre, 17,000-square-foot estate turned out to be a colossal disappointment. I thought it would be far more grand. Maybe it's just that, as a museum left exactly as it had been when the King died, it can't help being a fashion victim of the '70s. But really. One of the richest men in the country, a cultural icon no less, and he had Formica countertops?

As much as Graceland was a letdown, Memphis did provide us with an eye-opening visit to a stop along the Underground Railroad.

At its height in the first half of the eighteenth century, tens of thousands of slaves escaped through this extensive network of safe houses and secret routes, mainly to free states and Canada, but also to Mexico and overseas. "Underground" refers to the secrecy required and "Railroad" to the code words, all taken from train terminology, used to direct the fugitives. "Passengers," for example, would travel by foot or wagon at night, guided by "conductors" and stopping to rest at "stations" or "depots" in the homes of "stationmasters." (Harriet Tubman, after escaping to freedom herself, became a conductor for seventy slaves over thirteen separate trips, largely in Maryland. She boasted she "never lost a passenger.")

When German immigrant Jacob Burkle established the Memphis Stockyards two blocks from the Mississippi River, he built his house there, too, in 1849, complete with a cellar to hide escaping slaves. They would wait until a shipment of cattle arrived, then make their way to the river, hiding amongst the animals and hay. There they'd be transported over water to the free state of Illinois or even as far away as Canada. (Canada became a particularly desirable destination after 1850 when the Fugitive Slave Law was passed, allowing slave hunters to capture fleeing slaves from northern "free" states.) While Burkle hid his activities as a conductor on the Underground Railroad from his family for their own safety, slave catchers suspected him nonetheless, and at least once kicked in his door. Still, his activities did not cease until his death.

Today, Slave Haven Underground Railroad Museum resides in

Burkle's white clapboard house. A nonprofit surviving on admissions, gift shop sales, and donations, it was founded and run by Joan Nelson and Elaine Turner, sisters arguably Burkle's equal in energy and vision. As Joan showed us around the Burkle Estate (quite the misnomer—we nearly passed it right by), seemingly ancient history slapped us right into the present.

It wasn't just the old posters (including the original "Wanted: Dead or Alive. Reward $40" for Harriet Tubman), the whip hanging on a wall next to a picture of a slave's ravaged back, the nine-foot burlap sack which had to be filled with cotton, then emptied, then repeated all over again several times each day, the flyers advertising "one hundred good negroes" for sale, or the quilt patterns with escape routes or other messages stitched into them (it was illegal for slaves to read or write). It was Joan's sharing her own story of marching for civil rights in the 1960s with Martin Luther King, Jr., her arrest as a teenager, and her friendship with Emmett Till's mother, which gave it all a tragic continuity, an unbroken time line of hate and prejudice that, as unbelievable as it seemed when surrounded by those very artifacts of hate and prejudice, continues to today.

As psychiatrists, we've always been connoisseurs of quirky. And up until this point in our travels, this attraction to oddities had resulted in our learning about many ill-conceived, obsessive quests. Joan, however, made us realize that there is such a thing as a grand obsession (as opposed to silly ones like building heavy, uncomfortable furniture out of dead sea creatures or believing Jules Verne insane because we're already at the center of the earth), that there are some things worth developing a passion for and zealously pursuing. Meeting Joan, we wondered if either of us would ever find such a thing for ourselves. And more importantly, once found, if we'd possess this remarkable woman's determination to see it through.

As we left Memphis on I-40 West, traffic started building up. While I hoped our seven-hour trip to Dallas wouldn't be delayed too long, Tim for once was looking forward to driving in the dark—anything so that I would cease and desist my panic-stricken rant every time we passed one of the many construction signs along the way (not to mention the seemingly ever-present, and ever-dreaded, double Jersey barriers).

One particularly disturbing sign I'd never seen before had an arrow pointing up with the words "DANGER. POWER LINES." Tim tried to reassure me that they were meant for large excavator rigs which extended far higher than our bus's measly twelve feet six inches. He tried, really he did. Then all of a sudden, all oncoming traffic disappeared. Soon we saw why: A truck had jack-knifed, a car apparently hit it, and both were incinerated. There was no way to tell if anyone was injured, as the accident was clearly hours old. A hazmat team was on the highway, cleaning up the oil and who knows what else. We checked the odometer and kept looking down in disbelief: Traffic was backed up for ten miles and the cleanup was nowhere near complete.

If driving the bus had given Tim road rage, my "traffic rage" had always been present, whether in car or bus, as driver or passenger. It didn't even matter if I wasn't directly affected. Just seeing a bumper-to-bumper mess threw me into a tizzy. And heaven forbid, if I was going to get stuck, I would much rather drive an hour out of my way than sit in traffic for five interminable minutes. Maybe I'm just jealous of all that idling around me.

So for this, the worst traffic pileup I had ever seen in my life, it became my mission to warn as many oncoming vehicles as possible. I turned on the CB radio for the very first time, almost exactly six months into our trip, fiddled with the instruments, and got mostly static.

"Turn it to channel nineteen," Tim commanded. My hand hovered over the dial as I shot him a dubious look. He'd never owned a CB radio. But I changed the channel to 19 and, sure enough, truckers for miles around came in loud and clear.

"How the hell do you know this stuff?" I asked, incredulous. He just smiled and gave me a variation on his pat response, which always included a shrug and the word "everyone."

The truckers were already warning each other, so I just listened. Tim didn't want me to say anything, anyway. He was afraid I'd be a smart-ass and get us killed at a rest stop (he had to pull the bus over to pee sometime). Still, the soap operas on five axles were compelling: budding romances between drivers, sinners seeking blue-collared absolution in their mobile confessionals, litanies of fascinating family foibles.

"I want to talk," I informed Tim.

"I'm sure you do," he replied. I tried to ignore him, but just could not resist announcing what my handle would be: "Prevost Princess."

"Way to stay incognito," he said and absolutely forbade me from touching the mike. *Geez*.

While playing around with the CB was a pleasant distraction, my bus phobia only got worse about fifty miles from Texarkana, where it started pouring. To keep my eyes off the road, I tried to read.

"SHIT!" Tim shouted. By now, I had him trained not to use expletives for road rage or other routine matters, so I knew it was bad even before my head snapped up. Then I saw it: One of our windshield wipers was stuck.

Tim didn't want to keep the working wiper going, for fear it would burn out the motor and we'd be left with no wipers at all. (Why one working wiper could tax a motor more than two, he was happy to explain later in painstaking and excruciating detail.) He took the next exit and parked on the shoulder. I watched him fiddle around with the wiper in the downpour, then go get something from the bay. When he came back to the front, he had a wrench in his hand. Project Nerd to the rescue. He fiddled around some more, stood back, surveyed his work, then gestured to me to turn the windshield wipers on. *Right*.

"I've been leaving the driving to you, remember?" He rolled his eyes, came around to the driver's side, opened the ticket window, and turned them on himself. They were actually on the same doohickey as the lights—*just like in a car. Who knew?* When he got back in, I made the mistake of asking what had been the matter.

"Well, the acorn nut must have gotten loose and fallen off somewhere. It keeps the . . ." Ever since the Coral Palace, I had tried to at least feign interest in his mechanical musings, but we were standing on the shoulder of a highway exit lane in what can only be described as a torrential downpour. Seeing my eyes both glaze over and register fear (a feat, even for me), he stopped himself with a "I'll just have to get another acorn nut in Dallas. This should hold until we get there." *Should?*

The first thing we noticed about Texas is that Texans take their "Lone Star" moniker very seriously. There are stars (lone ones, natch) all over the place: on buildings, highway overpasses, and, of course, the state flag, which is where the whole lone star thing came from in the first place.

Our initial foray in Dallas was to the Sixth Floor Museum, housed in the former Texas School Book Depository. With all the conspiracy theories we'd heard all our lives, it was fascinating to see the site of JFK's assassination for ourselves. The museum gives a surprisingly balanced view of the events of 1963, with equal consideration not only to President Kennedy's achievements and legacy, but to alternative theories of the assassination. That's still not enough for some people, who then head around the corner to the aptly named Conspiracy Museum.

As a diehard fan of the TV show *Dallas*, I just had to see Southfork Ranch in Plano, about a forty-minute drive from downtown. I wish I hadn't. Kind of like I wish I'd never seen the third *Aliens* movie, for it, too, ruined everything that came before it. (Or the *Buffy the Vampire Slayer* movie, as it nearly ruined everything that came after it.) The cast of *Dallas* apparently only went to the ranch in the summers, filming all the outdoor shots they would need for the year. None of the interior of the ranch was ever used (those scenes were filmed in Los Angeles).

The only really interesting thing about the entire tour was how tiny the Southfork pool is. Our guide explained that when a cast member took a dip, she swam with a clear inner tube around her waist. (Actually, the guide said, "he or she" and "his or her." *Oh, please.* It was always either Linda Gray or Victoria Principal in a skimpy suit. Personally, I would love to have seen Howard Keel take a dip. *Seven Brides for Seven Brothers* is one of my favorite musicals.) The tube was then attached to cables held on to by crew members. As a result, it appeared as if it took Sue Ellen or Pam a long time to get to the other end. I wish we had saved the eight-dollar admission (a dollar more than either the Clinton or voodoo museums . . . no one ever said Texans lack moxie) and just viewed the ranch from the street. The only consolation was that our tour group consisted of people from all over the globe. Thus, Tim and I were able to feel quite superior as we commented to each other under our breaths, "At least *we* only drove forty minutes to get here."

Once Tim squirreled away an acorn nut for the windshield wiper, we got back on the road and headed to Houston. There, in a residential neighborhood on a small lot, we stumbled across the Orange Show, which, depending on your point of view, is either a whimsical or insane (we're professionals and we couldn't even decide) homage to all things orange, in all possible permutations and combinations. A former postman spent twenty-five years collecting, well . . . junk, in honor of his favorite fruit, to form this suburban maze of sculpture, balconies, and outdoor theaters. After his death in 1980, a nonprofit was formed to not only preserve the Orange Show but to promote creative thinking and making art more accessible.

This was not the only oddity we encountered in Houston: Downtown is home to one of the most unusual fountains we'd ever seen. It runs the length of a city block, spraying water high over trolley cars, automobiles, and pedestrians in an arc to the other side. At certain times of day, there's also a water video, which projects images on a sort of stone picture frame (think *Star Trek*–Edith Keeler–*City on the Edge of Forever* kind of thing). On windy days, we supposed everyone working in the vicinity brings raincoats. On very windy days (over 10 mph) it shuts down.

In Galveston, we were hoping to find a lovely spot to relax and enjoy the beach. Not so much. Galveston has clearly seen better days. We got a sense of its glorious past by viewing a short film about the devastating storm of 1900, which took six thousand lives and resulted in a six-year dredging effort to raise the grade of the town, complete with the construction of a ten-mile-long seawall.

Next door to the movie theater stood the Ocean Star, an offshore oil rig converted into a museum. (The Port of Galveston is one of the places these gargantuan structures come to be reconditioned.) Through videos, models, actual drilling equipment, and interactive displays, we learned everything we ever wanted to know (and in my case, so much more) about drilling for oil. I found it all just one big bore (hole). Tim was, of course, fascinated. But as much as he enjoyed all the exhibits, his favorite by far was the one where he made me put on an orange jumpsuit—what the roughnecks wear—undoubtedly on display for the sole purpose of encouraging husbands to make fun of their wives. Back in my usual (usually) less laughable outfit, we then drove along the seawall in our Jeep, but the beach was rather unattractive. Galveston has really clearly seen better days.

Austin, on the other hand, was our favorite Texas city, probably because it reminded us of our beloved Boulder, only a river runs through it. Normally, as we headed into a town, I'd haul out one of our telephone book–like guides to RV parks and figure out where to stay based on proximity to what we wanted to see as well as the amenities in the park itself. No Jacuzzi was usually an automatic no, as was no pets. (Some parks actually restrict dog size. So when asked what breed Miles was, I got used to responding, "Oh, he's just a poodle.") Then I'd phone to check availability. For Austin, I quickly settled on its highest-rated RV park called (what else?) Austin Lone Star RV Resort, which the ad boasted was only about a ten-minute drive from downtown. Once we checked in, we discovered that not only was it convenient to the highway (just off it, in fact) but even more convenient to the adult movie establishment next door.

While in Austin, we toured the state capital, which of course is the largest in the U.S. But it was also one of the loveliest we'd seen, both inside and out. The senators' walnut desks date from the 1880s, and have been modified to accommodate changing

technology: Microphones sit in the inkwells. The entire building was wired for gas lighting when it was built, just in case electricity was some fancy, newfangled, passing fad.

Perhaps the most important thing we took away from Austin
had to do with the roads; Austinites drive like maniacs. In retrospect, this is probably where Tim's road rage started to generalize
to when he drove the Jeep. I, of course, was thrilled at this new
development. *Thanks, Austin!*

The Alamo, in San Antonio, was a bit of a disappointment.
We should have boned up on our reading beforehand, as the
exhibits did a very poor job explaining the history behind the
thirteen-day siege, or the one-hour battle that ended it. We were
sure told that the theme of this "Shrine to Texas Liberty" was
self-sacrifice, specifically for the independence of Texas, but it
was frustrating not to get any kind of feel for what the defenders
actually did. Instead, we were left to make what we could of the
various displays. On a more positive note, we did get to see Davy
Crockett's vest, done in light tan leather with tasteful yet un-
derstated multicolored beading. How come all the history books
leave out that ole Davy was such a sharp dresser? Of course, he
always had a certain flair: After being defeated for reelection to
the U.S. House of Representatives, he told his constituents, "You
may go to hell, and I will go to Texas." He died at the Alamo less
than six months later.

By this point in our travels, we had learned to ask locals for
suggestions of interesting things to see or do, rather than rely on
a guidebook. Then we made the mistake of consulting the office
manager at our RV park, leading us to take a day trip in the Jeep
to some small, "quaint," hill-country towns. I complained bit-
terly. "I can't believe he recommended these shit holes." Then
I got a bright idea: I should write a tour book to prevent others
from making the same mistake.

"You could rate every place on a crapper system; lid down versus lid up," Tim offered.

On our way to Tucson, we stopped at a truck stop in Segovia, Texas, whose sign boasted "Fuel, food and pretty waitresses." I was a bit offended, until upon closer inspection, the word "old" became apparent between "pretty" and "waitresses."

In the nine-hour drive through the barren stretch of desert from San Antonio to El Paso, the most exciting thing I saw was the clock on my cell phone adjust from Central Standard to Mountain Standard Time. Then we passed a large cement-block building, surrounded by an electrified barbed-wire fence. Signs instructing drivers not to pick up hitchhikers dotted the highway.

"I guess if you have to live out here, prison isn't a bad option," I allowed.

Between our residencies and then starting our private practices, Tim and I spent nearly ten years in Tucson, so we were looking forward to revisiting some of our Old Pueblo haunts. Particularly our favorite Mexican restaurant (it's hard to get good Mexican food in Boulder).

We beat feet over to Sanchez Burrito Company our very first night, hoping they still had our favorites on the menu. They did. The place itself also hadn't changed a bit: small, sparsely decorated, abundant Formica. No waiters, no frills, no worries—never a bad meal. We perused the large, illuminated menu by the door and gave the young woman behind the counter our order. After getting our drinks, we settled into a booth, waiting for Tim's name to be called. We were the only customers in the joint and chalked it up to a Monday night. Surely Sanchez hadn't lost its touch? It only took a few minutes to confirm that it hadn't; our food was ready. Tim returned to the counter (no waiter, no frills) and brought the meals to our table on plastic trays. We dug in. *Yummmm . . . Huh?*

A man was yelling by the door. We figured the cook and the girl were just having some fun, until we heard her scream. My back was to the entrance, but before I could turn around, Tim looked up to see a hooded, bandana'd youth pointing a gun at the now empty counter. The girl had fled to the kitchen. Tim said quietly, although with an unmistakable urgency, "They're being robbed. He has a gun. Don't move." I froze in my seat. We knew the only way out of the place was past the guy. He glanced over at us. Tim caught his eye. I maintained my gaze at Tim, thankful he was the one facing the door, because I sincerely doubted I would have been able to muster that calm a look. But it was more than that. It was a look that said, "Do not. Whatever you're thinking. Just . . . do . . . not."

I suspect it was the same look he gave psychotic patients in psychiatric units who escalated to the point where they needed to be restrained for their own safety as well as everyone else's. Most psychiatrists called for the staff at that point and slunk over to the nurses' station to chart about the incident as it was unfolding. Not my Tim. He'd make sure he had help in case he needed it, but could usually de-escalate the patient just by his demeanor and words. On those rare occasions when a takedown was in order, he was always the one heading it up. When he'd recount the incident to me later, I'd shake my head, proud of him but also wishing he'd just act like a "normal" psychiatrist. Although he obviously knew what he was doing, I was afraid he'd get hurt. Now it seemed all that on-the-job training had been worth it.

The youth hesitated, then ran out the door.

Tim ushered me under a table and grabbed my cell phone. He

called 911 and told the operator we didn't know if the guy ran out back to get the girl or if he was planning to come back in to get us. I hadn't even considered the latter possibility.

"I'm going out front to look around," Tim informed me. "I won't be cornered like rats." For the first time in my life, rats didn't seem so . . . rodentlike. They seemed positively lovable. If one had been in the place, in fact, I would have scooped it up and kissed it on its adorable, whiskered lips, just to prove my point. Since there were none, instead I begged Tim not to leave. I was afraid he'd run into the guy. He insisted. I begged some more, pawing (rather ratlike, actually) at his arms.

Fortunately, just then, six cops surrounded the restaurant, which was all windows, brightly lit from the inside. Tim, realizing he could very well be the only male (and therefore suspect) in the place, put his hands up in the air and walked out to the parking lot. The girl, hearing the police, emerged from the back room, crying. As soon as the assailant had pointed the gun at her, she'd fled there, locked the door, and used the phone . . . to call her boss. (Look, I'd have run too if I were her, but I'd like to think I have the customer service skills to at least call the police.) The cops interviewed them both, but neither Tim nor she could give a good description.

We returned to our meal. Tim ate heartily. I had no appetite, and besides, my hands were shaking too much to safely handle the plastic silverware. I took a swig from his beer. A big swig. I hate beer. I didn't care.

As we left, Tim told the still-crying girl, "Wonderful burritos, but the floor show needs work."

Back in the Jeep, he wanted to go to a convenience store for a six-pack.

"Are you insane?" I exclaimed. "Convenience stores are even better targets for robberies! No way." I would not relent and instead offered to make him the martini of his choice. No problemo; I needed a few, myself.

In retrospect, our would-be assailant was none too bright. The counter was easily visible from the outside and if he had simply waited to make his move until the girl was near the till rather than toward the back, he might have gotten some money. Frankly, it added insult to injury to be so frightened by a robber who's such a moron. I would have felt better about the whole thing if he had been just a teensy bit higher up on the fast-food chain.

The next day, a package arrived for me at the RV park. My hands were still shaking, but I managed to steady them enough to get the wrapping open. *What in the world could it be? Oh. Of course.* A pair of Richard Tyler mules I purchased on eBay the week before. (Although I seemed not to shop in volume in malls anymore, I still enjoyed perusing for select designer duds online.) I stared at the shoes. Sure, I could appreciate the perfectly proportioned kitten heel, the stylish tortoiseshell hue, the exquisite workmanship of the leather buckle, the . . . I wrapped them up and never took them out of the box again.

For that moment, for however long that moment was to last, I didn't care about shoes. Tim and I were alive . . . and happy. I always knew I was loved and cherished by my husband (even as he callously upended my entire life to follow his bus dream), but I'd just witnessed him protecting me and putting my life before his. With all we had been through this year, shoes—even such a pair as this—were reduced to their proper place in my universe, one that allowed for a more detached admiration of *things* in general. With five months left on our trip, I found myself looking forward to discovering all the ways that particular emotional energy of mine which clung to objects could now become free to direct elsewhere.

Although we had planned on going to Sanchez frequently during our stay, we never did return. But there were certainly plenty of other excellent Mexican restaurants to choose from in Tucson—perhaps too many, judging from the state of my colon. Lying in bed one night, Tim lifted the covers and exclaimed, "Whoa, Warden! I haven't had my last meal yet."

Given that our trip thus far had ranged from the sublime to the ridiculous (along with far too many descents even farther into the death-defying), all with our marriage still very much intact, during our next stop, Las Vegas, we did what felt like the most natural thing in the world: renewing our wedding vows in the bus . . . with Elvis officiating.

That was to be only the second-craziest thing we did all year.

Chapter Ten

BUSING IN THE BUFF

Nudist Nectar

3 parts apple vodka
1 part apple schnapps
½ part butterscotch schnapps

Wearing a blindfold, measure and mix ingredients in shaker.
(It's not polite to look.)

From a two-armed, none-too-bright bandit we headed to the one-armed bandits and bright lights of Las Vegas . . . with a dying alternator.

Shortly after we left Tucson, Tim noticed the needle on the voltmeter drifting downward. What was a Project Nerd to do? Why, call on the vast knowledge he'd gleaned from his favorite National Public Radio show—*Car Talk*, of course. For PN, tuning in to Click and Clack every week was like being in direct electromagnetic linkage to the "automotive" branch of the

Project Prophet Pantheon—the other branches being "home improvement," "yard maintenance," and "crap my wife makes me do." He quickly realized the needle drooping on that gauge labeled "volts" meant . . . something. Nonetheless, he somehow resisted the temptation to stick black electrical tape over the pesky, if incessant, warning light.

Tim was able to explain that the voltmeter measures the output of the alternator, the electrical system that provides energy to pretty much everything on the bus except, unfortunately, me. With four hundred miles of desert to get through, an ailing alternator was not a good thing.

As we neared Las Vegas, the needle on the voltmeter sank steadily. With only thirty more miles to go, we approached Hoover Dam on U.S. 93. Like the road leading up to the haunted forest in *The Wizard of Oz*, this one was also lined with signs warning people to stay away. (There were so many and they were so insistent, I half expected one to say, "I'd go back if I were you," or at the very least, the Wicked Witch of the West skywriting on her broomstick, "Surrender, Dorothy!") The signs foretold of everlasting traffic and interminable congestion crossing the dam and suggested (some might say "commanded") an alternate, albeit much longer, route. Our alternator was not allowing for any alternate, so I swallowed my traffic rage and we soldiered on.

The reason for all the hullabaloo quickly became apparent: new security measures after 9/11. All big rigs had to be boarded. We turned in to the inspection area and awaited our turn. For once, gorgeous Shula did not merit so much as a glance, not one *ooh* or *ahh*, even from the female officer who entered our coach. Although we took some comfort in that, Shula seemed less than impressed.

Once we were in the gambling capital of the world, our luck decidedly changed. Tim called the manager of a Prevost repair shop we had previously frequented. He put us in touch with his brother who had taken over a truck repair place right in Vegas. Usually, truck mechanics eschew buses because the motor is stuck in a small, cramped compartment in back, rather than being easily accessible under the hood. But in deference to his brother, our new savior had been endeavoring to make his shop bus friendly and was even able to get us a rebuilt alternator, considerably lowering what we had expected to ante up. Then we landed at the Oasis—a true RV resort. It had two large pools and an adults-only hot tub that stayed open late. We immediately extended our stay.

We just enjoyed the ease of it all, from our full-of-frills campground to Las Vegas's no-hassle world travel. After all, where else can you stroll around Paris without breaking the bank to look chic, amble through New York without worrying about muggings, visit Venice's Grand Canal without gaining ten pounds on pasta, feel at home in ancient Rome without wrapping yourself in a toga, experience a volcano erupting without running for your life, watch pirates battle from the safety of a sidewalk (alas, without seeing Johnny Depp), or shop at a Middle Eastern bazaar without having to pretend you're Canadian.

Of course, we also did crazy rides wherever we found them. Our favorite had to be the Big Shot on top of the Stratosphere, propelling us 161 feet straight above the already 921-foot-tall hotel-casino, pulling four G's on the way up and negative G's (and for some, negative lunch) on the way down. The ride also provided me good payback: After it was all over, the helpful girl at the exit offered that we could go again, right away, for a steep discount. I immediately exclaimed, "Yeah!" only to turn around and see Tim glaring at me. At the risk of all eyes questioning his manhood, what else could he do but follow his wife, again?

Las Vegas is also where the company I've worked for the longest—over ten years—is based. I had been there before and met the staff, so this time I just had a few of them over for a "bus happy hour." Alison, a nearing-retirement nurse who shared my passion for fashion, had become Miles's long-distance aunt. Although they had never met, "Auntie A" got plenty of pictures of her furry nephew and frequently sent him treats in the mail, prompting Tim to observe wryly, "I needed someone my dog's never met to teach me he likes peanut butter." When they finally saw each other for the first time (and especially after we explained that this was the woman responsible for all the care packages), Miles and Alison became fast friends.

Ginny, another nurse, was one of the few people who could match my raunchy humor. As is the case with all insurance companies, the phone calls are "monitored for quality assurance," leading Ginny and me to often wonder if our dual firing was also assured.

A few days later, Alison invited us (come to think of it, she only invited Miles and I tagged along) to a Doggie Parade at the upscale District at Green Valley Ranch, where George Clooney keeps a condo. (Ironically, the condos, themselves don't allow dogs.) I thought I was being clever slapping a white bow tie on the poodle. Not so much; Miles was woefully underdressed, although as usual, he was a good sport. Although ever friendly with all manner of his species, he always seems to recognize kin, this time in the form of Jacques, a white standard poodle sporting a jaunty blue beret. While Alison appreciated the bichon frise with the pink bow in her hair and matching pink booties, my favorite was the terrier in a baseball shirt, cap, and sweatpants—complete with a hole cut out for his tail.

On past trips to Las Vegas, Tim and I had tried to see as many shows as possible, and although this one was no exception, it was the first time I feared being arrested for stalking. Always on the lookout for Motown cover bands, I found one, Sho Tyme, listed as playing in a small club in one of the hotels. Tim tried to get out of the cover charge—"Ladies free. Gentlemen $5"—by telling the woman at the door he was no gentleman. I'm pretty sure that only made her tack on an extra buck. Regardless, we became hooked and came back three more times. It would have been four, but during the last performance, I saw the lead singer glance our way with what can only be categorized as alarm on his face.

Another performer who should be alarmed at his fans but never seems to be is Jimmy Buffett. Even blocks from the MGM, where the concert was to start in two hours, hordes of Parrot Heads, dressing and acting bizarrely even by Las Vegas standards, combed the streets: There was the fireman wearing his helmet painted with a tropical scene, complete with stuffed parrot perched on top. The ten-year-old boy with his dad, dressed identically in grass skirts and coconut shell bras, prompting Tim to wonder if this was merely a sweet method of bonding or child abuse. The Elvis Parrot Head, a cultural commingling that would not even have qualified as a near miss anywhere else.

The revelry continued in the venue itself. Before the concert started, large beach balls bounced around the arena. Unfortunately, one of the bounces took the man next to me off guard, spilling his entire twenty-four-ounce cup of beer all over my favorite pants—pink Lillys with green martinis on them. His apology was so sincere and it truly wasn't his fault (after all, he hadn't had anything to drink yet), so we started chatting about all the Parrot Head functions he'd been to. His chapter, like so many others, not only has get-togethers but does charity work. Who knew?

Even though I was now effectively wearing my husband's favorite cologne, Tim wasn't focused on me when he returned from the vending area.

"I got these for free!" he proudly exclaimed, holding up two giant beers. Of course, I wanted to know how. He explained that the lines for that most essential part of the food pyramid—the beer group—had been so long, that a guy came up and offered Tim twenty dollars if he'd buy him a brew. Of course, my good-natured, some might say "rash," husband told the guy to just pay to fill a couple of go cups instead.

"You turned down twenty dollars?" I demanded evenly.

"But I got you a free beer," he protested.

"I don't drink beer," I said, even evener.

"Oh, yeah," he replied as he took big, alternating, two-fisted gulps.

Barring that, we enjoyed the show immensely, except the part where Jimmy observed how the concert was great group therapy for all the Parrot Heads in the audience, saying he'd "just saved you a bunch of money on psychiatrist bills." Fortunately, the crowd couldn't hear us boo.

Finally, yes, we did renew our vows on the bus with Elvis officiating. I booked him sight unseen and was pleased when Jeff Stanulis, a svelte, pre-drug-addled, pre-fried-donut King arrived. As he sang along to a boom box, his funny takeoffs on various Elvis standards left us all shook up and in no danger of ever losin' that lovin' feelin'.

Death Valley's hundred-year bloom was all over the news. And since we were in the area anyway . . .

We couldn't get a reservation for a campground in the park (well, we could have gotten a spot—maybe—if we'd lined up at 6 a.m. to try, and how likely was that?), so we stayed in nearby, charming Beatty, Nevada. OK, so it's only nearby. Beatty is a one-whorehouse town and it shows. Our RV park happened to be conveniently situated just down the road from Angel's Ladies, housed in a none-too-discreet, pink double-wide, complete with a large letter "A" branded on the hill above it.

On the plus side, the RV park fee did include access to any one of three private bathhouses on the property fed by Bailey's Hot Springs, each with a different temperature water (from the highest, 103 to 105 degrees, for the hardy, to the lowest, 98 to 101 degrees, for the completely wussy). We were only going to stay in Beatty four or five days, but ended up parked for a week. We were, after all, only feet from what we considered to be the biggest attraction in town (sorry, ladies), even though I was dubious of the hot springs at first. The rooms were so dark and passels of people seemed to be passing through. What about germs? Tim reassured me that little could survive in that heat. *Oh, yeah? That's what I thought about heating my lunch in the windshield.* I remained worried until the warm waters washed away my apprehensions. We took a dip every night.

Beatty did inspire us to come up with the "Top 10 Reasons You Know You're in a Shit Hole." You know you're in a shit hole when: 10. There's no grocery store in town but there is a whorehouse; 9. The whorehouse never seems to get any business; 8. The elevation is greater than the population—and the town is a stone's throw from Death Valley; 7. You can't even be bothered to think of seven more reasons.

In Death Valley itself, we took several short hikes not even short enough for me. Suffice it to say there's a bug in the desert so disgusting, I still don't know how it can stand itself.

"I know I always say you should get out more, but maybe that's not such a good idea," Tim was forced to concede.

Nevertheless, he did entreat me to accompany him on a "technical" hike through a rock formation. Not really understanding the word in the context of actually doing anything, I assumed "technical" meant I could simply, as always, tune out the details that didn't interest me. I started the hike in my usual attire: capri sweatpants, pink sneakers and sweatshirt, Chanel sunglasses (just because I hadn't bought new clothes didn't mean I threw out the old ones). As I arranged myself, all the while shooting dubious looks at the nonexistent path, Tim shook his head.

"It's known as Nail Breaker Canyon. Are you sure you're up to it?"

To our mutual shock, I actually enjoyed that hike. It wasn't the usual endless, mindless meandering over identical scenery, but much more interesting—challenging even, what with having to discern the best route over a constantly changing landscape of jagged rock formations. It kept my brain occupied, rather than emptying it out even more. At first, Tim tried to guide me, but quickly backed off when he realized how much I enjoyed figuring it out for myself.

At one point, we had to traverse a huge granite slab wedged into the ground at a forty-five-degree angle with nothing on either side for support. It was easy for my long-legged husband to simply bound through in one giant step. But for five-foot-two me . . . I studied the situation, taking into account the distance, the slope, and, most important, my attire. Not wearing hiking boots turned out to be an advantage, for I simply planted my feet together, hunkered down into a squat, and slid down the slab on the slippery soles of my sneakers, halting my descent by grabbing the trunk of a tree which conveniently jutted out from the ground below. Tim beamed his admiration.

"I was wondering how you were going to manage that!" He gave me a kiss, and for the first time in our relationship I understood the pleasure he derives from working with his hands, from puzzling something out and making it right. I even managed not to spoil the moment, keeping to myself my chagrin that the maneuver had, in fact, caused me to break a nail.

Of course we took other, less pleasant walks as well. I've never been a big fan of bugs. (Here Tim feels the need to interject, "But you're about to tell a spider story. They're not bugs. They're arachnids."

"They're bugs to me, sweetie.")

When we still lived in Tucson, our friend Butch came over one night to pick something up. I'd neglected to inform Tim, who was at the back of the house, that we were going to have a visitor. When the doorbell rang, realizing it was Butch, I opened the door . . . and let out a bloodcurdling scream. An enormous tarantula stood at his feet. (Actually, I think it was almost up to his knees.) Meanwhile, all Tim heard was the ring of the doorbell and what appeared to be the sound his wife would make if she were being brutally murdered. He ran to my rescue, realizing his last thought on this earth might very well be "Oh, God. This is really, really gonna hurt."

By the time Tim arrived, fists at the ready, I was in a crumpled heap, crying on the floor.

I don't like bugs.

Tim had to fetch what Butch had come for, but before he left, the poor man, who worked at our psychiatric hospital, mind you, was heard to murmur in a tone bordering on admiration, "Wow. I've never seen anyone lose it like that before." For the next year, I'd periodically find plastic spiders in my mailbox at work.

So the huge, buzzing flies on Death Valley's Salt Creek Trail (which we only bothered to traverse to see the endangered pupfish. And really, those things could disappear from the universe and no one would miss them) nearly did me in. One landed on Tim, then buzzed around me. Since I wasn't aware of any handy-dandy safety tips where flies were concerned (i.e., were you supposed to back away like with bears? Stand your ground like with mountain lions? Duck and cover like with nuclear bombs?) I reverted to my old trusty standby: screaming, crying, and running. I can report with confidence that none of that helps.

Since we were about to pass a group of children, Tim felt the need to perform his civic duty and warned me not to scare them by losing it again.

"Now, as we pass these kids, I want you to get ahold of—"

"Great idea!" I interrupted. "I'm sure that fly'd rather have a smaller, more manageable target." And I rushed over to my new decoys.

The completely bugless Scotty's Castle in the northern end of the park was much more my speed.

Scotty had been a huckster since he was a kid, leaving his home in Kentucky in 1883 at the age of eleven just because he thought school was a waste of time. To support himself in the Nevada desert, he sold donuts to railroad passengers until the restaurant at the depot ran him off. Getting back at the owners in true Scotty fashion, he tricked their customers into rushing out without paying by yelling, "All aboard." Then there was the time he got a local girl to whoop and holler at one end of the station as the train was leaving, so that when the male passengers poked their heads out the windows to see what the ruckus was all about, he could run up behind them from the other end, whacking their hats off with a stick. He then sold them to men on the next arriving train for two bits apiece.

His creative methods of supporting himself didn't end when he became an adult, and that's how he met Chicago insurance magnate Albert Johnson. Scotty managed to get investors, including Johnson, to shell out money for his "mine" in Death Valley by showing them gold nuggets he'd gotten from a real mine's tour. After hearing from Scotty for years about the many calamities preventing the delivery of any gold, all the investors pulled out—except Johnson. Instead, he decided to come to Death Valley to see the mine for himself. Scotty figured that after a few grueling days in the desert, the city slicker would give up and go home, but Johnson, sickly since a childhood accident, saw his health improve in the dry climate and stayed a month. By the time he realized there was no mine, he didn't care: He was smart enough to understand the value of what he got from his charming friend and call it good. He so valued their friendship, in fact, that when he decided to purchase property in the desert, he and his wife invited Scotty to stay. Of course, once Johnson started building the estate, Scotty told everyone it was *his* castle, but Johnson didn't mind that either; amused as ever by his colorful companion, he played along, telling folks he was merely Scotty's banker.

It seems that some of Scotty's bravado rubbed off on Johnson, who fought with the government for years over whether or not his castle sat on federal land. According to our tour guide, the two sides finally came to the agreement that Johnson could own the home during his lifetime as long as he didn't sell it. Since he had no heirs, Johnson agreed. But after his wife died, he founded a charity and *willed* the abode to it. After he passed away, the charity took care of both Scotty and the castle.

My psyche stripped naked to the core and my closet down to the bare bones, was it such a stretch that we stay at a nudist RV park? Although as a psychiatrist Tim is very much in tune with unconscious drives, hidden meanings, and deep-seated motivations, he is also a typical guy. And typical guys want to go to nudist resorts. Not being any type of a guy myself, I had always informed him I would never, ever, EVER, not in a million . . . *Oh, what's the use?* By now I had clearly lost any semblance of free will. I was, after all, living in a bus for a year. I didn't stand a chance. Not that I was nonchalant about this, mind you; I'd started Atkins in anticipation—just in case—as soon as we left New Orleans. I need not have bothered, for as I discovered, nudists are incredibly low-key. Unless, that is, you're trying to get into one of their parks. Then they can be just as big a pain in the ass as any prudes.

As we neared California, I checked around on the Internet. One place seemed particularly promising, so I called and asked if they were, indeed, clothing optional.

"No," the lady unequivocally answered.

"Oh. I'm sorry. I must have the wrong information," I apologized, hoping she didn't think me some weirdo. But something in her voice made me query further.

"So . . . people don't walk around naked?" I tried to confirm.

"Oh, yes, they do," she answered. *Is this place English optional, or what?*

"OK . . . but you're not clothing optional," I offered slowly, with impeccable pronunciation.

"No, we're nudist," she snapped. *Well, excuuuuse me.*

"I'm not sure I know the difference," I conceded. She explained that when inside the park, one is *required* to be naked. Now I got it. It was the *optional*, not the *clothing*, that was the problem with the whole *clothing optional* thing. Who knew? I proceeded with what I thought was a perfectly reasonable follow-up question.

"Can I wear shoes?" She guffawed, muzzled the phone, and called out to some other nudity-requiring linguiphile, "She wants to know if she can wear shoes!" For those as clueless as

I, the answer is yes. I decided she could keep her shod-optional accommodations and found a different park.

When we pulled into Olive Dell Ranch Nudist Resort near San Bernardino, I faced yet another dilemma: Usually, I headed to the office to check in while Tim stayed with the bus. Should I take my clothes off now? What if, in a variation on the universal nightmare, this was some god-awful joke and everyone was clothed but me? I was wearing earrings. Do I take them off, too? A valid question, methinks, even after the shoe debacle. I could have called on my cell phone and asked, but it seemed a mite like the shoes question and I didn't feel like being laughed at again just yet, especially as I was anticipating that reaction as soon as I stepped off the bus, anyway.

I kept my clothes on. The woman in the office had not. (If ever I can't work at home anymore, this could very well be my dream job, for even though I'd have to leave the house, I still wouldn't have to get dressed.) She told us where to park and that the owner would come by to show us around.

The campground itself is at the end of a long, winding road set on 140 acres up against a tree-studded hill with views of the surrounding countryside and valley. There are about two hundred members, half of whom are permanent residents, the rest weekenders, with about another fifty to a hundred visitors like us just passing through at various points in the summer to stay in the handful of cabins and RV spaces. After we parked, we saw the owner approach. He was in his forties and nude, but wore an open work shirt against the sun (and sneakers, I was pleased to note). We quickly donned (or, rather, undonned) similar gear and met him outside.

I soon discovered that none of my concerns mattered. In a nudist park, everything is stripped down, so to speak. As Tim observed, there's no macho, no pretense, no posturing. Your balls (and whether or not you have any) are out there for everyone to see. (Especially, as we would later discover, when partaking of naked karaoke.)

That first day, we hung out at the pool, relaxed, read, and met some of the locals. (No murmurs of "your rig or mine" to be heard.) As was my custom, if I got a call to do a review, I did it. I had already blogged about being in the nudist park, so after Alison and I finished discussing a case, she asked in a whisper, "Are you talking to me while you're naked?"

"Yep."

"You're kidding."

"Nope. I'm naked. Tim's naked. Bill, Sue, and Cameron are naked . . ."

"Oh, my."

In Boulder, I used to get a kick out of the fact that the doctors I reviewed probably assumed I was wearing a business suit in an office somewhere, instead of at home in my pajamas with a cat on my lap. (And, in fact, if Morty was in one of his talkative moods, I usually explained it away with "Someone brought her baby into work.") Olive Dell Ranch brought that titillation to a whole new level.

Our first night, Tim started closing all the curtains in the bus. I wondered why—we'd been nude all day, anyway. He explained he was about to start cooking and for his own safety needed to put on clothes; he didn't want to offend anybody.

We both had to dress, of course, to leave for our day trips to Joshua Tree National Park and Palm Springs. And each time during our weeklong stay, we did so reluctantly. This nudist resort was the friendliest RV park we'd ever stayed in. (It was also quite cheap, although we easily made that up in sunscreen.) Established in 1952, it has been owned and operated by two generations of the same family and the atmosphere was completely laid-back. The married owners, Bobby and Becky, grew up there in nudist families and now raise their own children in the park. Bobby, who is also the cook (working in the kitchen clad only in an apron), gave me his recipe for the best tuna salad I've ever tasted. Like every place on the planet, this one also has its eccentrics, including the woman who explained why she couldn't stop to chat, saying, "I have to catch my breath. I just had brisket." But our favorite had to be the maintenance guy who walks around nude except for his tool belt. An interesting effect, for every time he turned around, I nearly exclaimed, "Hey! You dropped your . . ." *Oops.*

"Letting it all hang out" certainly reinforced my newfound freedom going designer brand–less. For Tim, it underscored the resolve that led to the bus thing in the first place: to do what was right for him (taking a year off, part of it, as it turned out, naked) versus what was expected of him (working himself to death, albeit fully clothed). This further solidified his ideas about career for when we returned. Finally, being so stripped down, he also could not help but take his other hang-ups less seriously.

("Like what?"

"I'm not telling you. I don't want people reading about all my hang-ups. It's enough for them to know I took them less seriously.")

Between the two of us, Tim and I have several friends in this part of the country. We stopped and visited each one. While we haven't seen any of them in years and only rarely talk on the phone, somehow we're still close. In every single case, we picked up as if we'd just had dinner the night before.

Alene is one of my best friends from residency. We're about

as different as friends can be: She was never interested in private practice. She had no patience for patients with "issues." She wanted to go where the need was greatest, to treat the sickest of the sick, so she became the first female psychiatrist to work on San Quentin's death row. Now she's chief of psychiatry at Pelican Bay State Prison, which houses some of California's most dangerous inmates. And we're still about as different as friends can be: I wear designer duds. She wears a slash-proof vest. I go to Mr. Lai for tailoring. She gets her fittings at the armory. When I'm interviewed for a new contract, it's on the phone in the safety and comfort of my own home. When she interviews for a job, she must first sign a waiver acknowledging the "no hostage policy" (and this after passing the sign helpfully informing all comers "NO WARNING SHOTS FIRED"). She always laughed at me for my sheltered life. I always told her, "Thank God for sheltered." After the bus thing, I bet she thinks my life is less sheltered. Then again, maybe not.

We spent an afternoon with Alene and her partner, Debra, at their lovely home just prior to her promotion. As a dog person (who is also allergic to cats, but has acclimated to ours over the years), Tim could not understand their living with eight felines (they also had one very understanding terrier). I promptly informed him that if I were living alone, I'd probably have twice that number. He wasn't so much impressed as horrified. Debra, ever the caring hostess, laid out towels for us and offered the use of their shower and other indoor plumbing, thinking that surely living in a bus for a year meant we'd been roughing it. As I said, it's Alene and I who have been close.

Farther up the coast, we stayed at a campground just off Marina Dunes State Beach, a lovely, protected and uncrowded stretch of the Monterey Peninsula that was simply a pleasure to amble on, especially with camera in one hand and husband's hand (or dog's leash) in the other.

Joanne, another dear friend from residency, lived nearby and we had her over for a Tim-cooked feast. She's the one he loves for me to stay in touch with because he thinks her rotten luck in men makes me appreciate my man all the more. Even though she wasn't currently dating anyone (so, much to Tim's chagrin, had no new tales of horror to tell), we both loved seeing her.

We didn't just visit old friends, but a new one, as well. It's funny how people can come into your life. I "met" John years ago when I hired him to critique one of my screenplays. I had inauspiciously gotten his name out of a magazine, but it turned out to be an incredibly valuable experience. Over the years, I'd sent him additional scripts and we'd developed a friendship over e-mail and phone calls, discussing writing and life in general. I knew he and Tim would hit it off, so when we passed near Los Angeles, we all met for dinner. I was right. (Since then, John has visited us in Boulder.) It *is* funny how people can come into your life. And how, when you make the time, they stay there.

Finally, near San Francisco, we visited one of Tim's best friends from college, Dave, who he roomed with throughout his four years. He was the most easygoing kid Tim had ever known. Then he became the CFO of a major Silicon Valley company. In many ways, Tim had always admired Dave and I could see why: Dave seems to live his life deliriously happy with whatever he has, never feeling he needs to look any further. Early on while they were in college, he formulated exactly what he wanted to do and where he wanted to go. He then got exactly where he said he'd be and has been supremely satisfied with the results. But we always got the impression that even if he weren't quite so successful, he'd still be as happy. This again made Tim think about how his self-image had been riding on the profession of medicine, when now he couldn't be happier riding on three axles.

As we left the Bay Area to head for the Redwoods, we remembered the story of Scotty and his castle and realized that by putting such a high value on friendship, Albert Johnson had his priorities right. We thought of all the time spent at home doing . . . what? We didn't recall, but knew we'd always cherish these visits. *What in the world has been more important than connecting with these dear people?* We couldn't think of a thing.

Traveling farther up the California coast we passed the town of Prunedale. "Prunedale. Full of regular folk," Tim quipped.

Just before crossing into Oregon, I started talking to—well, OK, yelling at the TV. Tim wasn't too worried. After all, in our line of work, we see people doing that all the time. What did worry him was when the TV started talking back.

I'm boarded in forensic psychiatry, so I've always been fascinated with court proceedings. Throw in outlandish fashion, an old Motown connection, and really, how could I possibly resist the Michael Jackson trial? I watched the coverage on and off while I did reviews during the mornings we stayed in the bus. One day as I worked at my desk half watching Court TV, Tim sat in front of me on the love seat, reading the paper and eating his cereal. He had no interest in the proceedings, but given our small space, didn't have much of a choice in the matter.

I thought I had a really interesting point that none of the correspondents were making, so I e-mailed the anchor. Tim was by then very used to my railing at the TV when no one was saying what, in my opinion, they should be saying about the trial, so easily tuned it all out. That is, until one of the anchors said,

"We've gotten some very good viewer e-mails, especially this one from Dr. Doreen Orion, forensic psychiatrist."

Tim promptly spit up his milk. I promptly became spitting mad, for while the anchor attempted to make my point, she screwed it up so badly that it ended up sounding totally lame. When Tim could breathe again he said, while wiping milk from his chin, shirt, newspaper, and the love seat, "Did you really say that? It was totally lame." I dug up my brilliant e-mail and read it to him. He had to admit, "Good point." Then, not five minutes later, the same airheaded anchor did make my point, nearly verbatim, but without attributing it to me. I became apoplectic.

"That plagiarizing bitch!" I screamed. But I'm a benevolent vidiot, so decided to give her another chance. The very next morning, I e-mailed that little stinker with yet another brilliant point. This time, I read Tim the e-mail just before I hit "send." He went back to his cereal and newspaper with a barely indulgent sigh. Sure enough, within minutes, she made my point again (it was obvious she was listening to someone read it over her earpiece). Tim, hearing the exact same words come out of the TV that I had spoken only moments before, spit up his milk again, then whirled around to shoot me a questioning look. I nodded, assuring him of his sanity and we both waited with bated breath. Nothing. That plagiarizing bitch didn't even mention me this time. *Well, I'll show her.* I moved on to another anchor and cut the bitch off. *Let's see if she can find anything useful to say on her own. I'll have her begging, BEGGING, I say.*

I'm still waiting for her call.

Perhaps my psychotic break was partly precipitated by lack of sleep. The birds in this part of the country really need to get a life. At three o'clock every morning they'd start with the chirping. Only it wasn't just any old chirping. It was so utterly embellished with runs that even Paula Abdul would have told them

less is more. The only other birdcalls I'd ever heard that over-
the-top were from Indian scouts in old B-movie Westerns. After
several sleepless nights I'd finally had enough and shouted, "Attack the frigging fort already and let me get some sleep!"

Since we'd been to Oregon before, we mainly intended to just
pass through on our way to Washington. Yet it was my lunch
that nearly passed through—the wrong way—for much of our
drive through the state.

The hairpin turns up Highway 199 from California almost did
me in. On the plus side, the drive substantially enhanced my
clinical skills as it made me understand why psychotics engage
in what therapists term "self-quieting behavior" (rocking, word
repetition, twirling hair, etc.). This psychiatrist's mantra as we
twisted over Highway 199 became the rather unimaginative but
still evocative "Kill me kill me kill me kill me," the words somehow making their way to my lips before I was even aware they'd
formed in my brain.

Minutes went by until I even realized what I was saying. The
error was immediately apparent. *I'm not afraid of dying. I'm afraid
of dying like this.* My newest new mantra then became "Kill me,
but not like this . . . kill me, but not like this . . ." Soon I couldn't
take it anymore and rather dramatically announced I was going
to the back of the bus to kill myself. As always, Tim brought me
back to earth. This time with the observation "So I guess you'll
be in the bathroom, trying to slit your wrists with your electric
razor?" *The guy actually charges people for this stuff?*

To see somewhere I'd never been (and to get me away from
that road), we veered off near Medford and headed to Crater
Lake, Oregon. Tim had been there as a kid and remembered how

beautiful it was. Unfortunately, we never actually saw it. Not that we didn't try. It was snowing—in mid-May. The park ranger at the entrance informed us visibility was nil. I was about to ask, "Is it often that way?" when he handed us a printed sheet titled "Rainy Day Suggestions."

Still, it was a good thing we made the trip, as we found an excellent welding shop in the area when the last of our Peter-installed devices—this time the trailer hitch connecting the Jeep to the bus—collapsed. The welder said he'd never seen such shoddy work. We just shook our heads and figured that was only because he'd missed the opportunity, since we'd already purged the bus of the rest of what Peter had done.

We made a quick cut north on the interstate. Just north of Eugene, passing through Coburg, we saw Marathon Coach, just off I-5. If my mecca had been the Mall of America, this was Tim's, the epicenter of high-end Prevost conversions, where a brand-new, fully outfitted bus might run as high as two million dollars. As we passed by, I saw him steal reverential glances at the gleaming line of coaches beckoning from the lot.

"We could stop. See if they'll give us a tour," I offered. Tim shook his head. Sometimes, it's better just to dream.

Barreling through Scappoose, near Portland, we passed the "Peace Candle," really more of a peace silo, painted red with a giant, gaudy, fake flame on top. Tim said he could just feel the world drawing closer together as we whizzed by on 30 West.

We took a detour and headed for the coast, where we were treated to spectacular views, particularly when we stopped along the Columbia River gorge and climbed the 164 stairs of the 125-foot-high Astoria Column. Thankfully, after that trek, it was a clear day and we were rewarded with a view all the way to Mount St. Helens.

Before heading into Canada to catch the ferry to Alaska, we

stopped in Wenatchee, Washington, for a week to see Lisa and Jim, two of our closest friends. Jim had been Tim's "sponsor" in the dorm during his freshman year of college at Pomona and they had been close ever since. After Tim and I started dating, the four of us traveled together a few times and we spent a week every summer at their cabin in Wyoming. Even our dogs got along famously. Lisa and I hit it off right away and have become good friends of our own. So much so, I've told Tim if he ever divorces me, I get Lisa in the settlement.

It always reassured me that Tim felt so close to Jim, for he and I have much in common. Lisa, on the other hand, is much like my husband: a sweet, helpful, kind, and generous person. If the marriages were reshuffled, the relationships would become studies of inertia, both the implacable and impeccable kinds. Neither couple could ever get anything done, but for very different reasons: Jim and I would be waiting each other out. But good-hearted Tim and Lisa's life would be just as much of a living hell.

"What would you like me to cook for you tonight, sweetheart?"

"Oh, no! Let *me* cook for *you*."

"No, no. I insist. I'll cook."

"No, darling. *I* insist." The two of them would become skin and bones, only made worse by all the exercise they'd get cleaning the house.

We were, regrettably, nearing the end of our yearlong journey. And we were regretting our decision to go to Alaska. While we still wanted to see the state, we weren't really sure, given all the potential for new disasters, that we should do it in a bus.

"How 'bout a nice, tame cruise?" I wondered out loud. But we had also learned not to let fear, panic, or trepidation—no matter how justified—run our lives. So, like the morons we had become, off to America's Last Frontier we went.

Chapter Eleven

BUS-TED AT THE BORDER

Always Get Your Man

1 case Moosehead beer

Chill. Serve straight from bottle. Turn on hockey game. Keep mouth shut.

We had gotten our usual early start of noon when we left the campground in Washington to cross the border into Canada. There, we would drive for three days through British Columbia to catch a ferry to Alaska. Tim had never had a burning desire to go to the forty-ninth state. I was the one who declared oh so many months ago, "If we have to do this bus thing, we should at least go to Alaska." *What an idiot.* After nearly ten months on the road, I was still apprehensive—especially about heading "North to the Future." Just what did I ever think was so bad about the past, anyway? Especially a past that included a nice, safe, stationary home.

Although the state motto was full of promise, I wasn't exactly sure what that promise held. I had heard the roads in America's Last Frontier were not only terribly rutted, but dotted with the ominously termed "frost heaves." I could only surmise these occurred when iron-deficient, ice-age monsters, entombed during the original paving of the road, broke through the blacktop, grabbing at unsuspecting vehicles, of which buses driven by hapless men living their dreams were undoubtedly the easiest targets. And that was just along the paved parts. I was also, shall we say, just a wee bit "concerned" about hitting a moose, getting mauled by a bear (granted, that was more likely to occur outside our rig, but you never know), and since my bus phobia had by now generalized (a fancy-schmancy shrink term that means I'd become bat-shit crazy about being in anything that moved), I was also terrified of the ferries.

Taking the ferry up sounded like a good plan all those months ago when I made the reservations, as it would not only cut our driving time substantially, but allow us to make several stops along the Alaska Marine Highway in towns inaccessible by car. Now, however, as with my usual, run-of-the-mill bus phobia, the prospect of riding on the ferries had me fixating on the sound of our belongings careening and crashing. Never mind that our Prevost would be in the ship's hold with us topside for the entirety of each journey, so I would never actually hear anything—except perhaps what sounded like a giant can opener when our boat hit an iceberg.

I was half hoping we'd be turned back at the border, but we weren't. They didn't even ask about the pets' vaccinations and trusted us on the ridiculously minuscule amounts of alcohol we said we had. Tim assumed the border guards must figure no self-respecting terrorist would dress like me. (Pink cotton tracksuit with what I call my "slippy socks"—a bit of a misnomer, I admit, since they're really antislippy socks—big, pink, furry things with rubber on the bottom to prevent sliding. A necessary accoutrement for a Princess on the move.) Indeed, it took us only two minutes to cross. The Canadians didn't bother aboot us at all.

We would have avoided Canada altogether by catching the ferry in Seattle or Bellingham, Washington. But, since that would have nearly doubled the cost of our entire Alaska Marine Highway passage, we decided to drive the nineteen hours to the port in Prince Rupert. We were glad we did, as for most of the ride through British Columbia we were treated to stunning scenery, ranging from majestic peaks shrouded in mist to more barren vistas reminiscent of the Old West (no wonder Hollywood often films up there) to churning rivers fed by waterfalls twisting down mountains like the woven tassels on the white summer Chanel bag I'd left back home. (Do waterfalls ever feel unfashionable after Labor Day?) Fortunately, the roads were in excellent shape and had many more rest stops and large pullout areas than we were used to in the States. I relaxed. A little.

On June 11, we left the campground in Prince Rupert at the ungodly hour of 7 a.m. to board the *Malaspina* at the port just a half mile away. She would take us to our first stop in Alaska, Ketchikan, in under six hours. At over four hundred feet long, the *Malaspina* was one of the larger vessels in the Marine Highway's fleet, able to transport five hundred passengers and almost ninety vehicles.

We joined the other cars and rigs parked in the ticket holders' line and unhooked the Jeep from the bus. Then we ensured that everything was battened down and the pets supplied with ample food and water, since, as was the case for all the ferry crossings, we would not be allowed back in the car deck until we docked.

Tim was concerned that the deckhands guiding the bus would have an attitude, that they must be weary of directing hordes of inexperienced RV drivers to their spots in the cargo hold. (See? Even my angelic husband has his catty moments.) But he was pleasantly surprised, even more so when he realized that given the way the hold was organized, our bus had to be first or last, meaning everyone either watched him park from the dock while waiting their turn, or watched him park from the deck while waiting for the boat to sail. Meanwhile, I was fortunate nobody gave me a second look. The only time I've ever managed to parallel park was on my driving test at age sixteen. Since then, my parking ability has rivaled my navigational skills (and if I ever have to do both at the same time, well . . .). The deckhands must be used to such confluences of vehicular ineptitude, because their instructions to me in the Jeep were precise and easy to understand; none of this "turn the tires right" crap. I can't be bothered to figure out which way the tires go when I steer. And besides, does the instruction refer to the front or the back of the tires, which end up pointing in opposite directions, after all? Just tell me which way to turn the wheel. *Geez.*

During that first passage, we sat outside on deck chairs, letting ourselves be enveloped by the salty air as we took in the lush forest surrounding the calm waters of the sound, complete with snowcapped peaks in the distance. We read, snoozed, gazed, got sustenance from the cooler we brought, then repeated the whole process.

As we arrived at port in Ketchikan, population 10,000, we scanned the Tongass Narrows for a glimpse of our first Alaskan town. Finally, we found it: a dot sandwiched between hills thick with spruce and sea teeming with all manner of marine craft, from small fishing vessels cutting quick, determined paths across the water, to humongous cruise ships lumbering to and from port, to seaplanes flitting about to avoid everyone else. As we approached, Tim commented he'd never seen such dense forest.

I just nodded, for not having anything to compare to, I wouldn't know. But then we saw our first eagles, circling in the distance over the treetops in the hills south of town. Even though they were far away, we were mesmerized, watching their graceful arcs as they effortlessly rode the currents in the crisp northern air.

Disembarking the bus was as easy as getting on had been. I drove ahead in the Jeep, figured out (I firmly hoped) which way to turn to get to our campground, and waited for Tim and the bus at the terminal exit. (We couldn't use our cell phones to communicate; we would discover they did not work throughout most of the state.) There was no reason to rehook the Jeep (we didn't until we left our last campground on the Marine Highway three weeks later) since, as with all the stops we would make, it was only a few miles to the RV park.

Our site was right on the water, across from the RV "resort's" dock. When we checked in, the campground manager mentioned that he saw eagles in the park around sunrise every morning, so Tim, eager to get a closer look, immediately decided he'd get up early the next day. Since sunrise in summer in this part of the world is around 3 a.m., it was clear my husband would be on his own. The next morning, a bleary-eyed Tim reported that although he'd theoretically risen in time, he hadn't seen any of the majestic raptors. Then, that evening, we saw an eagle in the tree right next to our rig, proving my lifelong thesis that it never pays to get up at the crack of dawn. By our second day in Ketchikan, it seems we couldn't avoid seeing the things, including several perched on rocks near the Safeway (which was right on the water, its salad/sandwich/Chinese food bar offering seating with a view). Still, we didn't become jaded. Instead, we felt sorry for all the other birds.

That second day, we took our first hike in Alaska. Yes, I said "first." I figured since we were coming all the way up there I might

as well. The added advantage was imagining that this would ful-
fill my quota for the coming decade. But it was really Tim who
made the mistake of encouraging me to go, only worsening his
faux pas by picking the Perseverance Lake Trail. He loved it, of
course (being easy to please has its advantages), but I found the
endless steps of a boardwalk leading to an averagely scenic lake
endlessly tedious, although the rain forest we passed through was
lovely. But really. For mile after interminable mile—all three of
them—it was all pretty much the same. Even having camera in
hand couldn't redeem the trek. Enough was enough.

Although, it did inspire me to develop a hike rating system for
the couch potato spouses of outdoorsy folks, to let us Couchies
know if it's worth our effort. Instead of Easy, Moderate, and Difficult ratings for hikes, the CE (Couchy Equivalent) would be:
"Acceptable," What do you want from me?, and Why should I
suffer? The first entry, the Perseverance Lake Trail in Ketchikan,
would be a definite "Why should I suffer?" Not only does it need
an escalator (look, it has stairs anyway, so it's not like they'd be
introducing something *totally* foreign to an über-pristine environment), but a few waterfalls here and there would certainly
help. Truth be told, we could hear waterfalls, just couldn't see
them. Perhaps, then, the CE description should more accurately
reflect that some clear-cutting needs to be done.

Adding insult to injury, the entire time on the trail, I was
afraid we'd encounter a bear. Tim tried to calm me, saying he
didn't think bear like such dense undergrowth.

"Oh, great. They'll all be waiting for us at the lake. A regular
bear convention."

"Yup," Tim agreed. "And they've been promised a JAP as the
keynote squeaker." We let the only other person on the trail, a
young man, pass us. Beneficent me whispered to Tim, "Good.
Now he can startle the bear!"

The next day, Tim did the five-mile, nearly vertical Deer Mountain Trail with the poodle—not that they didn't invite me. In spite of the spectacular views of the town and harbor he reported on his return, as well as the wide grins on both their faces, judging by their mud-crusted, exhausted state, I was glad I had stayed in the campground, reading out on the dock.

With the heaviest annual rainfall in North America at 152 inches, Ketchikan is one of the wettest spots on earth. We could tell; it rained for part of every day we were there. If I had to walk around, I much preferred strolling through the downtown with its colorful history, where I could at least duck in and out of shelter when needed.

In 1903, Ketchikan's city council decided to root out the "bawdy houses" from "Uncle Sam's Wickedest City," ordering them all moved to Creek Street. Since more than two "female borders" constituted a house of prostitution under the Territory of Alaska law, most of the women chose to live alone or in pairs. Thus, sailors of the North Pacific halibut and salmon fleets found their favorites by the glow of porch light globes, inscribed with such names as: Frenchie, Prairie Chicken, Deep Water Mary, and Dirty Neck Maxine. More discreet customers would slink to their rendezvous under cover of hillside brush by way of the "Married Men's Trail." During Prohibition, booze was snuck into the establishments via trap doors over the creek which the Creek Street houses were conveniently located on. Thus, prostitution in Ketchikan flourished until 1954, when it was permanently banished. Some old-timers still grumble about honest women put out of business.

These days, Ketchikan's main industry is tourism and as many as four large cruise ships might be docked in the harbor at any one time, effectively doubling the population for the afternoon. That's why it seemed to us Ketchikan might be better called

Kitschikan. Some of our favorite tourist shop finds: a key chain with a plastic moose that when squeezed, seems about to extrude a dropping. (I still wish I'd bought that.) A five-fingered glove, each digit with a different native animal's head. A pillow with a picture of a moose reclining, its head and feet sticking out for a more realistic, 3-D effect. It sure looked real all right—like real roadkill.

The indigenous people throughout Alaska's southeast, the Tlingit, had a complex society that was blessed with an abundance of sea life and relatively mild weather for that part of the world. They even had a saying: "You have to be an idiot to starve." The Tlingit adhered to the notion of intellectual property rights well before modern Western laws came up with the idea; property belonged not to individuals, but to clans who claimed ownership of things like stories, songs, dances, artistic designs, and speeches.

They also held slaves as property, taken from other indigenous people in the surrounding areas. When emancipation came after the territory was purchased from Russia, they lost an important part of their economy and expected their new U.S. government to compensate them. The compensation never came. To shame those with unpaid debts, the Tlingit traditionally erected a totem pole with the welsher's likeness, and this time was no exception. In Ketchikan, at Saxman Totem Park, we saw the one with an unmistakable Abraham Lincoln perched on top.

When we walked into a Tlingit community house, daylight was creeping in between the vertical boards of the walls. Project Nerd made a brief appearance, muttering about the shoddy craftsmanship. But when we were informed by a guide that the boards, all hand-hewn from logs, were in fact intentionally engineered that way, both Project Nerd and Tim were duly impressed: We were there during a warm, (relatively) dry period and the boards had shrunk, the gaps allowing a natural ventilation. During the cold, wet time of year, the boards swell, creating an airtight seal. The clan house itself was a single large room with a central fireplace used to house the native community of several dozen people during the winter months. The sole entry consisted of a small door, requiring considerable stooping to get through, thus conserving heat and also making it easy to kill any enemies trying to enter. As a former New Yorker, I found this design immensely satisfying.

Before leaving Ketchikan, we splurged on a seaplane trip to Misty Fjords National Monument, as it was either that or a boat to get there (and we figured we'd be sick of boats all too soon). We flew on a six-passenger, DeHavilland Beaver for a two-hour flight that included forty-five minutes on the shore of one of the fjord lakes. There are no cars and no roads anywhere in this 2.3-million-acre preserve, so there was no one else around, although our pilot helpfully pointed out bear prints in the sand where we stood.

On the ferry from Ketchikan to Wrangell, I saw "DOREEN" written on the front inside cover of a book lying on a deck chair, its pages flapping in the wind. Soon, a Hispanic woman sat down and I asked if her name really was. We discovered we had something else in common; she's from Colorado, too, but the similarities ended there. About ten years previously, when her son was in first grade, he got suspended for having a knife in his sock. He told her he needed it for protection. So this single mother decided right then and there that they had to move to prevent his joining a gang. She did some research and settled on Wrangell (population 2,000), where they knew no one. That soon changed, as not only did her son thrive in the small town, but she married the great-great-great-grandson of one of the Tlingit chiefs. Doreen gave me her number and told me to call with any questions, or come by and she'd give us some salmon (her now teenage son makes four thousand dollars a week on fishing boats). Turns out, this sort of openness and hospitality is typical of people in the state. But since I doubted her offer included filleting, we didn't take her up on it.

With such a small population, we weren't going to Wrangell for the amenities. I'm not even talking about the fact that there are only a couple of restaurants and bars. Oh, no. In Wrangell, the grocery store closes at 6 p.m. and isn't even open on Sundays. We went to Wrangell simply because it's peaceful and gorgeous.

When we backed into our spot at Alaska Waters RV Park, I guided Tim with the improvised signals which had by now become our standard. It was a system that worked well for us, but inevitably, some man in the park would come on over to "help" the little lady with the wildly flailing arms who couldn't possibly be doing it right. I'm sure I wasn't, and Tim, being the only one whose opinion mattered, didn't care. This time, however, when the park manager started to help, he quickly stepped aside when he saw that I was doing just fine. After the bus came to a stop, he told me, "That was some really good signaling." We immediately became fast friends with him and his wife.

Jim and Joanne Silverthorn have had quite the colorful life. Former restaurant owners and developers of a super-secret pizza recipe that folks would drive hours to tiny Creede, Colorado, to sample, they were now in retirement, full-timing in their RV with their two cocker spaniels. They particularly love Wrangell and come up every summer, where they manage the campground for the owners. One night, they had us over to their rig for a fresh-off-the-boat salmon dinner. We brought the wine and salad and ended up talking until the wee hours. Before we left, Joanne blew us a kiss and gave me a lovely piece of slate she'd painted, to remind me of Wrangell. It reminds me of both the place and the Silverthorns when I see it on my desk every day.

The owners of Alaska Waters, Inc., are Washington native Jim Leslie and his wife, Wilma, who is of Tlingit and Haida decent (and, Jim proudly told us, also descended from a Haida chief). Jim was not only a wonderful resource for all things Alaska, but a true man of the bush and a sort of Candide of the North, to boot. As he propelled us in his jet boat along the Stikine River (the fastest free-flowing navigable river in North America), he pointed to the many places he'd been nearly killed by calving glaciers and large, angry mammals. Even more harrowing were the tales of his days owning logging camps, where at one time, three of the FBI's Ten Most Wanted were speculated to be in the area—and they weren't even the employees who ended up murdering each other.

While Jim's life leaves little room for what, as a psychiatrist, have been staples of mine—introspection and contemplation—*he* is the one who seems completely untroubled and totally satisfied with his existence. I had to wonder if spending so much of one's time under the stars and out in the vastness of the Alaskan wilderness (rather than just rooting around in the cramped confines of one's own brain) could not help but make any foibles in self or situation seem insignificant. Even though his life appears so much more complicated than mine (to start with, he dresses *and* leaves the house every day, not to mention hunts and fishes for his food, as well as the constantly staring death in the face thing), perhaps simple isn't all it's cracked up to be.

Our six-hour jet boat trip down the Stikine River included

two male guests from Louisiana also staying at Jim's RV park whose wives were too afraid to accompany them on the small boat. An older couple, Ivan and Gina Simonek, friends of Jim's, were also aboard. Ivan and Gina were born in Prague. After the Russians invaded in 1968, they asked their U.S. pen pals to help get them out. One in Wrangell sent airplane tickets.

At first, Ivan worked at a sawmill before he could earn a living as the gifted photographer he is. Both Tim's psychiatrist and Project Nerd within were fascinated by Ivan's story of working at the mill, where he found it impossible to true (flatten) the blades. His constant mistakes got him so angry, he was actually afraid he'd kill someone. Fortunately, the mill closed for a year and he had all that time to process what he was doing wrong. When he came back, he discovered "the saw would listen to me," allowing him to do whatever he wanted with it. It seems he learned an important lesson from that experience, because he's also become an accomplished naturalist.

"I like to learn about the things I take pictures of," he told us.

Pointing out an eagle's nest, Jim said that although monogamy is dominant, recent DNA samples from along the river discovered that they do fool around.

"Hey, honey," Jim joked, "I'll be back in a while . . . just going out to get some stuff for the nest." Birds with benefits, I guess.

At the end of the trip, Jim put the boat through a "Hamilton maneuver." I won't go into the physics of it (OK, fine. I couldn't even if I wanted to), but suffice it to say the boat turned end to end within a very short distance, resulting in G-forces better than an E ticket ride. He had told us to fasten our seat belts and hang on, or if we wanted to have an even wilder time, go to the back deck and brace ourselves on the railing. Tim and I immediately shot up and raced to the stern. During the first turn, I let out a scream. It wasn't so much fear as shock when the icy water hit me.

"Better hold on," Jim called out to me with a gleam in his eye. "That was only a practice run."

"Don't worry," I called back. "That was only a practice scream."

A Princess would not last a day in Jim's world. And, in fact, I nearly didn't. His boat had no head, so I managed not to pee for seven hours—it was either that, squat in the bush, or use the outhouse we encountered near one of the Park Service cabins. (I couldn't tell which would be worse: peeing in the former or sleeping in the latter. Come to think of it, peeing in the latter or sleeping in the former would have been just as bad. Fortunately, I had no intention of doing either.) As a result, I inadvertently became a celebrity of sorts amongst our little band, but by the time we got back to the bus, I was ready to explode.

Passing through the narrow Wrangell Strait (so narrow, cruise ships can't make it) for our next stop, we delighted in seeing the ferry's wake wash up on the nearby shore. We were on our way to Sitka, the former Alaskan capital. This eleven-hour leg was to be our only overnight in a cabin. Some hardy souls eschewed that "luxury" (this Pacific Princess can tell you the Love Boat it ain't) and pitched a tent on deck, instead. Scanning the color-ful, newly sprung slum of harnessed Gore-Tex straining against the wind, Tim asked, "Wouldn't that be fun?" He was actually serious.

At over 4,800 square miles (nearly half of which is water) Sitka is the largest city in the U.S.—by area. (The population is only around nine thousand.) By the early 1800s, after a series of battles with the Tlingit, Russia claimed Sitka for its capital in North America. For over a half century, the Russians then exploited the lucrative trade in sea otter pelts. By the time the U.S. purchased the territory for $7.2 million (less than two cents an acre), overhunting had destroyed the industry. The Alaska Purchase was not a terribly popular proposition in the Lower 37 and became known as "Seward's Folly" after Secretary of State William H. Seward, who spearheaded the effort.

When Seward visited Alaska two years later, in 1869, the Tlingit in Ketchikan threw him a potlatch—an elaborate celebration involving extravagant gifts which usually bankrupted the host. Tradition dictated that in return, the guest of honor must then throw one himself, allowing the original host to recoup his expenditures. Not knowing the custom, the secretary never did, leading the chief to erect a totem with an upside-down likeness of Seward on top, complete with red nose and cheeks, signifying a fool who does not repay his debts. In case anyone still didn't get the point, he's even perched on an empty box, signifying the gifts he never gave back. Some descendants of Seward's descended on the village a few decades back and asked that the totem be changed. The Tlingit refused—the debt still hadn't been repaid.

Although our RV park on Sitka was little more than a parking lot at the harbor, what a parking lot it was. We not only had a view of all the boats, but the tiny, one-runway airport just across the channel and snowcapped mountains farther across the sea. We spent several afternoons sitting on a patch of lawn with Miles, just soaking it all in.

Unfortunately, I had decided that if Wrangell Jim could live for days in a tree in the rain along the river, hunting moose, the least I could do was try hiking again, especially when our guidebook raved about one particular hike's views and photographic opportunities. Tim was thrilled . . . until we hiked. For it was on Sitka's Harbor Mountain that we took what I would come to term The Alaskan Death March. Although even I had to admit the scenery was spectacular (ocean, islands, distant peaks, yada yada) the lack of an escalator on the steep climb nearly did me in. And why should I suffer alone?

So I devised the Five Stages of Getting Grief from Hiking with Doreen: Denial ("We're not going all the way up there, are we?"); Anger ("I can't believe I let you take me on this stupid hike!"); Bargaining ("If we stop now, I'll have the energy to do another hike tomorrow. Really, I promise!"); Despair ("Oh, why did I ever let you talk me into anything over three miles?"); Acceptance ("Fine. But this is absolutely, positively, the last hike I will ever go on for the rest of my life!"). Recalling the disappointing Perseverance Lake Trail of Ketchikan, I felt compelled to add a sixth stage, one which only occurs in extreme circumstances, at a perfect storm of elevation gain, accumulated mileage, mud, and bugs: Confabulation ("Look at the dog! You're killing him!"). Finally, when I nagged enough to make even Tim agree to quit, I clutched the poodle to celebrate, beaming as I attempted to reinforce the wisdom of my husband's capitulation.

"I'm so glad you didn't make me continue to the top. This way, I could actually enjoy how beautiful it was. I'd even do it again."

"Really?" Tim retorted. "I wouldn't." Here, even I have to admit that I *would* do it again. I guess experiencing something that stupendous tends to erase memories of the hardships endured in experiencing them (kind of like childbirth, I'm told), especially when reviewing the fabulous shots I was able to take. If all hikes came with a guarantee that they were in surroundings so stunning, I might actually get an REI (Recreational Equipment Incorporated) membership. Lord help the REI folks.

Ever wonder what to do if you find an injured eagle? Wrap it in a blanket (it'll be calmer if it can't see) and get it to Alaska Airlines for its free, all-expenses-paid flight to the Alaska Raptor Center on Sitka (salmon crudités not included). There, it'll be nursed back to health or, if too severely injured, could become a permanent member of their Raptors-in-Residence program. The center started in 1980 in the backyards of two Sitkans who rescued an injured eagle and eventually grew into a nonprofit in a new location on seventeen acres. In a specially designed viewing corridor which keeps them hidden, visitors can see the birds put through their paces in the flight training center before being allowed to return to the wild, flying from tree to tree and swooping down into waterfalls and streams to pluck up a salmon dinner—sushi style, of course. There are even several flight conditioning areas, including vertical flight mews to test for lift and a flight tube to check stamina and maneuverability. Up until our visit to the Raptor Center, we had seen plenty of eagles from a distance, but it's up close that we could truly appreciate their immense scale. And those eyes. Those piercing, mesmerizing eyes that bore into your soul and make you wonder just who should be anthropomorphizing whom. This ain't your grandma's parakeet.

From the former Alaskan capital, Sitka, to the current one, Juneau, we caught a high-speed catamaran that cut the trip in half, to less than five hours. This was the only leg where we saw an abundance of marine life: humpback whales, orcas, and sea lions, not to mention the never ho-hum eagles.

All the ferries have a naturalist or park ranger aboard to provide programs and commentary. On this trip, the guide mentioned that humpback whales are as big as buses. Tim and I couldn't help beaming at her unknowing nod to one of our own, until she ruined the moment by mistakenly commenting that this meant they were fifty feet. The woman may know her wild-life, but she sure doesn't know buses. I wanted Project Nerd to get up and give a rebuttal, but for once, he demurred. The naturalist also pointed out an island just off Sitka with a rare species of pink flamingo, native only to that one tiny spot on the planet. Once we rounded the bend, there they were, a few dozen or so, scattered throughout some trees. They seemed a bit still. *Maybe they're sleeping.* It was only later, when she mentioned some other upcoming wildlife viewing and promised, "I won't be fooling you with plastic flamingos this time," I realized I'd been the butt of some uproarious Sitka humor. *Concrete as a sidewalk.*

Although by now we'd seen plenty of Alaskan glaciers (like with eagles, it's hard to become jaded about the things), the Mendenhall in Juneau was quite unique, its river of ice hovering over the city like a brooding uncle, menacing and beckoning at the same time. (I swear I could hear it purr, "Want some candy, little girl?") Standing so close to this towering, ancient behemoth (the Mendenhall is over thirteen miles long, up to one and a half miles wide, and 1,800 feet thick) I couldn't help but feel how transitory and insignificant our own lives were in the greater scheme of things. It made me appreciate, yet again, the time we had taken out for the bus thing from whatever minuscule time we'd been allotted in the universe. But even the seemingly venerable and invincible have their vulnerable moments: The visitors center at the glacier displays striking old photos from decades past showing how much the Mendenhall has retreated—about two miles—in this relatively short amount of time. To drive the point home even further, while walking the various trails in the area, we regularly encountered signposts announcing the year the edge of the glacier had reached that particular point.

Downtown at the state capitol (unlike most, it's rather plain, lacking a dome since it was originally built as a territorial building), we learned about a remarkable woman who championed civil rights for Native Alaskans in the 1940s. At that time, restaurants, hotels, movie theaters, and stores hung signs saying "No Natives Allowed" or sometimes even "No Dogs or Natives Allowed" and Native children could not attend public schools. A Tlingit, Elizabeth Wanamaker Peratrovich, lobbied for the passage of an antidiscrimination law.

In 1945, it came before the territorial council for the second time, having failed to garner enough votes two years earlier. The law seemed destined again for the same fate. Then one of the debating senators asked, "Who are these people, barely out of savagery, who want to associate with us whites, with five thousand years of recorded civilization behind us?" Peratrovich, who wasn't even scheduled to speak, rose from her seat and calmly answered, "I would not have expected that I, who am barely out of savagery, would have to remind the gentlemen with five thousand years of recorded civilization behind them of our Bill of Rights." She then went on to eloquently portray the effects of discrimination on people she knew. Her impromptu speech was greeted by resounding applause and the Alaska Civil Rights Act was overwhelmingly passed.

Before we took our leave of Juneau, we went to a salmon hatchery to see the heavenly humpies throw themselves up over rocks from Gastineau Channel to climb a fish ladder, thanks to their built-in, biologically powered GPS system, which routes them to their spawning site. (Do they have some know-it all lady's voice in their heads intoning, "In . . . four . . . hundred . . . feet . . . swim . . . left"?)

I sincerely do hate getting up early. Always have. In fact, I was so upset about having to wake up at 4:30 a.m. to catch the ferry out of Juneau that I hadn't slept well for months obsessing about it. I'm a bad sleeper anyway, as one poor hotel maintenance man in San Francisco can attest to.

In 1997 when my first book came out, the publisher decided to send me on a book tour. I was, of course, thrilled. Until I read the itinerary. While TV, radio, and bookstore appearances were scheduled, sleep did not appear to be. For five days I was to travel to five cities, staying long enough in each to appear on the local evening news, then take a flight out to arrive early enough to appear on the morning news in the next city. By my calculations, I would be lucky to get four hours of sleep a night, when more than double that is an absolute requirement for a Princess's beauty rest. I knew the thought of not getting enough sleep would further keep me awake on the trip to the point where four hours would seem a luxury, so I took a few sleeping pills with me.

At the end of the week, I arrived at the last stop, San Francisco, at one in the morning. I had to be up at 5 a.m. to get to the local television studio in time for my segment on the live broadcast. By then, I could adjust how much of the pill I had to take to be assured of various amounts of sleep, so rather than wait until I was already in the room, I bit off an appropriate piece as I was checking in at the front desk. I figured this would afford me an extra twenty precious minutes or so of shut-eye. My plan worked, until I was rudely awoken at 3 a.m. . . . . . by a cricket.

The chirping was unmistakable. I was incensed; this was not a rural burg, but a fancy, big-city hotel. The thing wouldn't stop. In my drug-addled state, I reached for the phone and managed to rouse the concierge.

"There's a cricket in my room," I slurred.

"Ma'am?" Surely I wasn't that unintelligible. The poor man must be deaf.

"A CRICKET! THERE'S A CRICKET IN MY ROOM!" *Why in the world did the hotel have deaf people manning the phones?*

"I'll send maintenance right up." I have no idea how much time passed, but a uniformed man (who I vaguely recall had a short straw in his hand) did indeed arrive at my door to find me sitting at the edge of the bed, head in hands.

"Kill the cricket," I moaned. He gave the room a quick once-over, a dubious look on his face. Then he heard it, too. *CHIRP.* His head snapped toward the ceiling. He beamed at me, triumphant.

"Ma'am, it's only the smoke alarm battery. I'll just—"

"KILL THE CRICKET," I pleaded.

"But, ma'am. It's the city code. I'll have to go get a new—" I would have none of it. This man was learning what my commoner husband had known for years: Do not get between a Princess and her beauty rest.

"KILL IT! KILL IT!" I chanted

"But, ma'am. If there's a fire . . . the code . . ." I let out a wail, which he undoubtedly understood to be only a taste of what was to come as punishment for disobeying royalty from the infamous Island of Long.

"I have to be up at five in the morning." I like to think it was sympathy at that last whine that compelled him to grab the battery and make haste out of my room never to be seen again. But I could be mistaken.

We boarded the ferry in Juneau at a particularly low tide. This was easy to discern, even for physics-impaired me, as the dock's ramp was at a much steeper incline to the boat than we had seen

before. I ungallantly (gallantry is a consort's lot, after all) wished
Tim luck and drove the Jeep into the hold as instructed by the
attendants. Neither of us could understand how the bus would
make it. Then, after every other vehicle was loaded, a deckhand
motioned Tim forward. The crew brought out four short ramps
and very efficiently stuck two under the tires to lessen the incline. As Tim slowly crept the bus to the end of one set of ramps,
the attendants put down the others, rotating them around, repeating the procedure three or four times. Of course, it seemed
to take forever and Tim felt with particular acuity the eyes of
all five hundred or so passengers upon him as he inched his way
onto the ship.

On July 5, almost three weeks after we'd boarded our first ferry
in Prince Rupert, Canada, we arrived at our final stop on the
Marine Highway, Haines. There we spent a delightful few . . . oh,
fine, I really have no idea how long, tasting wine at Great Land
Wines, Ltd. The vintner, Dave Menaker, has lived in Haines for
fifty years, and greets guests in a heavy pullover work shirt, jeans,
and work boots. He also operates a sawmill out back, hopefully
not running both businesses at the same time.

Dave's establishment proved a stark contrast to the wine tastings we did in Napa only a couple of months before, which were
complete with waitstaff in formal attire attending to the hordes
of tourists. Here, we were the only ones in the joint and the
generous samples flowed free and wild—onion, potato, blueberry,
raisin, rose petal, and dandelion wines were just a few of the se-
lections, with Triscuits proffered for palate cleansing. The wines
weren't cheap—ten to fifteen dollars for a small bottle—but the
fun was well worth it. I was totally blitzed by the time we left.
Fortunately, he also offers a carryout service—not for bottles, but
spouses.

After we discussed Dave's past life in the logging industry, we ventured into possibilities for future vintages, including a cat/ dog hair variety. I vaguely recall getting started on that when Tim thought "beet" wine was "beef" wine, which somehow led to "Why not make one out of pet hair?" I still think that's a fabulous idea, especially for crazy old broads like the one I hope to become, who might want to memorialize their dearly departed Flopsies by drinking a most personalized toast on the anniversary of their pet's death. The bottle's motto could be "You grow it, we'll ferment it." Or perhaps "Equal opportunity fermenter." Then there's always "Ferment it now, ask questions later." I said I was pretty well lubed.

On July 6 we finally saw our first (and only) Alaskan bear—a grizzly, at that. He was fishing on the Chilkat River just a few miles from town. We stood only fifty feet away watching him, but even I was not terribly worried as there were several elderly tourists doing the same who I felt confident we could outrun.

Just before we left Haines, I checked my e-mail. There was one from the Boulder Book Store and another from Denver's Tattered Cover, both locally owned institutions. I'm a longtime subscriber to their e-mail lists and saw no reason to unsubscribe while we were away, as I enjoyed reading about who was coming to town for book signings and other literary events. But now, as I scanned the August lists, it hit me with a jolt and not a pleasant one; I could actually attend this stuff. Our year was almost at an end.

Leaving Haines, we had to pass through Canada again to catch the Alaska Highway west into the interior. Since I was our travel agent, Tim never felt the need to keep up on our itinerary all that much. But I knew if we were questioned at the border, it would look a tad suspicious when the customs officer asked the driver, "Where are you going?" and "Where have you been?" only to have him snap his head around and shoot me a frantic look. So I made Tim memorize a few town names. Turns out, we were to have trouble of a different kind.

In spite of my attire (perhaps it was the not-so-chicly-coordinated contrast of *turquoise* slippy socks with my usual pink tracksuit that aroused suspicion), we got boarded by a female Mountie as we left Haines to enter British Columbia. Rather than cite me for a fashion infraction, she wanted to know how much alcohol we had. Since the limit was a bit ridiculous for people living in their vehicles (well, OK, for us living in our vehicle), we under-reported a wee bit. When she asked to take a peek, we knew we were screwed. And, indeed, she looked a bit taken aback when she opened our liquor cabinet.

"There's a lot in here," she said. I *guess*, since it took her a full fifteen minutes to catalogue it all. (My explanation that I had all those flavored liqueurs for various martinis, each of which I might only use a few times a year, so therefore really should not count, did not seem to make much of an impression.) We actually got off lucky. She ended up confiscating only two large, but completely innocent, unopened bottles of flavored vodkas (a vanilla and a strawberry) that had never done anybody any harm. I kept my musings about what a male Mountie might have taken to myself, along with my recipe for Strawberry Shortcake Martinis. Her loss.

Why did we lie? We kept asking ourselves. Well, that's what you *do* at customs. We didn't realize we could just have paid a duty. We thought that whatever was over the limit would be confiscated if we declared it. Tim was humiliated. It's not like him to lie, or act in any way that isn't above reproach. I was the one who had encouraged the untruth, and predictably, I was more angry than anything else. Don't these people have anything better to do? We already paid tax on this stuff in the U.S. I railed on and on about how we should have invaded B.C., not Iraq, to keep our borders duty-free. Tim just wanted to turn around and go home.

Our state of mind didn't improve once we hit the road again. The Alaska Highway was indeed, shall we say, a bit pockmarked, rutty, dippy, uneven, or any description you choose to denote a road that would strike fear into the heart of a bus phobic. To make matters worse, back in the States, I had purchased a copy of *The Milepost*, a truly indispensable resource for anyone driving to America's Last Frontier. *The Milepost*, which put out its first edition in 1949, is an annual guide taking readers through every road in Alaska that can possibly be driven, providing information ranging from locations of RV parks and gas stations, to lists of all turnouts (including whether they're paved, gravel, double-ended, or particularly wide or narrow), to where to look out for moose and caribou crossings (even where to look up and see an osprey nest in a tower), to every rut, dip, and frost heave in the road. It was this last bit of information that nearly did me in. For not only could I experience every road imperfection as it occurred, but anticipate each down to the tenth of a mile.

I was not having a good time. At one point, we swerved dangerously close to the edge (there was also no shoulder).

"What was that?" I cried.

"Freak gust of wind," Tim replied. That was all I needed to get me started.

"Freak gust of w—?" And with that, we hit a big dip. Strangely, I didn't feel quite so bad anymore.

"Freak gust of wind. Freak gust of wind. Freak gust of wind," I repeated and kept repeating for the three hundred miles to Tok, the hard consonants again dissipating a good deal of my terror, similar to how that other slice of self-quieting behavior, "Kill me kill me kill me," had done the trick along the Oregon coast.

We reached Denali National Park in a few days. The town

itself was rather underwhelming, but we were there, like most, to see Mount McKinley, the highest peak in North America. Only once we got to Denali, we found out that it's hard to see any of the mountain's 20,320 feet from within the park, or at least from as far within the park as we were willing to go. Traffic in Denali is strictly regulated and buses (unfortunately not ours) are the only way to get around. (Yeah, bicycles are allowed, but don't we know each other well enough by now to understand that was not in the cards?) So Tim and I made the mistake of taking a tour in an aging Park Service school bus.

It wasn't (just) that I was spoiled after spending the year in our luxury Prevost. Packed with forty-nine other people travers-ing narrow, winding, Park Service–maintained roads over which large animals routinely cross, I was horrified, but that had noth-ing to do with the bus. The rule on the tour was that anyone could yell STOP for anything at any time: animal sightings, pic-ture opportunities, bloody noses (this really happened. They sent the kid off the bus—to be eaten by a bear, I suppose. Or is that sharks?). Our overly helpful guide/driver even got walkie-talkies for us slobs in back, so that we could more easily communicate our wishes to him on this hell ride. Unfortunately, "Stop the bus. I'll catch a cab" was not one of the possibilities.

The problem started with the very first animal sighting, a cari-bou. An older woman across the aisle from us let out a bloodcur-dling scream. I thought perhaps the poor animal was being eaten by a bear. Since I had only seen the one Alaskan bear and there was little I could do to help poor Rudolph anyway, I craned my neck in the caribou's direction. But, no. He of the mega-antler bling (someone should tell those poor, misguided creatures there *is* such a thing as overaccessorizing) was placidly grazing in a wide-open meadow, oblivious to the commotion he was caus-ing in our claustrophobic space. He didn't even flinch when the woman let loose with what appears to be the Tourist Rallying Cry: "WALTER! GET THE CAMERA!" Tim and I hadn't been on organized tours in quite some time and as we shot each other pained looks, we remembered why.

"This is going to be a very long trip," we said in unison. What does Walter's wife do when she needs to get his attention for something really important? Like, say she's being strangled by a stranger, which I can assure you, nearly occurred several times during the nearly eight-hour ordeal. Then there were the Dall sheep. Someone would shout, "STOP THE BUS!" and we would . . . for dots of white on a hill, which we were told were frigging sheep. OK. Our guide didn't really say "frigging" sheep. Being a naturalist named (what else?) River, he called them Dall sheep. Was there really anyone on that entire bus who had never been to a farm?

"But they're mountain sheep," Tim protested the first time I made this quite excellent observation. By the sixth, he delighted in spotting the frigging sheep himself, only to withhold the information from the rest of our wool-crazed herd. At one point, River even stopped the bus on his own, struck a pose, and in a misguided effort at channeling Marlin Perkins, announced he was going to scan the mountain ridge with his binoculars for the, thus far, elusive bear. I rolled my eyes at Tim.

"If they're that far away, who gives a shit?" I asked. To which Tim replied, already half out of his seat, "Let me get the walkie-talkie for you."

The eight hours crawled by slower than I've often prayed Tim would take highway exit ramps. The boxed lunch didn't help. In fact, as we were exiting the bus, I left a soda can on my seat. Tim went back for it, chastising me with "This isn't an airplane." To which I responded, "Really? Couldn't tell from the lunch." But Denali had one more indignity in store. As we disembused,

River (whose name while working in the Lower 48 during the off-season is probably Bernie, Tim observed) apologized for the paucity of animal sightings.

"I think what's important to take away from today," he asserted, "even more than what we did see, is what we didn't: strip malls and coffee shops and restaurants and . . ." The rest of his words were drowned out by rousing applause from the entire load—except us. *Like Walter and Edna could survive more than a day without any of that stuff.*

Yet, at some point during the interminable trip, I realized I had not been afraid. Not once. How could that be? Compared to our Prevost, the Park Service bus was a nightmare, even without Walter and Edna. So, what was it? The ride was certainly rougher in the school bus. With all the talking from the other passengers, it was much noisier, as well. Only . . . the noise was different. There was no . . . I suddenly realized that there was more to my yearlong bus phobia than gnashed teeth and bitten nails. It was never about careening off the road, about life and death, but about the potential loss of *things*. That every time something bumped, clacked, or clanged on our bus, it reminded me of all we had put into it. But I had lost sight of the most important "thing" of all it carried: us.

The fire and armed robbery both made me realize how all-important *things* had become in my life. Spending nearly 24/7 for a year with Tim, then seeing all those dear friends we lost touch with underscored what the important things truly should be. Once I understood I had only been fearful on *our* bus and only because of the trappings it held, I was able to put everything into perspective: It's fine to like stuff (after all, who's going to give it all up and live like a monk? I'm sure even Richard Gere has a nice house) as long as one doesn't lose sight of placing feelings and experiences, family, friends, and self first, ahead of things.

Living on our bus allowed me to see how few things I really needed and, ultimately, what I actually valued. I truly hadn't appreciated how important my belongings had become, until I shed most of them and put the rest at risk—on the bus. And risk itself turned out to be exactly what I needed. While going with the crowd feels safer (even on a rickety old school bus), it's much more rewarding to take to the open road on your own, to determine your own course and have your own experiences.

I'd never realized how crucial it is to keep stretching and challenging oneself. My work, my life had become rote, routine, albeit comfortable. I thought I had all I ever wanted. That's why I had railed against the bus thing to begin with. But in 340 square feet of living space, especially as it brought trials and tests I survived and even thrived on with my beloved husband and my adored pets, I was happier than I had ever been.

Two days later, we left Denali and made the nearly five-hour trip to Anchorage. Since I was no longer placing such a premium on material possessions, my bus phobia was gone.

Chapter Twelve

CORONATION

Jubilee

1 bottle white wine
½ cup peach schnapps
¼ cup sugar
2 sliced peaches
½ cup raspberries
1 sliced orange
½ liter ginger ale

Combine all ingredients except last and chill. Just before celebration, add ginger ale. Sip daintily so as not to disturb tiara. Survey kingdom. Toss tiara away and dance your butt off.

As we were leaving Denali for Anchorage along the narrow, two-lane George Parks Highway, an oncoming truck flaunted its "wide load" sign, smugly daring all vehicles not to scurry aside. I sat in the buddy seat, trying to make sense of the map, an always futile endeavor that nevertheless appears to be my lot in this bus life.

"You're not going to want to look at this," Tim said. Without thinking, I did just that. And even as I saw the indeed very wide load a-comin', it didn't bother me. Not one bit. Nor did the tight turns, the moose warning signs (which, in a perverse twist on the notion of constructive criticism, announce how many have been hit on Alaskan roads thus far in the year), nor . . . anything. I even encouraged Tim to pull over into the turnouts multiple times so we could get various views of Mount McKinley, since due to weather patterns I did not understand (another of my many crosses to bear), like most visitors to Denali National Park, we hadn't been able to see it while there. For the first time since the meltdown cruise, but under decidedly different circumstances (i.e., the door wasn't flying open and I was in no danger of getting sucked out), I stood in the stairwell, craning my neck to discern if the wide spots whizzing by were worth a stop. When the dishwasher drawer slid open on a turn, causing all the plates and glasses to clink and clack, I calmly went back to shut it. When Tim passed a caravan of large, lumbering RVs, I coolly made myself a counter egg.

"What's with you?" Tim wondered. "You're doing amazingly well."

"It's the Prevost Kool-Aid, babe. I've finally drunk it."

Anchorage itself was like any big city—any big city with incredible views. We stayed a few days and sampled various brew pub fare, exploring the only place we'd been to in the state with a modern feel. Then we headed for the Kenai Peninsula, driving along the scenic Turnagain Arm, a stygian fjord which separates the Chugach Mountains from the peninsula proper.

The Kenai Peninsula juts into the Gulf of Alaska just south of Anchorage. With glaciers, various mountain ranges, ice fields,

fjords, rivers, and lakes, it is one of the most beautiful areas of
the state accessible by car. Because of its mild coastal climate, it
also happens to be one of the few places in this part of the world
with an adequate growing season. We were headed down the
Sterling Highway, one of only two on the nearly 26,000-square-
mile peninsula, this one going to the southwest corner, dead-
ending at Homer.

Homer (pop. 5,000) marks the end of the paved highway
system in North America and is pretty much what you'd expect from an end-of-the-road kinda place, especially one that's
known as "the cosmic hamlet by the sea." Or, as Tim's favorite
T-shirt of the trip proclaimed, "Homer—A quaint little drinking town with a fishing problem." It didn't even have any traffic
lights (although it would get its first within a year of our visit).

Homer reminded us very much of Boulder: funky, artsy, laissez-
faire but with a blue-collar overlay, instead of Boulder's Yuppie
one. We stayed at an RV park near the entrance to town and
not at the more popular Homer Spit, a four-mile gravel protru-
sion into the windy Kachemak Bay, which along with the harbor, houses, bars, restaurants, and souvenir shops. I was glad we
were parked in the more out-of-the-way spot, especially after I
saw all the tsunami warning signs along the Spit. During the
Great Alaska Earthquake forty years earlier, the resulting enormous waves from this, the most powerful quake in U.S. history
(a 9.2), caused deaths and destruction as far away as California.
Back in Homer, the tsunami destroyed much of the Spit, leaving
it devoid of vegetation.

Our RV park was on a different part of the bay, and during
low tide, we took Miles and walked along the vast expanse of
beach. The view of glaciers from our rig was so spectacular, I
even caught Morty sticking his head out the ticket window to
take a peek. Although I suppose he could have been more in-

terested in the smells emanating from this, the "halibut fishing capital of the world."

One day, we took the Jeep and drove the thirteen miles to the end of East End Road, counting eight glaciers along the bay. Then we stopped for lunch at a fish-and-chips joint on the Spit to try some of the halibut Morty had been hankering for. Quite the nose on that cat: The difference between this and the usual frozen stuff we were used to was astonishing.

The Kenai Peninsula has the largest concentration of moose anywhere in Alaska and as we left it, we finally saw a cow with her calf. Making our way east for the first time in a long time, we realized this was the official beginning of the end of the bus thing. While we still had many sights to see in our three-week trip home to Boulder, we were now going back, no longer forward. We firmly hoped that would only be true of the physical part of our journey.

After doubling back to Tok (apparently there aren't many roads heading "North to the Future" in our forty-ninth state) on the Alaska Highway, we took a quick, seventy-eight-mile jaunt over to Chicken, population 87. Chicken, boasts its website (yes, even tiny Chicken has a website), was the second town in Alaska to become incorporated. In the late 1800s, the enclave of miners there kept themselves alive by eating ptarmigan, which for some reason were abundant in the area. Ptarmigan (which resemble chicken—wonder if they taste like chicken, too) would later become the state bird. So when Chicken became incorporated, the name "Ptarmigan" was suggested. As the website says, "Many people liked the name, but felt the quotation marks were too presumptuous. The name was shortened to Ptarmigan." Apparently, no one could agree on the spelling, so Chicken was born.

Downtown Chicken (is there any other part? Perhaps a north wing or a south leg? *Groan*) has a café, bar, gift shop, salmon bake, and post office. The public restroom (really a fancy outhouse) is called (what else) the "Chicken poop." Even the post office gets into the act, sporting various chicken "art."

Busing out of Tok heading east into the Yukon, we passed through the tiny town of Destruction Bay. I'd read that the name dates back to 1942, when winds in the area destroyed parts of the U.S. Army's construction project. (The Alaska Highway was initially built in less than eight months as a supply route during World War II.) Not too long ago, I might have wondered if buses could also be blown away. Now I just trusted that if that sort of thing happened regularly, we wouldn't be allowed on the road.

We kept seeing various RV tow vehicles covered with cardboard, plastic bubble wrap, and the like. Sure, this part of the Alaska Highway was rather rough, but that seemed a bit of overkill—or so we thought until we stopped at our campground in Whitehorse, just within the southeast corner of the Yukon border. Our intrepid little Jeep was caked with dirt inside and out (we had inadvertently left the windows open a crack). Its windshield had more stars than an Alaskan winter's night sky. The Prevost was filthy as well, but the Jeep had clearly gotten the worst of it, dragged behind our behemoth of a bus, getting dirt kicked on it like a beach-bound ninety-seven-pound weakling who had yet to take the Charles Atlas course. And like that scrawny boy with the shattered eyeglasses, our poor, pip-squeak Jeep endured the added humiliation of two broken fog lights.

Project Nerd spent several hours cleaning both vehicles. We also got the cell phone number of Randy, a local windshield repair guy. We were told to just leave a message as "he's really busy."

Our Jeep thus revived, we crossed the border back into Alaska for a day trip south to Skagway. Skagway sits on the Taiya Inlet just across Lynn Canal (the northernmost fjord of the Inside Passage) from Haines, which had been our last stop on the Marine Highway exactly three weeks before. Although nowadays a tiny town with only 800 residents, Skagway seemed like a veritable metropolis compared to Chicken. And in the late 1800s, it actually was, thanks to the Klondike Gold Rush. Then, Skagway was the largest city in the territory, with a population of nearly ten thousand. Most of the residents had initially arrived to prospect for gold themselves, but surveying the treacherous mountain terrain, decided instead to stay behind and provide support services (I'm talkin' brothels and saloons here) along with food and equipment to miners who passed through town at the rate of a thousand per week.

Any place growing that quickly due to the singular, albeit elusive, pursuit of fabulous wealth was bound to become totally lawless. Skagway was no exception. In fact, one Canadian Mountie at the time described it as "little better than a hell on earth." The town's most "prominent" citizen was a notorious crime boss, Jefferson Randolph "Soapy" Smith, who originally hailed from the American West. His operation was so successful in Denver, where he paid off so many officials, that he was not afraid to boast to the press of his prowess as a con man.

"I consider bunko steering more honorable than the life led by the average politician," he said. He got his moniker "Soapy" after the Denver paper reported on his "Prize Package Soap Sell Swindle," an elaborate street con in which unsuspecting bystanders bought bars of soap, believing that one included a hidden hundred-dollar bill. Of course, the only folks who ever got any of the money were Soapy's shills, members of his "Soap Gang." Soon, this "king of the frontier con men" became too famous for his own good and even the large amounts of protection money he paid city officials couldn't shield him from the law.

Wanted for attempted murder, Soapy fled Colorado and soon set up shop in Skagway. There, as the head of an organized crime ring, he formed his own militia, developed a network of spies, and even controlled the deputy U.S. marshall. He conned and swindled as many miners as he could, from simple scams (his telegraph office charged five dollars to send a message anywhere in the world, only its wires dead-ended in the brush out back) to elaborate gambling operations. He finally met his maker at the hands of a vigilante group previously sworn to drive him out of town, after he refused to refund a miner money lost in a game of three-card monte. Soapy's last words were "My God, don't shoot!" But he seemed to be the only one with regrets; his purported assailant's tombstone bears the epitaph "He died for the honor of Skagway."

So many prospective prospectors came to the area unprepared for the weather and terrain that, trying to forestall widespread famine, the Canadian government began to require that each bring with him a year's worth (equaling one ton) of food and supplies. At the summit of White Pass, then, it fell to the North West Mounted Police to check that the stampeders had the requisite supplies. Snowshoes were quickly discarded, as the thousands of feet that had gone before had already packed down the trail. To transport that much equipment, each stampeder had to trek the nearly forty miles over the steep pass a few dozen times. The biggest casualties were the terribly overburdened pack animals. More than three thousand died one summer over the White Pass Trail, which then quickly became known as Dead Horse Trail. A journalist at the time wrote, "Yesterday a horse deliberately walked over the face of Porcupine Hill: Said one of the men who saw it, 'It looked to me, sir, like suicide. I believe a horse will commit suicide and this is enough to make them; . . . I don't know but that I'd rather commit suicide too, rather than be driven by some of the men on this trail.' "

The stampeders' other alternative, the Chilkoot Trail through the town of Dyea, wasn't much better; either way was brutal for both man and beast. As one prospector who had climbed both said, "Whichever way you go, you will wish you had gone the other." Soon, there was no choice. Adding to its enviable deep-water port, Skagway was chosen as the site of the new, narrow-gauge railroad. Coming on the heels of an avalanche which buried Chilkoot, the town of Dyea was doomed, its population dwindling to three. By the time the railroad was completed in 1900, the gold rush had largely died, as well.

Today, along with the Chilkoot Trail (at thirty-three miles, considered the world's longest outdoor museum), Dyea, and a visitors center in Seattle (a major outfitting and departure point for stampeders), Skagway is part of the Klondike Gold Rush National Historic Park. We spent a few hours strolling along the wooden sidewalks and poking our heads into the nineteenth-century buildings. Imagining the hustle and bustle of yore wasn't difficult in this well-preserved town, especially while trying to avoid the crush of cruise ship tourists.

Skagway reaffirmed how much our trip had changed me. As we toured a small museum devoted to the Klondike Gold Rush, I wondered if I, too, would have been drawn to the great white north by the promise of impossible riches. But as we wandered through, I was struck by the many old photographs depicting how cruel the stampeders had been to their dogs and horses and realized nothing could be worth losing one's compassion and humanity. As one packer put it, "I must admit that I was as brutal as the rest, but we were all mad—mad for gold, and we did things that we lived to regret."

When we left Skagway, we were leaving Alaska for good, although we sincerely hoped not forever. We made it back to British Columbia in a nearly ten-hour drive, ending up in the tiny town of Steamboat Mountain, which didn't seem to have much else but the RV park. Our standing joke the entire year had been "Let's get an early start," which usually meant 11 a.m.—if we were lucky. Well, we finally achieved one: After a quick overnight at this muddy, mosquito-infested campground with only 15 amps of power (for all systems to run smoothly at the same time, we needed 50, although 30 would do in a pinch), you might say we felt no pull to linger. Tim swore he'd have us out of there by 9 a.m.

"Oh, ye of little faith," he said to my skeptical look. Yup, that's me: Yee Orion. From the lost tribe of Asian Jews. We were gone by eight-thirty.

Before we left the campground, I chatted with the owner about the plethora of RV parks and restaurants for sale along the Alaska Highway, especially noticeable once we entered B.C. While we talked, her Australian shepherd head-butted me, trying in vain to herd. Well, maybe not so in vain. I suddenly found myself standing awfully close to the woman. She said they were going to sell, too; that it had been really hard to make a go of it, especially that year, with high oil prices driving down tourism. Adding to the difficulty, they have to generate their own power. Winters found them in nearby Fort Nelson (pop. 4,200) working for the oil rigs. She said it was a hard life. Not for the first time on our trip, I felt blessed.

The mosquito situation had been bad enough in Alaska, but in B.C., if anything, they seemed even bigger and badder. I mean, these things would make the new Airbus jealous.

On our way through Alberta, the bugs flew into our windshield like a squadron of kamikaze pilots.

"We're under attack!" Tim exclaimed. "Shields on full!"

"Aye," I responded. "Full power to the shields, sir. But she canna take much more a this!" We carried on like that for several miles, our own impromptu tribute to James Doohan, *Star Trek*'s Scotty, who had just passed away.

Our campground near Edmonton was notable for a particularly grotesque bug with more leg than a supermodel on stilts. With all my screaming, I'm sure I failed to do my bit to enhance the reputation of Americans around the planet. On the positive side, the city boasted that it had the world's largest mall—it was in the *Guinness Book* and everything (although apparently the year before, it had been eclipsed and was now only North America's largest). So we took the Jeep for a jaunt to the West Edmonton Mall. With hotels, an amusement park, water park (complete with a bungee jump over the wave pool), mini-golf, sea lions, sea caverns, arcade, casino, movie theater, replica of the *Santa María*, ice-skating rink, church (who said malls were godless places?), and, oh yeah, the over eight hundred stores, of course, we had to see it. *Change is good, but let's not get carried away.*

Still, I bought nothing.

After brief stops in Missoula, Montana (to visit some more e-mail buddies from work), and Pinedale, Wyoming (to visit Lisa and Jim at their cabin), we crossed into Colorado, where we happened to get gas at the same Flying J that had no place for us that awful, rainy first day of our meltdown cruise. There was still construction going on (*Hey, how come it took less than eight months to complete the nearly fifteen-hundred-mile Alaska Highway?*), but this time, it was easy to find (well, it *was* noon and sunny). Then we passed the exit for that community college whose parking lot had unwittingly hosted us. We could actually laugh about that night now, marveling at how far we had come.

About an hour or so from Denver, we stopped at an outlet mall. It was Tim's idea to shop and there was one specific store he had in mind: Carhartt. He wanted to buy work clothes for his new occupation. I stayed in the bus.

You don't need to be a shrink to figure out why, in spite of all I do recall about our trip, I really don't remember anything about how we debused for good. I suppose we landed back at Vanture's parking lot in Denver, loaded what we could into the Jeep, and made several trips back and forth to our house in Boulder. What I do remember is how I felt: Sad. Terribly sad. We both did. Our adventure had come to an end.

It took us weeks to unpack. I'm sure we could have done it all in a day, but it was as if by holding on to the containers that had been in the bay, we were holding on to our year, as well. I, for one, was astonished by how much I had taken on the trip and how much I'd ended up doing without. Seeing me in our master closet, which was about the size of our entire bus bedroom, Tim observed, "I had no idea you'd brought that many shoes." I had only worn six pairs the entire year, with one being sneakers and another, hiking boots. Even amongst *his* containers, Tim kept finding more of my stuff. I couldn't see where I could possibly fit it all in the bus, let alone our house. Finally, I couldn't take it anymore and pleaded, "Don't tell me when you find anything else of mine. Just give it to Goodwill."

"Sure thing," Tim agreed as he hunched over yet another container. Then I heard him mumble, "Who is this Richard Tyler, anyway?" I let out a primal scream and grabbed at the jacket in his hands.

Over the next few months, I did give a lot away (although not the Richard Tyler) and didn't buy one new thing. This was especially impressive as while we were gone, Boulder had gotten a brand-spanking-new mall. I hear it even has a Macy's. I wouldn't know—I've never been in it.

Although I don't shop much anymore, some things never change; I'm still concrete as a sidewalk—maybe even more so. The winter after our return, I was working at my desk and happened to see a headline on MSN.com that said, "Buffalo Hit by Snow." Not that I have anything against buffalo, mind you (I think they're even tastier than cattle), but I couldn't wait to get a break to click on the video of one being hit. Was it like . . . a snow meteor? Surely some form of killer projectile precipitation to fell such a beast. Then I glanced up and saw the same headline on CNN. Only the TV showed a blizzard in Buffalo, *the city*, and I finally got it. *"Buffalo Hit by Snow."* Oh.

One of the things I rediscovered about myself during the bus thing was my love of reading. I just hadn't made much time for it, for years, it seemed. Once we got back, as things naturally became more hectic with work and a stationary home, I found myself reading less again, so started staying in bed (with my phone turned off) for a half hour to an hour every morning with a book. And although Tim recently observed, "You're the only able-bodied person I know in danger of developing bedsores," I noticed that he'd been starting his days with a leisurely breakfast—while he reads.

While I still prefer to get my exercise in front of the TV, I find I don't watch reality shows so much anymore since I'd gotten out and experienced reality on my own for a year. (I'm still a sucker for *Project Runaway*, though.)

As for Tim, he embarked on his new work life as soon as we got back. First, he rented a warehouse next to the Vanture guys in which to store the bus. Then he refurbished an office space in that warehouse to see patients in, keeping his private practice small ("It's so small, nobody knows about it," he quips), only taking on cases he enjoys. Within a few weeks, he bought an old house and started fixing it up with Chris and John. Project Nerd was in heaven, working with the guys and learning all sorts of neat tricks he couldn't wait to try out at home. Just like Chris, he was waking up every morning looking forward to what the day had in store.

He also makes more time for developing and maintaining male friendships. Before we left for the year, one of his psycho-therapist colleagues stopped by Tim's office at the hospital to chat about a mutual patient and commented how sorry he was that he and Tim had somehow never made the time to develop more of a connection.

"I don't know what went wrong," he said. Tim took that to heart and, once we got back, made more of an effort to connect with Steve, as well as other men. Recently, they even attempted that most quintessential of male bonding experiences—going to a sporting event. I say "attempted" because that evening, the Rockies were unfortunately rained out. (I should also put "sport-ing" in quotes here, because really: How can it be a "sport" if even the beer-bellied players excel? Seems more like a skill, to me, like archery or bowling. Football and sumo wrestling are ex-empt from this rule of mine, by the way, as is any sport in which beer bellies actually enhance performance.)

I'd like to say that whenever Tim has a project, he now has several male friends to call on to help. And he does. It's just that, unfortunately, I'm still handier (in a proximity, not ability, sort of way, natch).

Of course, we both fall off the wagon now and then. When Lisa came to visit for a wedding, she wanted to head for an outlet mall, since there aren't any good ones where she lives. So I took her to my old haunts: The Rack, Needless Markup Last Call, and Saks Off Fifth. At first, I intended to just browse. I hadn't "gone shopping" in a very long time. Poor Lisa.

"I've lost my mentor," she said wistfully. Just to make her feel better, I bought a little something. Soon, I was buying a lot of little somethings. I got back into the swing of things so quickly, it became clear just how quickly I could swing back into old ways. I'm relieved to report I haven't gone shopping since.

Shula and Morty have maintained their uneasy truce. No longer hissing and spitting at each other daily as they used to, they've become able to tolerate sleeping on the same furniture at the same time, as long as they aren't touching. Even though, like her mother, Shula undoubtedly had no interest in stretching herself, the bus thing forced her to do just that, and she is clearly the better for it as well. She no longer runs and hides when people come to the house and she is certainly no longer intimidated by her brothers. Morty, in fact, seems to allow her a grudging respect, as even though he's still quite the alpha male with any strange animals, he generally leaves his sister alone—most of the time.

Miles, ever happy, just keeps poodlin' along, although he has slowed down quite a bit. We're glad we got to include him in our adventures and make one of his last years so rich and full of new experiences, not to mention new and varied smells, as well as the near-constant adoration he so richly deserves.

Not a day goes by that I don't count myself lucky to be married to Tim. That's something the bus didn't change, in spite of our being together 24/7 for a year. And I feel every single day how, improbably, he feels the same about me. If there is a heaven, this must truly be its essence: to be loved. Of course, Tim has always joked that I take our marriage vows, particularly the "till death do us part" part, very seriously—i.e., if he parts, he dies. While that might be just a wee exaggeration, I have always maintained, and still do, that if something ever happens to me, I want Tim to be happy and find another woman—provided, of course, that she's not younger or prettier than me and especially no thinner.

Tim still refuses to divulge exactly how he convinced me to go on the bus thing. I shudder to think what else he might get me to do. He continues to ponder living on a boat. I'd like to go on another land-based adventure—maybe Australia and New Zealand, maybe somewhere in Europe—and travel around in a rig for a year. I guess the destination really doesn't matter, after all. It seems all those people who say the journey's what's important may have a point. We just relish the fact that we can conceive of some potentially wonderful something, and know that we'll actually follow through.

We always assumed we needed to sell the bus upon our return. Instead, Tim now works on our stationary home as his next project to sell. It was our dream house, but the dream has changed: We want to live in the bus. We still love the house, but after all, it is just a house. We miss the bus life and no longer want to work to support an abode. While I'm still essentially a homebody, I get out more, experience more, and, in general, live a little more. Although I still don't understand the whole "fresh air" thing. While I'll now hike if certain stipulations are met—in writing (fabulous views, great photo ops, less than a five percent grade, and the whole thing under three miles), we do regularly walk downtown to get together with various people we've met.

Still, once we were home for several months, we noticed that life seemed less intense. When our living space was downsized, everything—from our relationship to the experiences we had, with all the danger, thrills, and joy—was magnified precisely because our horizons were endless. In that spirit, we started taking better advantage of all that our own town has to offer, from the arts and cultural festivals, to various classes and of course, spending time with dear friends. We've also managed to maintain the traditions started during the bus thing that became so meaningful to us: We never turn on the TV during dinner. There is not a meal in the freezer made by someone else at a factory. Tim continues to cook and I continue to watch, with a wineglass in my hand (I still enjoy my martinis but don't seem to drink as many since I don't require quite the anesthetizing I did during the bus thing), music playing in the background. And we still make time to dance.

One night, in fact, I decided to self-coronate (not coronary; that was when I still suffered from bus phobia). I figured that after surviving—nay, thriving—on the bus thing, I deserved a promotion from Princess. So we put on some Motown (the Queen of Soul seemed particularly apt), Tim cooked up my favorite dinner (pecan-crusted salmon in a spinach cream sauce—am I lucky or what?), and I made a special, fruity wine drink, which we used to toast the various memories of our trip, congratulating ourselves that the whole thing—even the disasters—had turned out so well.

Now I am truly Queen—of the Road—and proud of it.

Chapter Thirteen

TIM'S REBUTTAL

Mantini

gin
3 green olives
1 bottle vermouth (unopened)
ice

Combine gin and ice. (Put ice in first, then pour in gin to maximize its cooling. Remember, you're aiming for a drink chilled below 32 degrees because of the freezing point suppression afforded to the gin by the presence of alcohol.) Shake until well chilled. (All the talk about "bruising the gin" is an old wives' tale.) Glance at vermouth for dry martini. If you prefer it wet, leaving bottle sealed, tip it quickly over shaker. (Real men like it dry.) Pour into chilled glass. (Why go to all the trouble of chilling the martini just to add it to a warm glass? Chill the glass by adding both ice and water and letting it stand for several minutes. Just adding ice leaves air between the cubes, so the glass doesn't chill as well or as fast.) Add olives. (Real men also eat their vegetables.)

I am not an idiot.

(Project Nerd: "I am not an idiot, either!")

Special Places and People

Although some are not mentioned in the preceding pages, this doesn't make them any less so.

Chapter One

Bus Conversions magazine; www.busconversions.com

Vanture Coach Manufacturing; www.vanture.com; (303) 297–2708

Prevost; www.prevostcar.com

Chapter Two

Flying J Truck Stops; www.flyingj.com

Rapscallion; 1555 S. Wells Ave., Reno, NV; (775) 323–1211. Wonderful fish restaurant.

Louis' Basque Corner; 301 E. 4th St., Reno, NV; (775) 323–7203. For those who like spice in their food.

Chapter Three

International UFO Museum and Research Center, Roswell, NM; www.iufomrc.org; (505) 625–9495

Roswell, NM, UFO Festival; www.roswellufofestival.com

UFO Museum; 114 N. Main St., Roswell, NM

Jane Espenson's blog; former writer and co-executive producer of TV's *Buffy the Vampire Slayer* blogs on writing (and lunch). All Buffy fans should check this one out at www.janeespenson.com.

Caliche's Frozen Custard; 3009 N. Main St., Roswell, NM. Assimilate it into your intestinal tract. Resistance is futile.

Carlsbad Caverns National Park; 3225 National Parks Hwy., Carlsbad; (800) 967–CAVE for tour reservations; (505) 785–2232 ext. 429 for guided tour information; (505) 785–2107 for recorded information

Carlsbad KOA; 2 Manthei Rd., Carlsbad, NM; (800) 562–9109; www.carlsbadrv.com

Chapter Four

Black Hills Jellystone RV Park; 7001 South Highway 16, Rapid City, SD; (800) 579–7053

President's Alpine Slide at Rushmore Tramway; www.rushmorealpineslide.com; 203 Cemetery Rd., Keystone, SD; (605) 666–4478

Ruby House Restaurant; 124 Winter St., Keystone, SD; (605) 666–4404

Wall Drug Store; www.walldrug.com; 510 Main St., Wall, SD; (605) 279–2175

Crazy Horse Memorial; www.crazyhorse.org; 12151 Ave. of the Chiefs, Crazy Horse, SD; (605) 673–4681

Firehouse Brewing Company; 610 Main St., Rapid City, SD; (605) 348–1915. Tim says the beer is "really, really good."

Town and Country Campground; www.townandcountrycampground.com; 12630 Boone Ave. S., Savage, MN; (952) 445–1756

Lord Fletcher's Old Lake Lodge; 3746 Sunset Dr., Spring Park,
MN 55384; (952) 471–8513. Fabulous restaurant and bar right
on the lake. Get your own captain to take you.

Chapter Five

Cedar Point Amusement Park; www.cedarpoint.com; 1 Cedar
Point Dr., Sandusky, OH; (419) 627–2350. "The roller coaster
capital of the world."

Cornell Chimes; http://chimes.cornell.edu/about.html

Collegetown Bagels; www.ithacabakery.com; 415 College Ave.,
Ithaca, NY; (607) 273–0982

The Chariot; 420 Eddy St., Ithaca, NY; (607) 273–0081. Simply
the best pizza in the world.

Moosewood Restaurant; www.moosewoodrestaurant.com; 215 N.
Cayuga St., Ithaca, NY; (607) 273–9610. If you love the cookbooks, you'll love the restaurant.

Finger Lakes in upstate NY; www.fingerlakes.org. Tell the Romulans I said, "I came in peace."

Wegmans Food Markets, Inc.; www.wegmans.com; currently
found only in NY, NJ, VA, MD, and PA. You'll wish you lived
there—and I don't mean in those states.

Ben & Bill's Chocolate Emporium; www.benandbills.com; 66
Main St., Bar Harbor, ME; (207) 288–3281. For lobster ice
cream and other, even more delectable treats.

The Lobster Pound Restaurant; www.lobsterpoundmaine.com; U.S.
Route 1, Lincolnville Beach, ME; (207) 789–5550

The Black Frog; www.theblackfrog.com; Pritham Ave., Greenville,
ME; (207) 695–1100

Mount Washington, NH; www.mountwashington.org

Chapter Six

Nick Arrojo; www.arrojostudio.com; 180 Varick St., New York,
    NY; (212) 242–7786

Natural Bridge; www.naturalbridgeva.com; on Route 11 between
    exits 175 and 180 from Interstate 81; (800) 533–1410

Carolina Brewery Brewpub and Restaurant; www.carolinabrewery
    .com; 460 W. Franklin St., Chapel Hill, NC; (919) 545–2330.
    Named "Best Brew Pub" by *Beer Magazine*, but more impor-
    tantly, noted by Tim to have "really, really good beer." Even I
    liked their seasonal Santa's Secret, made with cinnamon and
    nutmeg (it didn't taste like a brew at all).

Burwell School Historic Site; www.burwellschool.org; 319 N.
    Church St., Hillsborough, NC; (919) 732–7451. Katherine
    wins the award for best tour guide of our year.

Basnight's Lone Cedar Café; 7623 S. Virginia Dare Trail, Nags
    Head, NC; (252) 441–5405

Chapter Seven

Mr. Friendly's New Southern Café; 2001 Greene St., Columbia,
    SC; (803) 254–7828. Out-of-this-world haute Southern cuisine.
    Try the tuna or filet mignon with creamy cheese grits. And
    don't even get me started on the chocolate pecan pie. Tim said
    several beers on their huge microbrew selection were "really,
    really good." Service excellent as well.

Atlanta Cyclorama; www.bcaatlanta.org; 800 Cherokee Ave. S.E.,
    Atlanta, GA (in Grant Park); (404) 624–1071. "The Longest
    Running Show in the Country."

Joseph's Salon and Spa; 116 W. Jones St., Savannah, GA; (912)
    236–8515. *Sigh.*

Chapter Eight

Fox Theatre; www.foxtheatre.org; 660 Peachtree St. N.E., Atlanta, GA; (404) 688–3353. For a tour of this unusual, historic theater, www.preserveatlanta.com.

Atlanta Fish Market; 265 Pharr Rd.; (404) 262–3165. Fabulous fish restaurant.

The Varsity; www.thevarsity.com; 61 North Ave.; (404) 881–1706

Prevost Car, Inc.; 6931 Business Park Blvd. N., Jacksonville, FL; (904) 886–4555

Café Versailles; 3555 S.W. 8th St., Miami, FL; (305) 444–0240. Ah, *ropa vieja*.

Casa Panza; 1620 S.W. 8th St., Miami, FL; (305) 643–5343

Coral Castle; www.coralcastle.com; 28655 South Dixie Hwy., Homestead, FL; (305) 248–6345

Robbie's of Islamorada; www.robbies.com; 77522 Overseas Hwy., Islamorada, FL; (305) 664–9814. Go tarpons!

Hogfish Bar and Grill; www.hogfishbar.com; 6810 Front St., Stock Island, FL; (305) 293–4041. Share a little something with Gray Cat.

Schooner Wharf Bar; www.schoonerwharf.com; 202 William St., Key West, FL; (305) 292–9520. Stop by for the "dropping the wench in the harbor at midnight" on New Year's and bring your dog anytime.

Chapter Nine

New Orleans Historic Voodoo Museum; www.voodoomuseum .com; 724 Dumaine St., New Orleans, LA; (504) 680–0128

Brennan's Restaurant; 417 Royal St., New Orleans, LA; (504) 525–9711. Get me the recipe for Filet Mignon Stanley, OK?

Slave Haven Underground Railroad Museum; 826 N. 2nd St., Memphis; (901) 527–3427

Laura's Creole Plantation; www.lauraplantation.com; 2247 Highway 18, Vacherie, LA; (888) 799–7690

Prevost Car, Inc.; 15200 Frye Rd., Fort Worth, TX; (817) 685–
0250

Sixth Floor Museum; www.jfk.org; 411 Elm St., Dallas, TX; (214)
747–6660

Conspiracy Museum; 110 Market St., Dallas, TX; (214) 741–3040

Fort Worth Stockyards National Historic District; www.fortworth
stockyards.org. Among other things, see the only daily long-
horn cattle drive in the U.S.

Orange Show; 2401 Munger St., Houston, TX; (713) 926–6368.
Whimsy or insanity? You be the judge.

Battleship Texas State Historic Site; 3527 Battleground Rd., La
Porte, TX; (281) 479–2431. Take a fascinating self-guided tour
of the world's only remaining dreadnought battleship. Get Tim
to tell you what a dreadnought is.

Goode Company Texas Barbecue; 5109 Kirby Dr., Houston, TX;
(713) 464–1901

Ocean Star; www.oceanstaroec.com; Pier 19, Galveston, TX;
(409) 766–STAR

Iron Works Barbecue; 100 Red River St., Austin, TX; (512)
478–4855

La Calesa; 2103 E. Hildebrand, San Antonio, TX; (210) 822–
4475. Best mole sauce we've ever had. So good, Tim doesn't
even remember the beer.

Chapter Ten

Sho Tyme. Fabulous Motown cover band. We saw them at Jerry's
Nugget. Check local Las Vegas listings. You won't be sorry. (See
if you recognize their youngest member from the semifinals of
one of *American Idol*'s first seasons.)

Oasis RV Resort; 2711 W. Windmill Ln., Las Vegas, NV: (702) 260–2020. Pamper yourself . . . and your rig.

Bootlegger Bistro; www.bootlegger.com; 7700 Las Vegas Blvd. S., Las Vegas, NV; (702) 736–7080. Stellar Italian cuisine with a neighborhood, family feel. Multiple beers on tap for the Tims in your life. Live music most nights.

Jeff Stanulis; (702) 737–7793. Elvis impersonator extraordinaire.

Olive Dell Ranch Nudist Resort; www.olivedell.com; 26520 Keissel Rd., Colton, CA; 909–825–6619

Great American Fish Company; 1185 Embarcadero, Morro Bay, CA; (805) 772–4407

Windows on the Water; 699 Embarcadero No. 7, Morro Bay, CA; (805) 772–0677

Eel River Brewing Company's Taproom and Grill; 1777 Alamar Way, Fortuna, CA; (707) 725–2739; www.eelriverbrewing.com. Guess what Tim said about this place?

Pelican Pub & Brewery; www.pelicanbrewery.com; 33180 Cape Kiwanda Dr., Pacific City, OR; (503) 965–7007. Ditto.

Chapter Eleven

Alaska Ferry; www.akferry.org; (800) 527–6731

All the regulations about travel in the 49th state, including pet vaccines: http://www.alaskaone.com/welcome/planning.html

Border cam!: http://www.wsdot.wa.gov/traffic/border

Clover Pass Resort and RV Park; www.cloverpassresort.com; 708 N. Point Higgins, Ketchikan, AK; (907) 247–2234

Tongass Trading Co., Inc.; 201 Dock St., Ketchikan, AK; (907) 225–5101; www.tongasstrading.com. Poopin' moose key chain, et al. What more could you want?

Ocean View Restaurant; www.oceanviewmex.com; 1831 Tongass Ave., Ketchikan, AK; (907) 225–7566. I know you didn't come all this way for Mexican food, but it's the hands-down food find of Ketchikan. (They've also got Italian and Greek choices.) Don't pass up the sangria or Halibut Olympia.

Bar Harbor Restaurant; www.barharborketchikan.com; 2813 Tongass Ave., Ketchikan, AK; (907) 225–2813. Another fab food find.

Island Wings Air Service; www.islandwings.com; (888) 854–2444. Fly with owner-pilot Michelle Madsen.

Alaska Waters, Inc.; www.alaskawaters.com; Wrangell, AK; (800) 347–4462. Jim recently got a brand-new boat, so no more headless trips, for any Princesses out there considering.

Ivan Simonek. Check out his amazing photography at www. alaskan.smugmug.com.

Alaska Raptor Center; www.alaskaraptor.org; 1000 Raptor Way, Sitka, AK; (800) 643–9425

The Hangar on the Wharf; www.hangaronthewharf.com; 2 Marine Way, Juneau, AK; (907) 586–5018. Fish, prime rib, pool tables, beer, bands. Life is good.

Oceanside RV Park and Canal Marine; www.oceansiderv.com; (907) 766–2437

Great Land Wines, Ltd.; www.greatlandwines.com; 817 Small Tracts Rd., Haines, AK; (907) 766–2698

Chapter Twelve

The Milepost; www.themilepost.com. Essential guide for driving any vehicle in the 49th state.

Chicken, AK; www.chickenalaska.com

Fast Eddy's Restaurant; Mile 1313 Alaska Hwy., Tok, AK; (907) 883–4411

The Pump House Restaurant and Saloon; www.pumphouse.com; 796 Chena Pump Rd., Fairbanks, AK; (907) 479–8452. Fine dining in a National Historic Site.

Alaska Native Heritage Center; www.alaskanative.net; near the
    intersection of Glenn Hwy. and Muldoon Rd., Anchorage, AK;
    (800) 315–6608. Plan to spend at least a half day exploring
    the exhibits, exhibitions, workshops with Native artisans, and
    traditional Native dwellings.
Simon and Seafort's Saloon and Grill; www.r-u-i.com/sim; 420 L
    St., Anchorage, AK; (907) 274–3502

Miscellaneous

Good Sam Club; www.goodsamclub.com. For RVers of every stripe.
FMCA (Family Motor Coach Association), www.fmca.com. Ditto.
Prevost Prouds; www.prevostprouds.com. For Prevost owners.
www.myRVspace.com. Free social networking, information,
    and entertainment site for RVers.
www.passportamerica.com. Discount camping club.
Prevost Owners Group; www.prevostownersgroup.com. For anyone
    interested in the Prevost experience.

Books Enjoyed on the Bus and Beyond

Because one of the changes we made on our bus year was reading more, I thought I would share some of the books Tim and/or I particularly enjoyed on the road and since we've been back. So, in no particular order:

Eat, Pray, Love: One Woman's Search for Everything Across Italy, India and Indonesia by Elizabeth Gilbert

A Walk in the Woods: Rediscovering America on the Appalachian Trail by Bill Bryson

The Kite Runner by Khaled Hosseini

The Sparrow and *Children of God* by Mary Doria Russell

Plum Lucky by Janet Evanovich

Water for Elephants by Sara Gruen

Skinny Bitch by Kim Barnouin and Rory Freedman

The Golden Compass, The Subtle Knife, and *The Amber Spyglass* by Philip Pullman

The Road by Cormac McCarthy

Musicophilia: Tales of Music and the Brain by Oliver Sacks

The Glass Castle: A Memoir by Jeannette Walls

Born Standing Up: A Comic's Life by Steve Martin

Into the Wild by Jon Krakauer

The Tipping Point: How Little Things Can Make a Big Difference and *Blink: The Power of Thinking Without Thinking* by Malcolm Gladwell

Freakonomics: A Rogue Economist Explores the Hidden Side of Everything by Steven D. Levitt and Stephen J. Dubner

The World Is Flat: A Brief History of the Twenty-first Century by Thomas L. Friedman

The Geography of Bliss: One Grump's Search for the Happiest Places in the World by Eric Weiner

Zen and the Art of Motorcycle Maintenance: An Inquiry into Values by Robert M. Pirsig

The Places in Between by Rory Stewart

Honeymoon with My Brother by Franz Wisner

Marley & Me: Life and Love with the World's Worst Dog by John Grogan

Look Me in the Eye: My Life with Asperger's by John Elder Robison

An Unquiet Mind: A Memoir of Moods and Madness by Kay Redfield Jamison

A Heartbreaking Work of Staggering Genius by Dave Eggers

The Lovely Bones by Alice Sebold

On Writing by Stephen King

The Other Boleyn Girl by Philippa Gregory

The Memory Keeper's Daughter by Kim Edwards

The Sex Lives of Cannibals: Adrift in the Equatorial Pacific by J. Maarten Troost

White Teeth by Zadie Smith

The Secret Life of Bees and *The Mermaid Chair* by Sue Monk Kidd

The Jane Austen Book Club by Karen Joy Fowler

Running with Scissors, *Dry*, and *Magical Thinking* by Augusten
   Burroughs
Up Country by Nelson DeMille
Good Dog. Stay. and *One True Thing* by Anna Quindlen
Any Place I Hang My Hat by Susan Isaacs
Nature Girl by Carl Hiaasen
Stiff: The Curious Lives of Human Cadavers by Mary Roach
The Orchid Thief: A True Story of Beauty and Obsession by Susan
   Orlean
The Time Traveler's Wife by Audrey Niffenegger
The Devil in the White City by Erik Larson
The Tender Bar by J. R. Moehringer
I Like You: Hospitality Under the Influence by Amy Sedaris
Me Talk Pretty One Day and *Naked* by David Sedaris
Ulysses by James Joyce
Drop City and *The Tortilla Curtain* by T. C. Boyle

Acknowledgments, Disclaimers, and Trip Insurance

Some names in this memoir have been changed to protect the idiotic (although not Tim's, in spite of his repeated requests). Some events and dates have likewise been time-warped and wormholed for clarity and narrative sake (not that I can think of any off the top of my head, and since I took Physics for Non-Majors the chance of me actually doing such things is rather slim, but I suppose I must have, so there you go).

With all the controversy surrounding memoirs these days, if doubt ever arises about the veracity of what is contained in these pages, rest assured I can provide appropriate documentation, including but not limited to: emergency room charts, police records, and AAA bills. Many of these can be found on my website, www .doreenorion.com. (Well, not really, but it does have my blog dating back to the start of our trip, slick shots of our travels and our bus, oodles of requisite and yet somehow always adorable pet pictures, several photojournalistic attempts at documenting our various disasters, along with considerably more than just a tad of fun stuff in the form of articles, martini recipes, contests, news, podcasts, and, last but not least, video "reenactments" of our various adventures—poor Tim, even I'm starting to feel sorry for him.)

And, speaking of my website, I have Steve Bennett at www .AuthorBytes.com to thank for designing it. (How you were able to capture the spirit and tone of the book so well when you're a guy, and not even that into shoes, is beyond me.)

To my parents, especially my mother, who insisted that if I allowed her to read the pages involving her beforehand, she would not utter one word of protest. Perhaps, then, I am truly giving thanks for the fortitude Gertrude and Henry apparently instilled in me, as when I offered, "Why can't you just read the book when everyone else does?" and she responded with the time-tested Jewish mother retort: "If I live that long," I nonetheless held firm.

To my beta readers, Robbie Barr, whose sound judgment I much appreciated, and Doug Roemer, cousin and grammar savant extraordinaire. To my writers' group—Barbara Cohn, Joan Knobb, and Sue Mcmillan—who put up with reading so many incarnations of the first two chapters in the proposal stage (when the book was titled *Leave the Driving to Him*); I'm surprised they didn't cry, "Why don't you just leave the reading to him too, while you're at it?" To my book group "goyles": Susan Wientzen, Sheryl Allen, Eileen Gilday, Jane Ann Hebert, Kathryn Lynch, Deborah Ramirez, and Robbie Barr, who provided support and feedback at crucial junctions. Susan also gave me invaluable assistance (due in equal measure to her background in marketing and to her being really, really sharp) in getting the word out about this book.

To my wonderful agent, Mollie Glick of the Jean V. Naggar Literary Agency. I wish I had something funny to say here, but your faith in this project and supreme skill in guiding it along were never a laughing matter. Kudos as well to Jennifer Weltz at the agency for her considerable expertise with foreign and other rights.

To my editor and polar opposite, Stacy Creamer. I remain utterly perplexed as to why you wanted to publish me, given what an incredibly active (she does triathlons!), accomplished (she's a VP at Doubleday!), well-rounded (she still makes time to needlepoint and be a mom!) woman you are. Ah, of course. Silly me. We shrinks call it "reaction formation." I always suspected people like you unconsciously yearned to be lazy sloths like people like me. I feel better now.

To Julie Sills and Ellen Folan at Broadway Books for wonderful work with marketing and publicity, respectively. To Kim Dower (Kim-from-L.A.) for taking this project on with such enthusiasm and seeing it through with such imagination and tenacity.

To Liz De Ridder, Queen of the Copy Editors, for not only doing a stellar job of fixing my mistakes, but actually making copyediting (sorta, kinda) fun. (Those hours of hilarity I spent trying to look up what a smiley face means in my copyediting guide were particularly memorable.)

To Bella Stander (the world's best consultant for authors) for hand-holding when I needed it, sound advice when I asked for it, and a wonderful sense of humor all the time.

Everyone should have a memoir mentor (even if you have no intention of ever writing one). I somehow lucked out and got Kathryn Black. I hesitate to name her here, however, for fear she will be swamped with potential mentees. Therefore, know this and know it well: I've got first dibs.

To John Rainy, for his friendship as well as teaching me much about writing in general.

To Alexandre Philippe for wonderful writing workshops throughout the years and appearing in my nightmares (for needed instruction only—although there was that thing with the headless chicken . . .) more than once.

To Boulder's Liquor Mart for . . . do we really need to get into that? And, speaking of which, to my guinea pigs/taste testers, Lisa Cook and Jeanette Buckingham. (I thought I told you two it was a "working happy hour"? *Geez.*)

And finally, to my (some might insert here "long-suffering") husband, Tim. When Mollie first read my proposal, she commented, "You know, this isn't a travel memoir. It's a love story." She couldn't have said it any better. So for once, I'll let someone else have the last word.

Oops.

Dear Readers

I hope what comes across in *Queen of the Road* is that this book has been a labor of love. After I wrote each chapter, Tim would read it and we'd reminisce about our travels. In a way, then, it felt like our amazing adventure was extended far beyond the measly (funny, early on I might have said "interminable") year. I like to think that even if I knew no one else would ever read it, I'd still have written *Queen of the Road*. But once I had a publisher, I truly found myself waking up every day marveling, "I can't believe I get to write this book!"

Thank you for reading it. Really. And to *really* thank you, I'd love to be invited to your book group. (I just invited myself, didn't I? How rude! Just ignore me, if you like.) If I'm in the area, I'd love to attend in person. (Here I go again.) If not, I'll attend by speakerphone. I've been in a wonderful book group myself for over a decade and would greatly enjoy visiting yours and answering any of your questions. Please go to my website, www .queenoftheroadthebook.com, to arrange a visit or "visit," see pictures from the *Queen of the Road* trip, and learn what we're up to now.

Readers' Guide

1. What would you do if you could take a year off? How do you think it might change you? Is there a life lesson you'd want to learn? Is it hard to incorporate lessons learned while traveling or on vacation into your daily life? What could you do to improve that disconnect?

2. How would it be to spend 24/7 with your significant other for a year? Would a life on the road appeal to you?

3. Doreen said she would "never, ever, EVER live on a bus." She said the same thing about going to a nudist RV park. Are there things you thought you'd never do in your life but ended up doing anyway? How did they work? Are there things you're certain you'll never do now? Why?

4. Are there any "things" you feel you couldn't live without? Why? Did Doreen's changing relationship with material possessions make you feel any differently about your own?

5. Discuss how Tim's experiences growing up may have contributed to his "working himself to death" and thus became the catalyst for the whole "bus thing."

6. Doreen says she and Tim are "polar opposites." How does that affect their relationship for better or worse? What do you think each sees in the other?

7. How did Doreen and Tim change during their trip, and how did you see that change progress through the journey? Do you feel their relationship changed as well? What do you envision their future life will be like, and how would that be different had they never done the bus thing?

8. Who do you think is the most inspirational person Doreen and Tim met or learned about on their trip? Did he or she make you think about doing something differently in your own life?

9. Did the book make you want to visit any particular place in it? Why?

10. The bus seemed to have a "will of its own." How did Doreen and Tim's relationship with it change during their yearlong adventure? What was the significance for each of them of the challenges it presented along the way?

11. Did your perception of psychiatrists change through reading this book? How did this memoir about married psychiatrists differ in its portrayal of the profession from that of pop-culture movies and TV shows?

12. Why do you think Doreen included her martini recipes in the book? What did the recipes represent for her? What self-soothing traditions have you experienced in your own life?

13. Doreen writes of their dog: "Miles was all about simple pleasures: It was enough in life to have a bowl of food and a small, quiet place to himself, surrounded by people who loved him. Why ask for anything more?" She also writes that he could "teach me a lot." What have you learned or what do you think you could learn from your pets?

14. The bus thing seems to have given the lives of all the travelers more balance. How do you think their future plans reflect this? Are you happy with the balance in your life and, if not, what could you do differently?

15. Doreen "self-coronates" on their return. Do you think she deserved the promotion from Princess to Queen? What experiences during their year especially contributed to her elevated royal status? What obstacles have you overcome that you are most proud of?

About the Author

DOREEN ORION is a triple-boarded psychiatrist on the faculty of the University of Colorado Health Science Center. She is an award-winning author, has lectured throughout the United States, and has been interviewed in major national media (*Larry King Live*, *48 Hours*, *Good Morning America*, and *People* magazine, to name a few). In spite of all this, Doreen considers her greatest accomplishment to be that her bus was featured as the centerfold for *Bus Conversions* magazine (for which she is the travel writer), thus fulfilling her lifelong ambition of being a Miss September.